The Dollar Crisis

Causes, Consequences, Cures

Revised and Updated

The Dollar Crisis

Causes, Consequences, Cures

Revised and Updated

Richard Duncan

John Wiley & Sons (Asia) Pte Ltd

Other Wiley Editorial Offices

John Wiley & Sons, Inc, 111 River Street, Hoboken, NJ 07030, USA
John Wiley & Sons Ltd, The Atrium, Southern Gate, Chichester PO19 8SQ, England
John Wiley & Sons (Canada) Ltd, 22 Worcester Road, Rexdale, Ontario M9W 1L1, Canada
John Wiley & Sons Australia Ltd, 33 Park Road (PO Box 1226), Milton, Queensland 4064, Australia
Wiley-VCH, Pappelallee 3, 69469 Weinheim, Germany

Library of Congress Cataloging-in-Publication Data:
ISBN 978-0-470-82170-1

Typeset in 10.5/13 points, Times Roman by Linographic Services Pte Ltd
Printed in Singapore by Saik Wah Press Pte Ltd
10 9

Contents

Preface to the Revised Edition

The principal flaw in the post-Bretton Woods international monetary system is its inability to prevent large-scale trade imbalances. The theme of *The Dollar Crisis* is that those imbalances have destabilized the global economy by creating a worldwide credit bubble. In the two years and three months since the first edition of the book was written, those imbalances, and the risk to the global economy of them coming unwound, have grown enormously. The U.S. current account deficit has ballooned by 40% and become the most hotly debated issue in international economics. Total international reserves, the best measure of global money supply, have surged by US$1.2 trillion, or 50%, with the world's central banks creating paper money at a pace never before attempted during peacetime.

This heightened disequilibrium in the global economy was the outcome – indeed, the goal – of the policy response to the worldwide economic slump that followed the implosion of the New Paradigm technology bubble. Policymakers in the United States applied unprecedented fiscal and monetary stimuli to pull the world out of the ensuing economic downturn and to ensure that deflation did not take hold in America as it has in Japan. Three large tax cuts took the U.S. budget from a surplus of US$127 billion in 2001 to a deficit of US$413 billion in 2004; and the federal funds rate was cut to 1%, a four-decade low. As interest rates fell in the United States, property prices soared, creating a wealth effect that was more than sufficient to offset the losses from the stock market crash. Equity extraction from homes fueled consumption, consumption fueled imports, and imports reflated the global economy. It was economic management through bubble creation.

Nearly every asset class appreciated in value except one – the U.S. dollar. With the U.S. current account deficit approaching 5% of U.S. GDP in 2002, it became clear that the "strong dollar trend" was unsustainable. Private investors dumped dollars in such quantities that the United States would have faced a balance of payments crisis had Asian central banks not intervened in the foreign exchange markets, bought up all the dollars the private sector wished to unload, and then reinvested those dollars in dollar-denominated assets in the United States. Japan's intervention amounted to US$320 billion, requiring the Bank of Japan to create money equivalent to 1% of global GDP, in what was effectively one of the most aggressive experiments in monetary policy ever conducted.

To date, the results of these efforts to reflate the global economy have been impressive. In 2004, the world economy grew at the fastest rate in nearly 30 years. Economic bubbles are easier to create than to sustain, however. The United States is the world's engine of economic growth because it imports 75% more from the rest of the world than it exports. The result is a current account deficit of US$640 billion that even Fed Chairman Alan Greenspan has described as unsustainable. There are no sources of global aggregate demand capable of substituting for the U.S. current account deficit. When that deficit corrects, as it inevitably must, the global reflation it brought about in recent years will give way to global deflation, as the capacity that has been put in place to fulfill the demand from an expanding U.S. trade deficit goes unutilized.

The policy options then will be to endure a very severe and protracted global economic slump, or to provide a new round of stimulus. Conventional policy tools are nearly exhausted, however. Therefore, an unconventional approach must be anticipated. The Federal Reserve, terrified of deflation, has spelled out what that response is likely to be: fiscal stimulus financed by money creation. If applied aggressively enough, that approach is likely to succeed in staving off the slump for some time by creating an even greater bubble; but ultimately it will all end very badly. If helicopter money were a viable policy option, it would have been discovered a long time ago and we would all be living in a world of infinite prosperity today.

Seven new chapters have been added to the revised edition of this book as Part Five to describe the extraordinary evolution of this crisis between September 2002, when the first edition was completed, and the end of 2004, as the second edition goes to print. Part Five also considers how the dollar crisis is likely to unfold over the years immediately ahead, the likely policy response to the crisis, and why that response cannot succeed. The dollar standard is inherently flawed and increasingly unstable. Its collapse will be the most important economic event of the 21st century.

Richard Duncan
March 2005
Hong Kong

Introduction

Then the Gods of the Market tumbled, and their smooth-tongued wizards
Withdrew, And the hearts of the Meanest were humbled and began to believe
It was true That All is not Gold that Glitters, and Two and Two make Four
And the Gods of the Copybook Headings limped up to explain it once more.

— Rudyard Kipling, 1919

When the Bretton Woods international monetary system broke down in 1973, the world's financial officials were unable to agree on a new set of rules to regulate international trade and monetary relations. Instead, a new system began to emerge without formal agreement or sanction. It also remained nameless. In this book, the current international monetary system which evolved out of the collapse of Bretton Woods will be referred to as the dollar standard, so named because U.S. dollars have become the world's core reserve currency in place of gold, which had comprised the world's reserve assets under the Bretton Woods system as well as under the classical gold standard of the 19th century.

The primary characteristic of the dollar standard is that it has allowed the United States to finance extraordinarily large current account deficits by selling debt instruments to its trading partners instead of paying for its imports with gold, as would have been required under the Bretton Woods system or the gold standard.

In this manner, the dollar standard has ushered in the age of globalization by allowing the rest of the world to sell their products to the United States on credit. This arrangement has had the benefit of allowing much more rapid economic growth, particularly in large parts of the developing world, than could have occurred otherwise. It also has put downward pressure on consumer prices and, therefore, interest rates in the United States as cheap manufactured goods made with very low-cost labor were imported into the United States in rapidly increasing amounts.

However, it is now becoming increasingly apparent that the dollar standard has also resulted in a number of undesirable, and potentially disastrous, consequences.

First, it is clear that the countries that built up large stockpiles of international reserves through current account or financial account surpluses experienced severe economic overheating and hyperinflation in asset prices that ultimately resulted in economic collapse. Japan and the Asia Crisis countries are the most obvious examples of countries that suffered from that process. Those countries were able to avoid complete economic depression only because their governments went deeply into debt to bail out the depositors of their bankrupt banks.

Second, flaws in the current international monetary system have also resulted in economic overheating and hyperinflation in asset prices in the United States, as the country's trading partners have reinvested their dollar surpluses in U.S. dollar-denominated assets. Their acquisitions of stocks, corporate bonds, and U.S. agency debt have helped fuel the stock market bubble, facilitated the extraordinary misallocation of corporate capital, and helped drive U.S. property prices to unsustainable levels.

Third, the credit creation that the dollar standard made possible has resulted in over-investment on a grand scale across almost every industry. Over-investment has produced excess capacity and deflationary pressures that are undermining corporate profitability around the world.

The U.S. economy, rightly described as the world's engine of economic growth, is now beginning to falter under the immense debt burden of its corporate and consumer sectors. The rest of the world has grown reliant on exporting to the United States and, up until now, has allowed the United States to pay for much of its imports on credit. However, record bankruptcies and accounting fraud at the highest level of corporate America raise serious doubts about the creditworthiness of the United States. The trading partners of the United States now face the choice of continuing to invest their dollar surpluses in U.S. dollar-denominated assets despite very compelling reasons to doubt the security of such investments, or else converting their dollar surpluses into their own currencies, which would cause their currencies to appreciate, and their exports and economic growth rates to decline. Neither choice is appealing, particularly considering the economic fragility of most of those countries and the huge amounts required to finance the U.S. current account deficit – currently US$50 million an hour, or 5% of U.S. gross domestic product (GDP) per annum.

In recent years, severe boom-and-bust cycles have wrecked the financial systems and government finances of countries with large balance of payments surpluses; excessive credit creation has fueled over-investment and culminated in strong deflationary pressures around the world; and the reinvestment of dollar surpluses into dollar assets has facilitated reckless debt expansion in the United States that has impaired the creditworthiness of its corporate and consumer sectors to such an extent as to preclude that country from continuing to serve as the world's engine of growth.

In short, the world economy is in a state of extreme disequilibrium and is at risk of plunging into the most severe downturn since the Great Depression. The purpose of this book is to demonstrate that flaws in the international monetary system are responsible for that disequilibrium; to show that the unwinding of those imbalances will soon culminate in a collapse in the value of the U.S. dollar and a worldwide economic slump; and to describe what can be done to re-establish equilibrium in the global economy and to lay the foundations for sustainable economic growth in the decades ahead. The dollar standard has failed and has begun to collapse into crisis. This crisis will be referred to as the dollar crisis, both because it originated from the excessive creation of dollar reserve assets and because it must culminate in the collapse in the value of the dollar.

The Dollar Crisis is divided into five parts. Part One will describe the nature of the extraordinary imbalances in the global economy and explain how they came about. It will be shown that trade imbalances, and in particular the U.S. trade deficit, resulted in the excessive credit creation responsible for the economic bubble in Japan in the 1980s, the Asian Miracle bubble of the mid-1990s, and the New Paradigm bubble in the United States in the late 1990s.

Part Two will demonstrate why the disequilibrium in the global economy is unsustainable and must result in a collapse in the value of the U.S. dollar and elimination of the U.S. current account deficit.

Part Three will show how a severe recession in the United States and the elimination of the U.S. current account deficit brought about by a collapsing dollar will cause a severe global economic slump.

Part Four will propose measures that could help restore balance in the global economy and mitigate the extraordinary damage that now seems likely to result from the implosion of a worldwide credit bubble.

Part Five, newly added to the revised edition of *The Dollar Crisis*, describes the extraordinary impact that the 40% deterioration in the U.S. current account deficit and the 50% increase in the global money supply have had on the global economy in the short time since the first edition went to print, as well as what can be expected next as the dollar crisis continues to unfold.

PART ONE

The Origin of Economic Bubbles

The global economy is in a state of extreme disequilibrium. Excess capacity across most industries has brought about deflationary pressures that are undermining corporate profitability, while the collapse of a series of asset price bubbles has created financial sector distress in many countries around the world.

Part One will demonstrate how the international monetary system that evolved following the collapse of the Bretton Woods system facilitated the development of a worldwide credit bubble. It will be shown that the U.S. current account deficit flooded the world with dollar liquidity, as well as how that liquidity caused excessive credit creation and economic overheating in those countries with large trade or financial account surpluses. It will also establish that a similar chain of events culminated in the Great Depression of the 1930s.

Chapter 1 will show that an extraordinary surge in international reserves took place once the restraints inherent in the Bretton Woods system were eliminated when that system collapsed. Next, the mechanics of the Bretton Woods system and its predecessor, the gold standard, are briefly described in order to demonstrate that both systems contained automatic adjustment mechanisms that prevented persistent trade imbalances between countries. The primary flaw of the dollar standard, the current international monetary system, is that it lacks any such adjustment mechanism. Consequently, trade imbalances of unprecedented magnitude and duration have developed. It will be made clear in following chapters how those trade imbalances have destabilized the global economy. Finally, the reader will be made familiar with the terminology used to describe the balance of payments between countries and be shown that extraordinary imbalances on the current and financial accounts have left surplus countries holding an enormous amount of U.S. dollar-denominated debt instruments and turned the United States, the primary deficit country, into the most heavily indebted nation in history.

Chapter 2 describes how those countries with large current and/or financial account surpluses have been blown into bubble economies as those surpluses enter their domestic banks and set off a process of credit creation in the same way as if the central banks of those countries had injected high-powered money into those banking systems. Japan and Thailand are taken as examples of how countries with large surpluses and a corresponding rapid accumulation of international reserves were transformed into bubble economies as their trade or financial account surpluses entered their banking systems and unleashed an explosion of credit creation that caused economic overheating and hyperinflation in asset prices.

Chapter 3 demonstrates how the United States has been destabilized by its own enormous current account deficit. It will be shown that the foreign capital inflows into the United States that finance the current account deficit are, to a large extent, merely a function of the U.S. current account deficit itself. The trading partners of the United States have accumulated large reserves of U.S. dollar-denominated assets with their trade surpluses, rather than converting those dollars into their own currencies, which would have caused their currencies to appreciate and their trade surpluses and economic growth rates to slow. Consequently, their acquisitions of U.S. dollar-denominated stocks, corporate bonds, and U.S. agency debt have helped fuel the stock-market bubble, facilitated the extraordinary misallocation of corporate capital, and helped drive U.S. property prices higher.

Chapter 4 explains how the breakdown of the classical gold standard at the outbreak of World War I set off a chain of events remarkably similar to that which has occurred following the collapse of the Bretton Woods system. Once the discipline inherent in the gold standard was removed, trade imbalances swelled and international credit skyrocketed. The result was prosperity ... followed by depression.

Part One shows how trade imbalances have destabilized the global economy by flooding the world with dollar liquidity and causing economic bubbles in Japan, the Asia Crisis countries, and the United States. Part Two will explain why the disequilibrium that has resulted from those imbalances is unsustainable.

Chapter 1

The Imbalance of Payments

There is no means of avoiding the final collapse of a boom brought about by credit expansion. The alternative is only whether the crisis should come sooner as the result of voluntary abandonment of further credit expansion, or later as a final and total catastrophe of the currency system involved.

— Ludwig von Mises, 1949[1]

During the three decades following the breakdown of the Bretton Woods international monetary system, trade imbalances have flooded the world with liquidity, causing economic overheating and hyperinflation in asset prices, initially within individual countries and now on a global scale. This chapter will illustrate the extraordinary surge in international reserves that came about once the restraints inherent in the Bretton Woods system were eliminated when that system collapsed. Next, the mechanics of the Bretton Woods system and its predecessor, the gold standard, are briefly described in order to demonstrate that both systems contained automatic adjustment mechanisms that prevented persistent trade imbalances between countries. The primary flaw of the dollar standard, the current international monetary system, is that it lacks any such adjustment mechanism. Consequently, trade imbalances of unprecedented magnitude and duration have developed. It will be made clear in the following chapters how those trade imbalances have destabilized the global economy. Finally, the terminology used to describe the balance of payments between countries will be explained in order to demonstrate how extraordinary imbalances on the current and financial accounts have left surplus countries holding an enormous amount of U.S. dollar-denominated debt instruments and turned the United States, the primary deficit country, into the most heavily indebted nation in history.

INTERNATIONAL RESERVES

International reserve assets consist of external assets that a country may use to finance imbalances in its international trade and capital flows. In earlier centuries, gold or silver fulfilled that function, but today foreign exchange comprises the vast majority of the world's reserves. As Figure 1.1 shows,

Figure 1.1   Total international reserve assets, 1949–2000

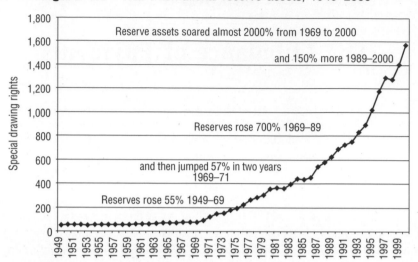

Source: International Monetary Fund (IMF), *International Financial Statistics Yearbook 2001.*

there has been an extraordinary surge in reserve assets since the early 1970s when the Bretton Woods system began to fall apart.

This chapter will demonstrate that this surge in reserve assets has been comprised of foreign exchange, primarily U.S. dollars; that those reserve assets have come into existence as a result of the widening trade imbalances between the United States and the rest of the world; and that this multiplication of reserves is indicative of the extraordinary expansion of credit that those trade imbalances have facilitated. Chapter 2 will document how countries with large balance of payments surpluses have experienced severe economic overheating and hyperinflation in asset prices as those surpluses stimulated credit creation through their commercial banking systems. Chapter 3 examines how the U.S. economy has become overheated and heavily indebted, as its trading partners have reinvested their dollar surpluses in U.S. dollar-denominated assets. Chapter 4 will show that a remarkably similar pattern of credit expansion, economic boom, and crisis occurred following the breakdown of the gold standard in 1914.

International reserve assets expanded at a relatively slow pace before 1970 and at a very rapid pace afterwards, as shown in Figure 1.1. It is extraordinary to note that the world's reserve assets increased more in the four years between 1969 and 1973 as the Bretton Woods system collapsed than during all preceding centuries combined. During the 20 years from 1949 to 1969, the world's reserve assets increased by 55%. During the next 20 years, they expanded by 700%. Altogether, between 1969 and today, international reserve assets have increased approximately 20-fold. The impact that this extraordinary expansion of reserve assets has had on global capital markets has been phenomenal.

Prior to 1970, gold had comprised the majority of total reserve assets and had been the foundation stone of the Bretton Woods system. Afterwards, as shown in Figure 1.2, the role of gold diminished rapidly as foreign exchange became dominant within reserve holdings. By the end of 2000, gold represented only 2% of total reserves.

This shift is particularly significant because all the major national currencies also ceased to be backed by gold after 1970. Consequently, as time passed, the world's reserve assets were not only no longer comprised of gold, they became comprised primarily of currencies that were also no longer backed by gold. Paper money replaced gold as the foundation stone of the international monetary system. Over the following pages, it will be shown how the abandonment of a gold-based regime of international trade and monetary relations sparked off an explosion of credit creation that has destabilized the global economy.

THE ERA OF PAPER MONEY

Rampant international credit creation began in 1973 with the first oil shock.

Figure 1.2 The breakdown of international reserve assets, 1949–2000

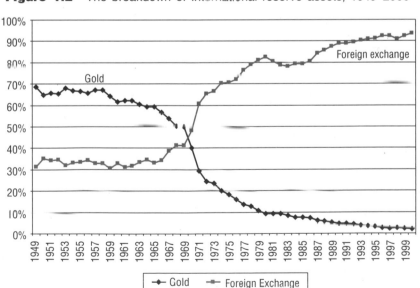

Source: IMF, *International Financial Statistics Yearbook 2001*.

The recycling of petro-dollars from the oil-producing nations to South America and Eastern Europe via the New York banks sparked off the first boom-and-bust crisis of the post-Bretton Woods era. The tripling of oil prices created enormous trade deficits in most oil-importing countries. However, the ability to settle those deficits with debt instruments rather than gold reduced the severity of the adjustment process – even though that relief came at the cost of several years of double-digit inflation. Then, beginning in the early 1980s, the United States began experiencing annual current account deficits exceeding US$100 billion. From that time on, those deficits replaced the oil shocks as the main source of global economic disequilibrium.

The evolution of the global economy would have been very different had Bretton Woods, or a similar monetary system based on gold, remained in place. First of all, the recessions following the oil shocks would have been much more severe than they were, since credit would have had to contract in the oil-importing nations as gold left those countries to pay for oil. Afterwards, the U.S. current account deficits that began in the 1980s could not have persisted for more than a few years before gold outflows produced a recession and brought about their end. Therefore, a short explanation of how the classical gold standard functioned is required to show how the global economy became inundated with credit once its successor, the Bretton Woods system, collapsed. The mechanics of the gold standard are not difficult to grasp.

Over the ages, gold had come to be accepted as the principal store of value and the preferred medium of exchange in commerce. The classical gold standard began to take shape from the end of the Napoleonic Wars and was fully in place by 1875. From then until the outbreak of World War I, the currencies of all the major trading countries in the world were fixed at a certain price to a certain quantity of gold. This thereby resulted in fixed exchange rates between the currencies of those countries. Gold coins circulated in daily use as the medium of exchange. Commercial banks accepted gold as deposits which they, in turn, re-lent. Those banks were able to create credit by lending out more than the original amount of gold deposited; however, they were compelled always to maintain sufficient gold reserves on hand in order to meet the demand of their depositors for withdrawals. Banks dared not lend out too great a multiple of their reserves for fear of insolvency should they be unable to repay deposits on demand.

The gold standard prevented imbalances in countries' trade accounts through a process that acted as an automatic adjustment mechanism. A country experiencing trade surpluses would accumulate more gold, since gold receipts from exports would exceed gold payments for imports. The banking system of the surplus country could create more credit, as more gold was deposited into that country's commercial banks. Expanding credit would fuel an economic boom, which, in turn, would provoke inflation. Rising prices would reduce that country's trade competitiveness, exports would decline and imports rise, and gold would begin to flow back out again. Conversely, countries with trade deficits would experience an outflow of gold. As gold left the banking system, credit would contract. Credit contraction would cause a recession, and prices would adjust downward. Falling prices would enhance the trade competitiveness of the deficit country and gold would begin to flow back in, until eventually, equilibrium on the balance of trade would be re-established.

Under the gold standard, trade imbalances were both unsustainable and self-correcting. They were unsustainable because of the recessionary pressure they brought about in the deficit country. At the same time, they were self-correcting through changes in the relative prices of the two countries.

The gold standard also deterred governments from incurring budget deficits. With only a limited amount of credit available, government borrowing would drive up interest rates with negative consequences for the economy as the private sector found it more difficult to borrow and invest profitably as the cost of borrowing rose. This process came to be known as "crowding out," because government borrowing crowded out the private sector from the credit market. Government budget deficits also tended to result in trade deficits and gold outflows. Initially, higher government spending would stimulate the economy and result in greater demand for foreign products because the propensity to import tends to increase in line with the economic growth rate. However, once again, as economic growth accelerated and a trade deficit developed, gold would leave the country, interest rates would rise, and credit would contract until recession and falling prices would once again restore that country's trade competitiveness and its balance of trade. Recognizing these undesirable side effects of deficit spending, governments generally strove to maintain balanced budgets – at least so long as the country was at peace.

The Bretton Woods system had been a close substitute for the gold standard. Established during the final months of World War II to ensure the smooth functioning of the post-war international financial system, the Bretton Woods system created a fixed exchange rate system in which the U.S. dollar was pegged to gold at $35 per ounce and all other major currencies were pegged to the dollar at fixed rates. The value of the dollar was backed by the gold reserves of the U.S. government, and foreign governments were able to exchange US$35 for one ounce of gold on demand.

One of the goals of this system was to prevent countries from devaluing their currencies in order to gain advantages in trade, since the devaluations undertaken by numerous countries during the 1930s were believed to have contributed to the rise of trade barriers and the collapse of international trade that characterized that decade.

The arrangements put in place at Bretton Woods worked exceptionally well for more than 20 years, but began to come under strain in the second half of the 1960s. At that time, a number of factors, including heavy investment by U.S. corporations overseas and the United States' rapidly increasing military expenditure in Vietnam, contributed to a deterioration of the country's balance of payments. Other countries, which found themselves holding increasing amounts of dollars, began exchanging their dollar reserves for gold at the U.S. Federal Reserve. Initially, there was little concern as the amounts involved were relatively small, but, in the second half of the 1960s, they began to cause unease in Washington. By 1971, the trickle of gold leaving Fort Knox had become a torrent. In August of that year, President Nixon suspended the convertibility of dollars into gold. Subsequent attempts to patch up the system failed, and in 1973, the major trading powers agreed to allow their currencies to float freely against one another. The Bretton Woods era was over.

Like the classical gold standard, the Bretton Woods international monetary system contained inherent adjustment mechanisms that acted automatically to prevent persistent trade imbalances. Any such imbalances resulted in cross-border transfers of an internationally accepted store of value (either gold or dollars fully convertible into gold) and changes in national price levels in a manner that eventually restored equilibrium to the trade and fiscal balances. When Bretton Woods collapsed in the early 1970s, those automatic adjustment mechanisms ceased to function. In their absence, government budget deficits increased dramatically and current account imbalances between nations became immense and unyielding. In 1982, the U.S. budget deficit surpassed US$100 billion for the first time (see Figure 1.3). Two years later, the U.S. current account deficit did the same (see Figure 1.4). A long series of triple-digit deficits was to follow.

Such enormous budget and trade deficits would have been impossible under either the gold standard or the Bretton Woods system because of the inherent self-adjustment mechanism at the core of those systems. Under the gold standard, so much gold would have left the United States that the government would have been forced either to take measures to re-establish a balance of trade or else to suffer a devastating contraction of credit that would have thrown the economy into depression. Under the rules of the Bretton Woods system, the huge outflow of gold would have forced the government to take corrective measures or else withdraw currency from circulation since every dollar was required to be backed by a fixed amount of gold. A sharp reduction in currency in circulation would also have thrown

Figure 1.3 U.S. government budget balance (including off-balance-sheet items such as Social Security receipts), 1980–2000

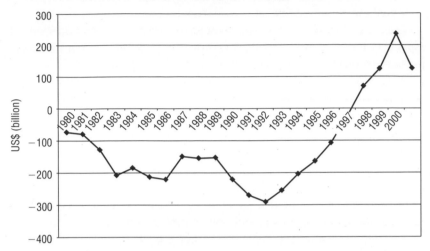

Source: Executive Office of the President of the United States, *Budget of the United States Government*, Historical Tables.

Figure 1.4 United States: Balance on the current account, 1980–2001

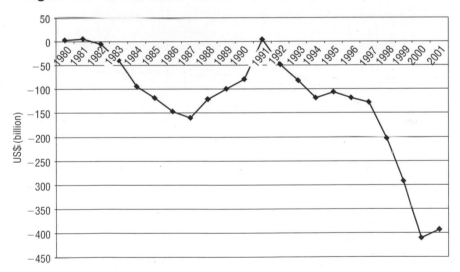

Source: Bureau of Economic Analysis.

the economy into depression. Under either system, the government would have had no choice but to restore the balance of trade.

The focus here is on the United States, not because it was the only country to experience trade deficits. It wasn't. Instead, the U.S. was unique in two other ways. First, the absolute size of its trade was extraordinarily large. Second, the United States was the only country able to finance its growing level of indebtedness to the rest of the world by issuing debt instruments denominated in its own currency.

When the United States refused to abide by the rules of Bretton Woods by suspending the convertibility of dollars into gold, the adjustment mechanism that had previously prevented persistent imbalances ceased to function. As if by magic, the constraints that had previously kept the trade deficits of the United States in check seemed to just disappear. The country was no longer required to pay for its imports with gold, or even with dollars backed by gold. Henceforth, the United States could pay for its imports with dollars with no backing of any kind, or with U.S. dollar-denominated debt instruments. The age of paper money had arrived and the amount of U.S. dollars in circulation began to explode. Figure 1.5 clearly demonstrates this point.

During the three decades since the collapse of Bretton Woods, the United States has incurred a cumulative current account deficit of more than US$3 trillion. As that amount of dollars entered the banking systems of those countries with a current account surplus against the United States, it set in motion a process of credit creation just as if the world had discovered an enormous new supply of gold. That creation of credit backed only by paper reserves has generated a worldwide credit bubble characterized by economic overheating and severe asset price inflation. That credit bubble is now

Figure 1.5   U.S. currency held by the public, 1890–2000

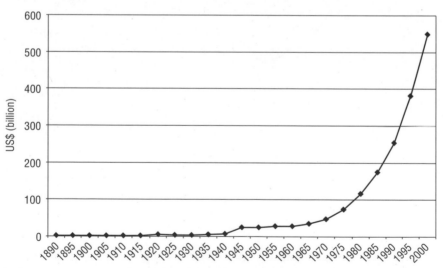

Sources: 1890–1970: U.S. Department of Commerce, Bureau of the Census, *Historical Statistics of the United States: Colonial Times to 1970*. 1975–95: IMF, *International Financial Statistics*, IMF Statistics Department. 2000: The Federal Reserve, *The Flow of Funds*, Table L.108.

precariously close to imploding, because much of that credit cannot be repaid. The economic house of cards built with paper dollars has begun to wobble. Its fall will once again teach the world why gold – not paper – has been the preferred store of value for thousands of years.

IMBALANCE OF PAYMENTS

As discussed at the beginning of this chapter, there has been explosive growth of the world's central bank reserves. This surge in international reserves has been comprised primarily of U.S. dollars and other U.S. dollar-denominated debt instruments that have become reserve assets as a result of the widening trade imbalances between the United States and the rest of the world over the last three decades. This multiplication of reserves is indicative of the extraordinary expansion of credit that those trade imbalances have facilitated (see Figure 1.6).

The enormous surge in foreign exchange held by central banks came about chiefly because of the large, persistent current account deficits experienced by the United States during this period. In those countries where central bank reserves increased most sharply, Japan in the 1980s and most of the other countries in Asia in the mid-1990s, excessive credit expansion caused an investment boom and asset price inflation in equity and property prices. Eventually, over-investment produced overcapacity, falling prices and

Figure 1.6 Total international reserves: All countries, 1949–2000

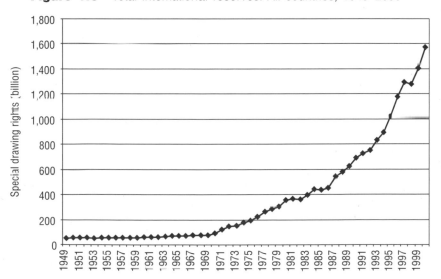

Source: IMF, *International Financial Statistics Yearbook 2001*.

falling profits that culminated in stock market crashes, corporate bankruptcies, bank failures, and deflation. By the end of the 1990s, a surge of capital inflows washed back into the United States, creating a stock-market bubble and a credit boom there. A repetition of the pattern established in Japan and replayed in South East Asia of stock market crashes, corporate bankruptcies, bank failures, and deflation is now under way in the U.S. The mechanics of the boom-and-bust cycle are the topic of Chapter 5. Here, we are interested in the origin of the worldwide economic bubble that is now beginning to implode.

This book contends that trade imbalances and trans-border capital flows are responsible for the current extraordinary disequilibrium in the global economy. As these imbalances are most easily understood using the balance of payments framework, a discussion of the concepts underlying balance of payments statistics is therefore necessary at this juncture. The balance of payments, the current account, the capital and financial account, the overall balance, and reserve assets are all concepts that require some explanation, as does their relationship to one another.

The International Monetary Fund (IMF) publishes a breakdown of every country's balance of payments in a monthly periodical, *International Financial Statistics*.[2] Those statistics are presented based on the methodology detailed in the fifth edition of the IMF's *Balance of Payments Manual*,[3] which was published in September 1993. That manual defines the balance of payments as "a statistical statement that systematically summarizes, for a specific time period, the economic transactions of an economy with the rest of the world."

The balance of payments (BOP) is comprised of two main groups of accounts, the current account and the capital and financial account. The current account pertains to transactions in goods and services, income, and current transfers between countries. The capital and financial account pertains to capital transfers and financial assets and liabilities. It measures net foreign investment or net lending/net borrowing vis-à-vis the rest of the world.

For the sake of simplicity, and without involving too much inaccuracy, the current account can be thought of as involving the trade in goods and services between countries, whereas the capital and financial account is concerned with capital flows between countries. A country with a current account surplus sells more in goods and services to other countries than it buys from other countries. A country with a surplus on its capital and financial account has experienced more capital inflows than capital outflows.

The following is a condensed outline of the standard components of the balance of payments:[4]

Standard Components of the Balance of Payments:
I.   **Current Account**
    A. Goods and Services
    B. Income
    C. Current Transfers
II. **Capital and Financial Account**
    A. Capital Account
    B. Financial Account
        1. Direct Investment
        2. Portfolio Investment
        3. Other Investment
        4. Reserve Assets

The following relationship between the standard components is also give in the manual:[5]

CAB = NKA + RT

Where

CAB = current account balance
NKA = net capital and financial account (i.e., all capital and financial
       transactions excluding reserve assets)
  RT = reserve asset transactions

This equation shows that the current account balance is necessarily equal (with sign reversed) to the net capital and financial account balance plus reserve asset transactions. This relationship shows that the net provision (as measured by the current account balance) of resources to or from the rest of the world must – by definition – be matched by a change in net claims on the rest of the world. For example, a current account surplus is reflected in an increase in net claims, which may be in the form of official or private claims, on nonresidents or in the acquisition of reserve assets on the part of the monetary authorities.[6]

This relationship is demonstrated in Table 1.1, which provides a summary of the most important items in the balance of payments for Japan, as given in the IMF's *International Financial Statistics* (*IFS*).

Table 1.1 Japan's balance of payments breakdown, 1993–97 (US$ billion)

	1993	1994	1995	1996	1997
Current account balance	131.64	130.26	111.04	65.88	94.35
Capital account balance	−1.46	−1.85	−2.23	−3.29	−4.05
Financial account balance	−102.21	−85.11	−64.98	−28.10	−118.05
Net errors and omissions	−0.50	−18.03	13.78	0.64	34.31
Overall balance	27.47	25.27	58.61	35.14	6.57
Reserves and related items	−27.47	−25.27	−58.61	−35.41	−6.57
Reserve assets	−27.47	−25.27	−58.61	−35.41	−6.57
Use of fund credit	−	−	−	−	−
Exceptional financing	−	−	−	−	−

Source: IMF, *International Financial Statistics Yearbook 2001.*

The term "overall balance" is defined in the introduction of *IFS* as "the sum of the balances of the current account, the capital account, the financial account, and net errors and omissions."[7] It is shown as line 78cbd in *IFS* in the breakdown of the BOP for each country. Throughout *IFS*, the line for the overall balance is immediately followed by the line showing reserves and related items (line 79dad), which is identical in amount to the overall balance. Reserves and related items are comprised of (1) reserve assets, (2) use of fund credit and loans, and (3) exceptional financing. As funds categorized under the latter two items are generally only utilized as emergency measures to fund the overall balance in case of crisis, most of the time the overall balance is equal to the change in the country's reserve assets.

In other words, whenever the current account is not exactly offset by the capital and financial account, the difference between the two appears as the overall balance. That overall balance is equal to the change in that country's reserve assets during that period.

The IMF is particularly concerned with situations where a country's reserve assets decline over an extended period. Its *Balance of Payments Manual* describes in some detail the IMF's opinion as to the appropriate policy response to such a situation. However, the manual offers much less on the subject of a protracted build-up in reserve assets, only: "The opposite situation (namely, a persistent current account surplus, inflow of capital, and substantial accumulation of reserve assets) occurs less often and generally does not pose as severe a problem for economic policy."[8]

There are two very important errors in that statement. First, there has been an extraordinary "accumulation of reserve assets" since the breakdown of Bretton Woods. All the "dragon" and "tiger" economies of Asia built up

Figure 1.7 Bubble fuel: Total reserves minus gold, 1970–96

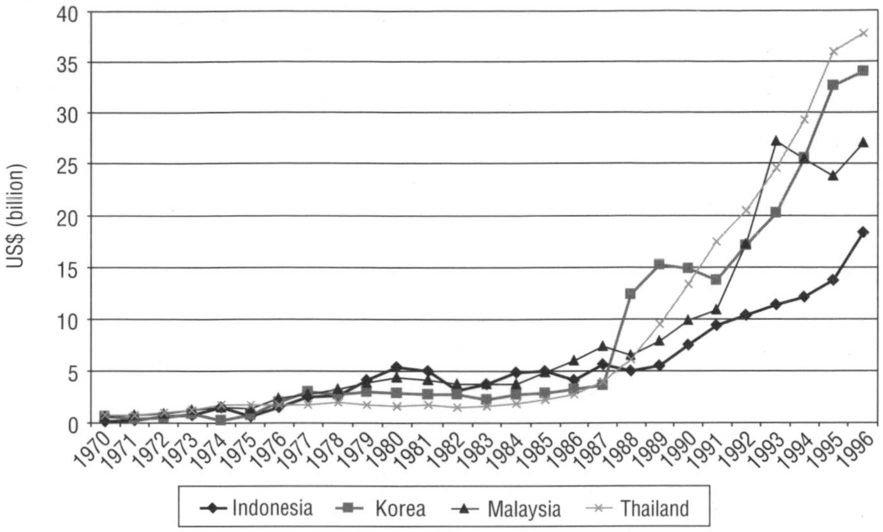

Source: IMF, *International Financial Statistics Yearbook 2001*.

enormous reserve assets in the 1980s and 1990s. So, to downplay the accumulation of reserve assets is misleading.

Second, the accumulation of reserve assets does pose a severe problem for economic policy. Policymakers in Japan and across much of the rest of Asia were unable to control the inflationary pressures inherent in imbalances in trade and capital flows that resulted in the accumulation of those reserves. As a consequence, bubble economies, characterized by extreme economic overheating and hyperinflation in asset prices, developed in their countries and then burst, leaving their financial sector in tatters and their governments deeply in debt.

The IMF statements regarding the substantial accumulation of reserve assets were made in the fifth, and most recent, edition of the *Balance of Payments Manual* which was published in 1993, before the Asia Crisis exposed "the Asian Miracle" as just one more credit bubble. Before the sixth edition is published, it is to be hoped that the IMF will come to recognize the significance of the link between the accumulation of reserve assets and liquidity (that is, credit) creation and to understand how and why the imbalances on the current account and/or the capital and financial account that result in a rapid build-up in reserve assets also cause economic overheating and hyperinflation in asset prices.

The reserve assets of a country rise when the overall balance of that country's balance of payments is in surplus or, expressed differently, when more money enters the country than leaves it. Such a situation can arise through a current account surplus, or because of a surplus on the capital and financial account. When more money enters a country than leaves it, that money (unless it is hidden in a mattress or destroyed) is almost always deposited into that country's banking system. When exogenous money enters a banking system, it sparks off a process of credit creation unless the central bank takes action to sterilize the capital inflows. When the sums entering a country are very large, and when the monetary authorities fail to absorb that inflow by issuing a sufficient amount of bonds to soak up the additional liquidity, the outcome is a rapid expansion of the money supply and the emergence of an economic bubble. That is what occurred in Japan and in the crisis-affected countries across Asia. Extraordinary amounts of foreign capital entered those economies, the money supply in those countries expanded rapidly, and bubble economies developed and then popped.

Up until those crises erupted, it was argued that monetary authorities across Asia had taken appropriate measures to prevent the inflow of foreign capital from disrupting their economies. In retrospect, however, the emergence of bubble economies in Japan and elsewhere in Asia is conclusive proof that the monetary authorities failed to take sufficient measures to prevent capital inflows from wrecking the economies they were responsible for regulating. Generally, in the crisis-affected countries in Asia, the surplus on the overall balance was so great and extended over so many years that it would have been expensive and impractical for the central bank to issue enough bonds to absorb the liquidity that those surpluses created. Moreover, it is always politically difficult for a central bank to cool down an economy that is overheating or to snuff out an asset price bubble as it develops. The events of the late 1990s show this to be no less true in the United States than it was in Japan in the 1980s or in Thailand in the early 1990s. Corrective measures tend not to be taken. Instead, the money supply is allowed to grow too quickly and concepts such as the "Asian Miracle" and the "New Paradigm" are allowed to develop to justify the excessive money supply growth. Eventually, the economic bubble pops, asset prices deflate, and the banking system becomes seriously impaired with non-performing loans.

Then, faith in economic miracles evaporates. However, even when it is understood that the recession came about because of the excesses inherent in the preceding boom, the origin of the boom generally remains unidentified. For example, what was the official explanation for the cause of the booms that preceded the implosion of the bubble economy in Japan, the Asia Crisis, or the crash of Nasdaq? Such explanations are rarely forthcoming. The explanation is obvious, nonetheless: the origin of almost every large-scale economic boom is credit creation. This brings us back to the concept of reserve assets.

Here, some further discussion of reserve assets is required. When the world was on a gold standard, gold was the only reserve asset. It was well understood that if much more gold entered a country than left it, economic overheating and inflation would occur. However, an adjustment mechanism was inherent within that system. When prices rose in the surplus country, its exports would decline and its imports would rise until balance was re-established.

Things have become much more complicated following the breakdown of Bretton Woods. To understand why, it is necessary to understand how the nature of reserve assets has changed. Today, gold only makes up a small percentage of the world's reserve assets. The bulk of the reserves are now comprised of foreign exchange. The *Balance of Payments Manual* provides the following list of components that make up reserve assets under the current international monetary arrangements.[9]

The Composition of Reserve Assets

Reserve Assets:
1. Monetary Gold
2. Special Drawing Rights
3. Reserve Position in the Fund
4. Foreign Exchange
   a. Currenty and Deposits
      i. With Monetary Authorities
      ii. With Banks
   b. Securities
      i. Equities
      II. Bonds and Notes
      iii. Money Market Instruments and Financial Derivatives
5. Other Claims

Clearly, there is a very great difference between reserve assets under the gold standard and reserve assets today. Under the gold standard, reserve assets were comprised of gold. Today, reserve assets are comprised of currency and deposits, and equities, bonds, and money market instruments. The crucial difference between the reserve assets then and now is that gold could not be created by a government or by any other entity to finance a balance of payments deficit, whereas currency, deposits, equities, bonds, and money market instruments are all financial instruments that can be created, either by a government or by the private sector.

Today, it is not necessary that such instruments be created specifically for the purpose of financing a balance of payments deficit. It is only necessary that such instruments exist and that those countries with a balance of payments surplus are willing to hold such financial instruments. Only when surplus countries acquire such instruments from deficit countries do those assets become reserve assets. Expressed differently, in the earlier period, deficit countries were required to pay for their deficits in gold; today, deficit countries may settle their deficits with debt – as long as the counterparty surplus countries are willing to hold their debt as reserve assets.

As the preceding paragraphs make clear, the nature and composition of reserve assets today are very different from those that characterized reserve assets under the gold standard. Those changes make a tremendous difference in how the global economy functions. The substitution of financial instruments in the place of gold as an acceptable means of settling balance of payments deficits has allowed international trade to expand much more rapidly than would have been possible under a gold standard, because it has allowed the United States to accumulate a cumulative current account deficit of more than US$3 trillion since the collapse of Bretton Woods. Current account imbalances were not sustainable under a gold standard. Then, surplus countries experienced inflation as gold reserves caused their money supply to expand and deficit countries experienced deflation as their gold reserves contracted and caused the money supply there to contract. Through this change in relative prices, the balance of trade was restored.

The global economy has benefited in many ways from the acceleration of international trade made possible by the breakdown of the Bretton Woods system. Nevertheless, there are three fatal flaws in the current system under which countries accept debt instruments as reserve assets. One of those flaws should be obvious to anyone who witnessed the rise and fall of the Japanese bubble economy or the Asia Crisis. That flaw is this: the current international monetary system produces credit bubbles that inflict severe damage on national economies when they burst. Just as occurred under the gold standard, countries with large, multi-year overall balance of payments surpluses develop overheated economies and extreme asset price inflation as foreign capital enters the domestic banking system and causes excessive credit creation. This is what happened in Japan in the 1980s and the other crisis-affected countries in Asia in the 1990s. Exactly how this process unfolded will be demonstrated in the next chapter.

However, the converse – that is, credit contraction and economic depression – did not occur in the major deficit country, the United States, because it was not required to settle its current account deficits in gold, but was permitted to pay with debt instruments instead. Consequently, the current international monetary system is lopsided. The adjustment mechanism that prevented protracted current account imbalance under the gold standard does not exist in the present international monetary arrangements. The present system has allowed current account imbalances to arise that are unprecedented in both their size and longevity. Over the last two decades, many countries in the world have grown to be dependent on exporting more to the United States than they import from that country. However, those countries that have been most successful at this strategy of export-led growth, the same countries that have built up enormous foreign exchange reserves comprised of U.S. dollar-denominated debt instruments, have suffered tremendously from the economic overheating and hyperinflation in asset prices that were by-products of their surpluses.

While the United States did not suffer credit contraction and an economic slump, as it would have under a gold standard, it has accumulated a tremendous amount of debt to the rest of the world. Its net international investment position is now approximately US$2.3 trillion in the red, an amount equivalent to 23% of its GDP (see Figure 1.8). That brings us to the second major flaw in the current international monetary arrangement. Much of the world has grown dependent on exporting more to, than they import from, the United States, but the rapid increase in the indebtedness of the U.S. to the rest of the world, which is the flip side of other countries' surpluses, is not sustainable. At present, the U.S. current account deficit is approximately US$50 million an hour. That is roughly the rate at which its indebtedness is rising. How much longer will the rest of the world be willing

Figure 1.8   The net international investment position of the United States (at market costs), 1982–2001

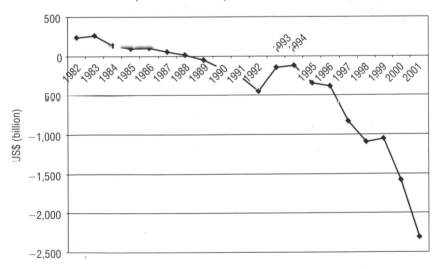

Source: Bureau of Economic Analysis.

to accept debt instruments from the United States in exchange for real goods and services? It is only a matter of time before the United States will no longer be considered creditworthy. In fact, it really is only a matter of time before the United States will *not be* creditworthy. This is the reason that a dollar crisis is inevitable. Before the passage of too many more years, the dollar will depreciate very sharply against other currencies and gold. The era of export-led growth will then come to an end. From that time on, the U.S. current account deficit will no longer be able to function as the engine of global growth as it has for the last two decades.

Finally, the third major flaw in the dollar standard is that it generates deflation at the consumer price level. By flooding the world with dollar liquidity, this system has facilitated an extraordinary surge in credit creation around the world, which has permitted over-investment and a tragic misallocation of capital. That over-investment is now culminating in falling product prices across most industries. Falling prices are undermining corporate profitability and resulting in widespread corporate distress. Deflation has once again become a serious threat to global prosperity for the first time since the 1930s.

To summarize, the current international monetary system has three inherent flaws that will eventually cause it to collapse in crisis. First, it allows certain countries to sustain large current account or capital and financial account surpluses over long periods, but it causes those countries to experience extraordinary economic boom-and-bust cycles that wreck their banks and undermine the fiscal health of their governments. Its second flaw is that this system has made the well-being of the global economy dependent on a steady acceleration in the indebtedness of the United States, a state of affairs that is obviously not sustainable. The third flaw is that it generates deflation.

CREDIT CREATION

To complete the argument set forth in this chapter that trade imbalances have caused excessive credit creation, it only remains to demonstrate how an overall balance of payments surplus causes money supply to expand.

It has been shown above that the surplus on the overall balance is equal to the change in reserve assets.[10] Thus, when the overall balance is in surplus, a country's reserve assets increase. Reserve assets are those "external assets readily available to and controlled by monetary authorities." Therefore, when a country's overall balance is in surplus, the external assets readily available to and controlled by its monetary authorities also increase.

The *Balance of Payments Manual* indicates that reserve assets may, in some cases, include external assets owned by commercial banks, as well as those directly owned by the monetary authorities.[11] However, the *IFS* statistics on reserve assets do not provide a breakdown between those directly owned by the monetary authorities and those which are merely readily available to and controlled by them. Therefore, two possibilities exist. Either the monetary authorities have acquired those external assets directly, or those external assets are actually owned by commercial banks, although the monetary authorities have some control over their use. The question to be resolved is, "What impact does rising reserve assets have on the money supply under each scenario?"

In the first instance, where the monetary authorities own the reserve assets, it would have been necessary for those assets to have been acquired by the monetary authorities. Monetary authorities acquire assets by paying for them with newly created currency, sometimes referred to as high-powered money. Clearly, then, the money supply must increase when monetary authorities issue new currency to acquire foreign assets. In such instances, the monetary authorities could reverse the impact of such transactions by issuing bonds in the same amount as the newly created currency. The consequences of this method of absorbing liquidity will be discussed below.

In the second scenario, where the reserve assets are actually owned by commercial banks, the impact of an increase in such assets on the money supply is even more direct. When foreign assets enter the banking system as deposits, being exogenous to the system, they will cause the money supply to rise as they are lent, redeposited, and re-lent numerous times. In this way, they have the same effect as that of high-powered money injected into the banking system by the monetary authorities, in that they set off a process of credit creation through the commercial banking system that results in expanding money supply growth. Here, too, by issuing an equivalent amount of bonds, it is possible for the monetary authorities to neutralize the impact that the increase in the foreign assets owned by commercial banks has on the money supply.

The method of neutralizing the impact of rising reserve assets on the money supply is the same regardless of whether those assets are owned directly by the monetary authorities or by the commercial banks. As explained above, it requires the monetary authorities to sell an equivalent amount of bonds to the public to soak up the undesired liquidity. However, such an exercise can become very expensive when large amounts are involved, because such bonds must offer a rate of interest in line with other debt instruments in order to attract investors. When reserve assets are growing at a rapid rate, as was the case in Japan in the 1980s and in much of the rest of Asia during the 10 years preceding the Asia Crisis, the interest expense involved in issuing bonds can be prohibitively high. That must explain, at least in large part, why the monetary authorities in Japan and the other crisis-affected countries in Asia failed to prevent the excessive money supply growth that led to economic overheating and hyperinflation of asset prices in their countries.

Other policy mistakes may also have been involved in the emergence of the bubble economies across Asia. It is not necessary to analyze all of them here. The point of this chapter has been to demonstrate how large balance of payments imbalances have caused global economic disequilibrium. In Chapter 2, the crises in Japan and Thailand will serve to provide concrete examples of how this occurred. The crucial characteristic that those crises, as well as those in the other crisis-affected Asian countries, had in common was that in one way or another, either through trade surpluses or extraordinary capital inflows, foreign assets entered the banking system of the country affected and, acting as high-powered money, sparked off, through a process of credit creation and over-investment, an unsustainable surge in asset prices and economic activity that ended in severe recession, a systemic banking crisis, and drastically higher government debt.

► REFERENCES

1   Ludwig von Mises, *Human Action: A Treatise on Economics* (Yale University Press, 1949).
2   International Monetary Fund (IMF), *International Financial Statistics*, prepared by the IMF Statistics Department.
3   IMF, *Balance of Payments Manual*, 5th edn. (1993).
4   Ibid., Appendix I, Table 7, p. 132 (abbreviated).
5   Ibid., Appendix V, p. 160.
6   Ibid.
7   IMF, *International Financial Statistics Yearbook 2001*, p. xxiii.
8   IMF, *Balance of Payments Manual*, op. cit., p. 165.
9   Ibid., Appendix I, Table 7, p. 138.
10 Except in unusual circumstances when "use of fund credit and loans" or "exceptional financing" occurs.
11 IMF, *Balance of Payments Manual*, op. cit., p. 98.

Chapter 2

Effervescent Economies

Bubble: Something insubstantial, groundless, or ephemeral, especially:
a. A fantastic or impracticable idea or belief; an illusion.
b. A speculative scheme that comes to nothing.

— Dictionary.com

Chapter 1 demonstrated how U.S. balance of payments deficits undermined the Bretton Woods international monetary system and caused a dramatic rise in international reserve assets comprised primarily of U.S. dollars. For individual countries, the rapid accumulation of reserves has proved to be a curse rather than a blessing, however. Those countries that have experienced a sudden, sharp growth in reserves became caught up in a domestic investment boom accompanied by rampant asset price inflation that eventually ended in financial calamity. The bubble economy that developed in Japan during the second half of the 1980s perfectly illustrates this point, as does the Asian Miracle bubble that followed in the 1990s.

▶ THE GREAT JAPANESE BUBBLE

By the end of the 1980s, land prices in Japan had risen to such an extent that the Imperial Gardens in Tokyo were said to be worth more than the state of California. Property prices were not the only evidence of Japan's bubble economy. Share prices commonly traded on price-earnings multiples of over 100 times. The Nikkei Index peaked above 38,000 in 1989. Recently, it fell below 9,000. Clearly, asset prices were extraordinarily inflated. Surging credit expansion was responsible for the runaway asset price inflation; and the unprecedented trade surpluses Japan had accumulated in the years following the breakdown of Bretton Woods had made that expansion of credit possible. As the surpluses were deposited into the banking system, money supply expanded remarkably, economic growth accelerated, and asset prices skyrocketed. The extraordinary surge in the Japanese stock market is shown in Figure 2.1.

Japan had become a major exporting power by the late 1960s. By then, it had fully recovered from its defeat in World War II and had once again become a formidable industrial power. The country's rising international

Figure 2.1   Japan's share price index, 1968–97 (1990 = 100)

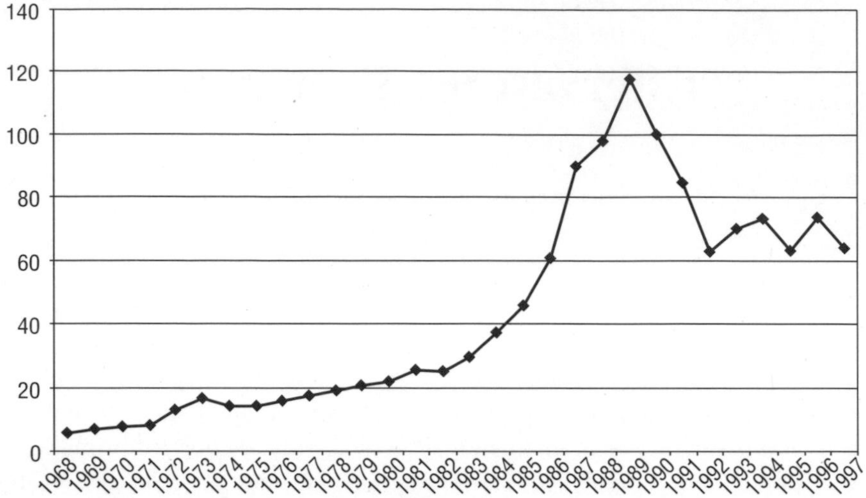

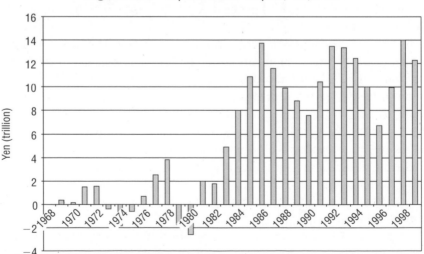

Source: IMF, *International Financial Statistics*.

reserves bore witness to the success of Japan's strategy of export-led growth. During the 1970s, the two oil shocks held Japan's trade surplus more or less in check, but from 1981 onward the country began to record an uninterrupted string of trade surpluses (see Figure 2.2). As those surpluses were deposited into Japan's banking system, they acted as high-powered money and set off an explosion of credit creation.

Figure 2.2   Japan's trade surplus, 1968–99

Source: IMF, *International Financial Statistics*.

Japan's trade surpluses in the 1970s appear small compared with those of the 1980s. However, relative to the size of the Japanese economy and monetary base at the end of the 1960s, they were nevertheless very significant. Furthermore, Japan also attracted net capital inflows during this period. These, too, not only boosted international reserves, but also entered the banking system as deposits and contributed to the growth of money supply and credit creation.

Between 1968 and 1978, Japan's international reserves (total reserves minus gold) soared 1,146% (see Figure 2.3). Japanese money supply (money plus quasi-money) increased by 356%.

Therefore, it is important to keep in mind that when the period of extraordinarily large trade and current account imbalances began in the early 1980s, they had been preceded by a 10-year period when Japan's money supply had already expanded at a galloping rate (see Figure 2.4).

In 1977, Japan began publishing a much more detailed breakdown of its balance of payments. From that point on, it is much easier to visualize exactly how foreign capital entered and left the country. That information is summarized in Figure 2.5.

As Japan's current account surplus began to expand at an extraordinary rate in the early 1980s, the country began to export capital in amounts that were almost as large as its current account surpluses. So long as capital exports (shown as the financial account deficit) were as large as the current

Figure 2.3   Japan: Total reserves minus gold, 1968–78

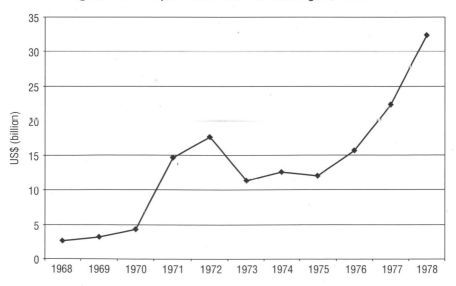

Source: IMF, *International Financial Statistics*.

Figure 2.4   Japan: Money supply, 1968–78

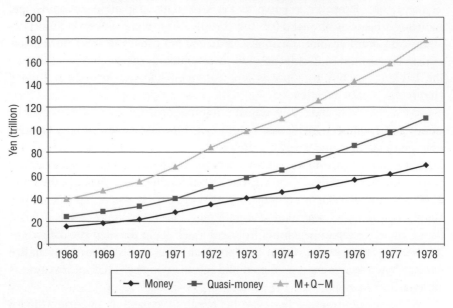

Source: IMF, *International Financial Statistics*.

Figure 2.5   Japan: Breakdown of balance of payments, 1977–99

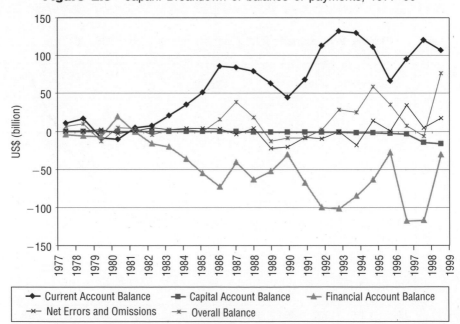

Source: IMF, *International Financial Statistics*.

account surplus, there was little impact on the country's overall balance of payments, meaning that the international reserves held by Japan remained unchanged. However, in years when capital exports were insufficient to offset the current account surplus, such as 1986–88, then the overall balance went into surplus, causing international reserves to rise.

As can be seen in Figure 2.6, Japan's inability to export sufficient capital to offset its current account surplus resulted in its international reserves rising by 260% between the end of 1985 and the end of 1988. With more money entering the country than leaving it, it is not surprising that money supply growth also accelerated during this period, growing at the fastest rate since the 1970s (see Figure 2.7). In 1989, quasi-money grew by 15%, a rate of growth last experienced in Japan in 1975. Nor is it surprising that, after so many years of trade surpluses, rising international reserves, and swelling money supply, a new surge in all these factors in the mid-1980s would cause such drastic overheating of the Japanese economy in the late 1980s.

One of the themes of this book is that when national economies are flooded with foreign capital inflow, regardless of whether the capital enters the country as a result of trade surpluses or capital account surpluses, it causes economic overheating and asset price inflation.

How differently the Japanese economy would have evolved had it not accumulated such large trade surpluses year after year. The country's

Figure 2.6   Japan: Total reserves minus gold, 1978–88

Source: IMF, *International Financial Statistics*.

Figure 2.7   Japan: Money supply growth, 1982–91

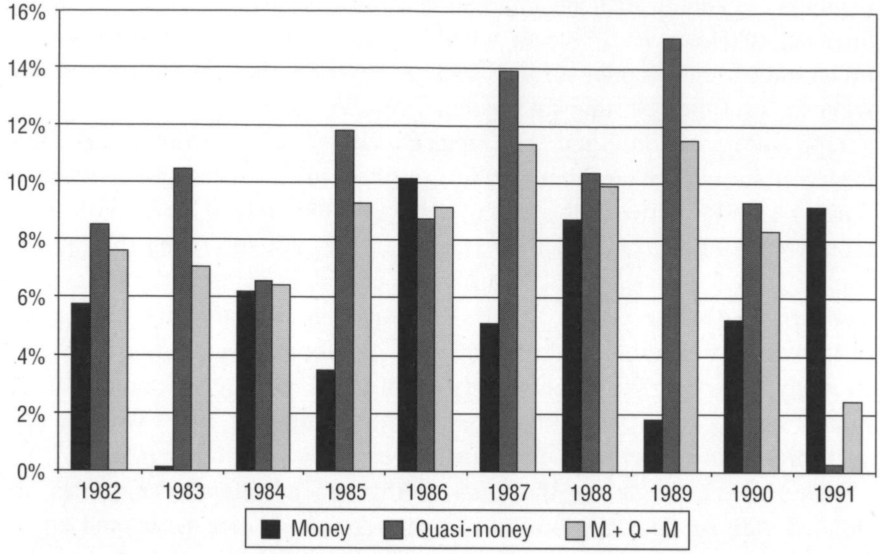

Source: IMF, *International Financial Statistics*.

cumulative trade surplus between 1968 and 1989 was ¥75 trillion. Over the same period, its international reserves expanded from US$3 billion to US$84 billion.

There can be no question that those trade surpluses directly benefited Japanese exporters and the people they employed. Clearly, there would also have been a multiplier effect, as those firms and their employees spent money in the domestic economy. Without the purchasing power derived from the trade surplus, Japan's economy would have grown at a much slower pace. This is very well understood.

What is much less appreciated is the expansionary impact that those surpluses had on domestic credit as they were deposited into the Japanese banking system. Each year that foreign capital entered Japan's banks, it acted as high-powered money and permitted credit creation. The rapid credit growth that Japan experienced during the 1970s and 1980s (see Figure 2.8) would not have been possible without those foreign capital inflows. There simply would not have been sufficient deposits to permit so many loans.

The rapid rise in deposit growth, money supply, and credit was only possible because of the surge in foreign capital entering Japan. Moreover, once deposited into the banking system, the foreign capital could be lent not only once, but, because of the process of credit creation through the banking system, the original amount could be lent and re-lent multiple times. So, while

Figure 2.8   Japan: Domestic credit growth, 1971–89

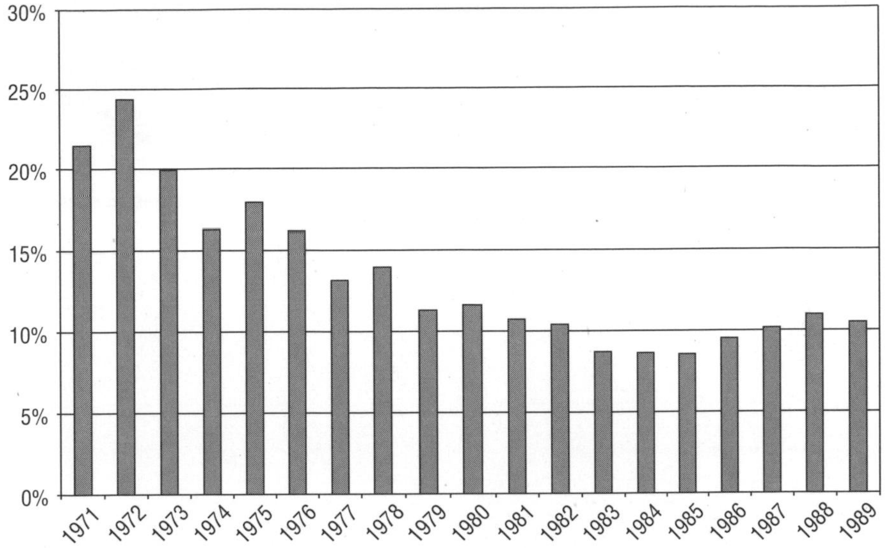

Source: IMF, *International Financial Statistics*.

there is no question that the Japanese economy was boosted by the direct benefit that exporters and their employees reaped from the trade surplus, that was not what caused Japan's economy to overheat. Instead, it was the capital inflows into Japan's banks and the extraordinary credit creation that those inflows permitted that caused the great Japanese bubble economy.

The role of credit in creating the bubble is illustrated in Figure 2.9, which shows that the ratio of domestic credit to GDP in Japan rose from 135% in 1970 to 265% in 1989.

All credit bubbles ultimately end in deflation because the purchasing power of the public does not increase quickly enough to absorb the surge in production that results from extended periods of easy credit. In other words, the ability of the public to buy does not increase in line with the capacity of industry to produce. When product prices begin to fall, debtors find they are no longer able to pay interest on their debt. Bankruptcies follow, credit contracts, and the economy enters recession. The Japanese bubble ended the same way.

The surge in domestic credit brought about a sharp rise in gross fixed capital formation, share prices, and property values. Japanese industrial production rose 25% between 1986 and 1989 (see Table 2.1).

The phenomenon of asset price bubbles also plays an important role in boom-and-bust cycles. As credit expands, asset prices rapidly inflate,

Figure 2.9   Japan: Domestic credit as a percentage of GDP, 1970–89

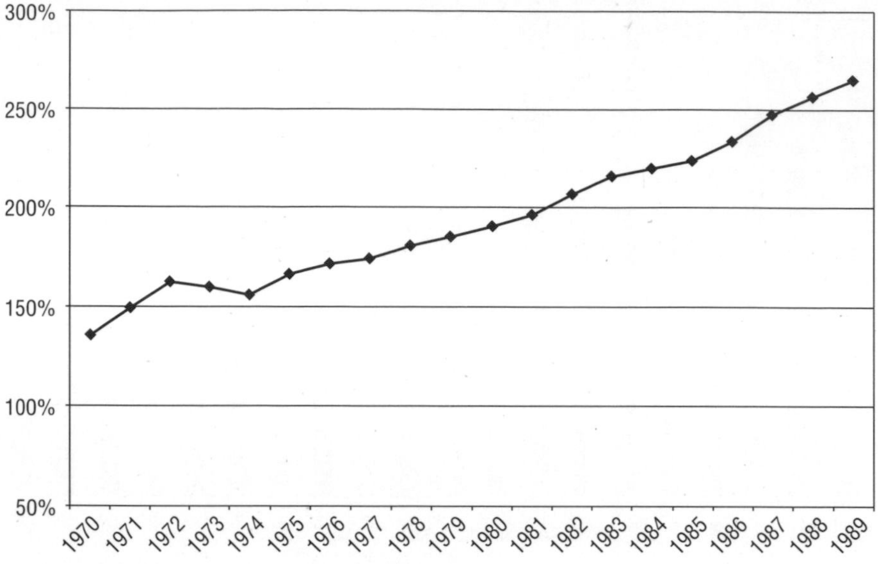

Source: IMF, *International Financial Statistics*.

creating a positive wealth effect that spurs consumption and causes the rate of economic expansion to accelerate. Eventually, however, prices rise so much faster than overall income that it becomes impossible to pay the interest on the credit that financed the acquisition of those assets. Then, bankruptcies surge, financial sector distress begins, credit starts to contract, and asset prices plunge, creating a negative wealth effect that deters consumption and undermines the rest of the economy.

The bubble in Japan popped in 1990 because over-investment had created overcapacity throughout the domestic economy. Excess capacity exerted downward pressure on prices and profits. Slowing earnings were incompatible with frighteningly inflated share prices. When the Nikkei Index began to plunge in 1990, the game was up and the bubble began to implode. Industrial production rose 1.8% in 1991 and then declined 10.4% over the next two years. Wholesale prices, which had been exceptionally weak in the mid-1980s due to the collapse in oil prices, rose 0.2% in 1991 and then fell steadily through 1995, a decline of 8% over four years that was a clear indication that the supply of goods exceeded demand at the wholesale level. Credit growth slowed sharply, reflecting a lack of viable investment opportunities in Japan's glutted markets in spite of rapidly declining interest rates. Finally, the stock market and property prices began to collapse in a slump that has subsequently reduced stock prices by 75% and property values by more than 50%.

Table 2.1 Japan: As reserves expanded, the economy boomed, 1981–92

	Total reserves minus gold (% change)	Domestic credit (a) formation (% change)	Gross fixed capital index (% change)	Industrial production (% change)	Share price index (% change)	Wholesale price index (% change)
1981	14.6	9.8	4.1	1.0	16.6	1.4
1982	−17.4	9.2	1.0	0.3	0	1.8
1983	5.6	8.1	−0.1	2.9	17.9	−2.2
1984	7.3	8.1	5.4	9.5	25.9	−0.2
1985	1.1	9.2	5.6	3.7	22.2	−0.1
1986	58.4	9.1	3.8	−0.2	32.8	−9.2
1987	91.5	15.4	8.7	3.4	47.9	−3.7
1988	19.4	13.1	12.0	10.0	8.9	−1.0
1989	−13.1	12.3	10.5	5.8	20.4	2.6
1990	−6.5	10.5	11.4	4.1	−15.1	2.0
1991	−8.2	6.3	4.9	1.8	−15.5	0.2
1992	−0.6	4.6	−0.1	−6.1	−25.9	−1.5

Source: IMF, International Financial Statistics.

This pattern of extraordinary foreign capital inflows leading to an acceleration of lending, over-investment, overcapacity, and asset bubbles followed by falling prices and economic collapse was repeated all across Asia from the mid-1980s to the mid-1990s. It had been called an economic miracle, but, in its later stages, it was only a credit bubble. Developments in Thailand clearly demonstrate this sequence of events.

THE ASIAN MIRACLE BUBBLE

The most miraculous thing about the Asian Miracle was how big the economic bubble in Asia became before it popped. It should have surprised no one that small economies grow very rapidly when inundated by enormous amounts of foreign capital. Almost everyone, however, including government policymakers, the IMF, bankers, and stockbrokers, failed to understand that the foreign capital inflows were creating an unsustainable economic boom. Even now, the unwillingness of those players to admit they were misguided has prevented the obvious explanation for the crisis from becoming commonly understood and accepted. Consequently, the most prevalent theory is still that the Asia Crisis was caused by the sudden outflow of foreign capital in 1997, when, in fact, it was not the outflow of capital, but the huge inflow of foreign funds during the preceding 10 years, that had created the bubble in the first place. The outflow of funds was only part and parcel of the panic that occurred as the Asian credit bubble imploded.

The pattern of events was quite similar in all the crisis-affected countries: Thailand, South Korea, Malaysia, and Indonesia. Here, Thailand will be used as the case study to illustrate how the Asian Miracle inflated and then popped.

As in the case of Japan, Thailand's economic bubble was characterized by rapid economic growth and rapid asset price inflation. The boom began in the mid-1980s when Japan, in response to a sharply appreciating yen, began to relocate its manufacturing capacity to the rest of Asia. Direct foreign investment from Japan put an end to the 1984 recession. By 1986 the boom had begun. Money supply accelerated and GDP expanded at double-digit rates. By 1990, property prices across the country had risen between 400% and 1,000%, and the surge in the stock market had exceeded all past records (see Figure 2.10).

Unlike what had occurred in Japan, however, Thailand's bubble economy came about not due to a trade or current account surplus, but rather despite an impressive string of current account deficits (see Figure 2.11).

Nevertheless, just as in Japan, the bubble in Thailand was caused by extraordinary amounts of foreign capital entering the banking system and

Figure 2.10 The Stock Exchange of Thailand Index, 1988–2001 (year end)

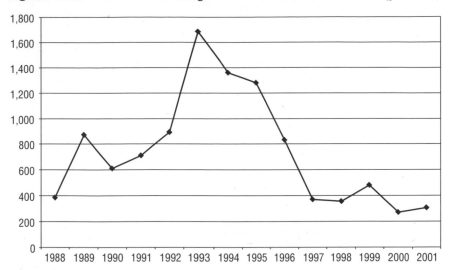

Source: Bloomberg.

Figure 2.11 Thailand: Current account balance, 1980–96

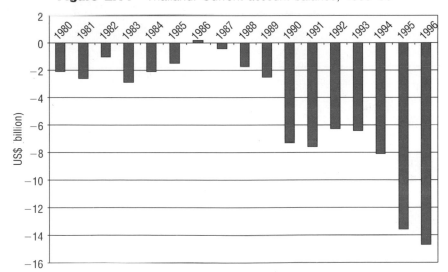

Source: IMF, *International Financial Statistics*.

resulting in excessive credit creation. In Thailand's case, this did not result from trade surpluses, but rather from surpluses on the financial account (see Figure 2.12).

Figure 2.12   Thailand: Financial account balance, 1980–96

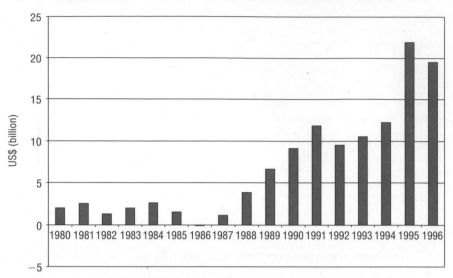

Source: IMF, International Financial Statistics.

Foreign capital entered the kingdom in various ways: as direct foreign investment, as portfolio investment in the stock market, as bank loans, and as deposits which were placed in Thai financial institutions to take advantage of the high interest rates on offer. These capital inflows were so large that they more than offset the country's large current account deficit and resulted in an extraordinary build-up in foreign exchange reserves. The annual increase in international reserves is reflected in Figure 2.13 as the surplus on the overall balance.

Thailand's international reserves rose from US$1.9 billion in 1984 to US$37.7 billion in 1996, an increase of 1,884% over a 12-year period. It is little wonder that a credit bubble developed (see Figure 2.14).

Regardless of the original reason that the money entered the country, eventually that money entered the banking system and, as it was deposited into Thai banks, money supply exploded (see Figure 2.15).

This rapid expansion of Thailand's money supply was not due to the Bank of Thailand printing money. As Figure 2.16 demonstrates, most of the increase was in quasi-money, defined as time, savings, and foreign currency deposits. Deposits multiplied as unprecedented amounts of foreign funds entered the country.

Before demonstrating how this flood of capital inflows transformed Thailand's economy, it should be noted that the largest part of the capital entering Thailand came from Japan, which attempted, but ultimately failed,

Figure 2.13 Thailand: Breakdown of the balance of payments, 1980–96

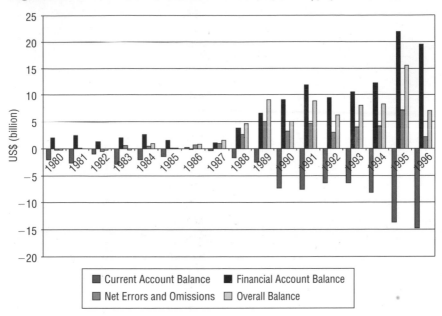

Source: IMF, *International Financial Statistics*.

Figure 2.14 Thailand: Total reserves minus gold, 1984–96

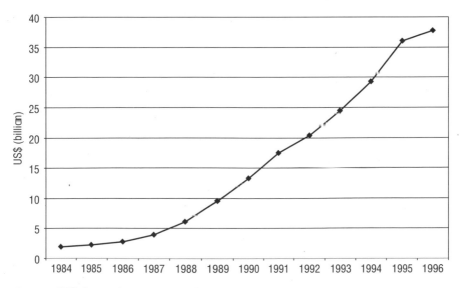

Source: IMF, *International Financial Statistics*.

Figure 2.15 Thailand: Growth in money plus quasi-money, 1984–96

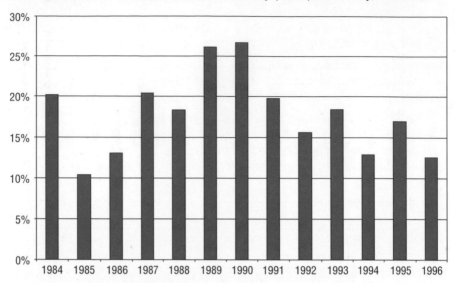

Source: IMF, *International Financial Statistics*.

Figure 2.16 Thailand: Money supply, 1983–96

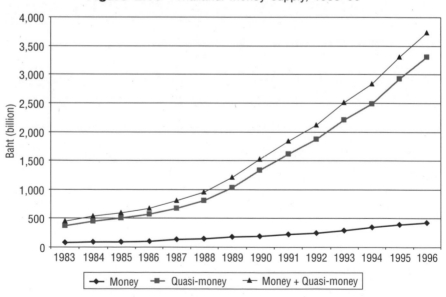

Source: IMF, *International Financial Statistics*.

to prevent its enormous current account surpluses from causing domestic overheating by exporting huge sums of capital abroad. It must be recognized that Japan's giant current account surpluses after 1982 not only created the bubble economy in Japan, but were also responsible for the bubble economies which later developed all across Asia.

As Table 2.2 and Figure 2.17 illustrate, Thailand's boom began in earnest in 1987 after the country's international reserves began to surge in 1986.

In 1988, when domestic credit expanded by 29%, Thailand's GDP increased by 13.3%. Over the next seven years, up through the end of 1995, this astonishing economic expansion continued. The annual growth in central bank reserves averaged 29.5%, domestic credit growth averaged 28.7% annually, and the GDP increased by approximately 9% on average – and all this despite serious social and political unrest in 1991 and 1992!

Beyond all question, this was a credit bubble of terrifying proportions. Initially, direct foreign investment and portfolio investment in equities combined were a more important source of foreign capital than bank loans. By 1993, however, debt began to swamp equity as the primary source of foreign capital entering the kingdom (see Table 2.3). Thai corporations found they could raise large sums on the international bond market, and foreign banks became increasingly eager to lend in Thailand. By then, much of the incoming capital was in the form of "non-resident deposits" – that is, short-term "hot money" deposited in Thai financial institutions in order to benefit from the high interest rates on offer there. Equity investment also became increasingly short-term and speculative in nature. For instance, a

Table 2.2   Thailand: The relationship between reserves, credit, and GDP, 1984–95

	Total reserves minus gold (% change)	Domestic credit (% change)	Gross fixed capital formation (% change)	SET Index (% change)	GPD (% change)
1984	18.8	14.9	7.0	5.9	5.8
1985	15.8	9.8	1.6	−5.2	4.7
1986	27.3	4.5	1.8	53.5	5.5
1987	42.9	20.0	23.0	37.5	9.5
1988	52.5	29.3	33.2	35.7	13.3
1989	55.7	33.6	34.4	127.3	12.2
1990	40.0	36.3	37.2	−30.3	11.6
1991	31.6	22.7	18.2	10.1	8.1
1992	16.6	24.8	6.7	25.6	7.6
1993	20.1	26.3	12.1	88.4	7.8
1994	19.6	31.2	13.4	−19.2	8.0
1995	22.9	26.0	16.5	−5.8	8.0

Sources: IMF, *International Financial Statistics*; Stock Exchange of Thailand; NESDB.

Figure 2.17 Thailand: Domestic credit growth, 1984–2000

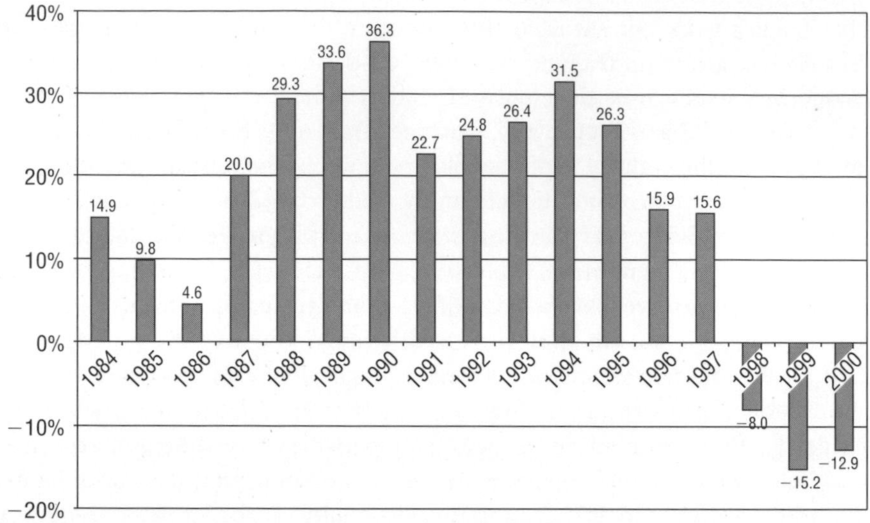

Source: IMF, *International Financial Statistics Yearbook 2001*.

Table 2.3 Thailand: Sources of foreign capital, 1984–95

	Direct investment	Portfolio investment		Bank loans
		Equity	Debt	
	(US$ bn)	(US$ bn)	(US$ bn)	(US$ bn)
1984	0.4	0.03	0.1	0.1
1985	0.2	0.04	0.9	−0.4
1986	0.3	0.1	−0.1	−0.6
1987	0.4	0.5	−0.2	0.2
1988	1.1	0.4	0.09	1.0
1989	1.8	1.4	0.06	0.7
1990	2.4	0.4	−0.5	1.0
1991	2.0	0.04	−0.1	0.2
1992	2.1	0.5	0.5	1.8
1993	1.8	2.7	2.8	6.6
1994	1.3	−0.4	2.9	14.3
1995	2.1	2.1	2.0	13.2

Source: IMF, *International Financial Statistics*.

sudden surge in hedge fund-driven foreign investment in listed equities drove the stock-market index up 75% in the last quarter of 1993 alone.

A tightening of interest rate policy in the United States in early 1994 caused a sharp correction on the stock market that year but did nothing to slow foreign bank lending, which more than doubled from US$6.6 billion in

1993 to US$14.3 billion in 1994, an amount equivalent to more than 8% of the size of the entire Thai economy.

A credit-driven investment boom of this magnitude was clearly unsustainable. Domestic industries of all descriptions dramatically increased their capacity as quickly as they could obtain new funds. Overcapacity became pervasive. Oversupply was most obvious in Bangkok's glutted property market, where an extraordinary building boom brought about an increase in supply of office space on the order of 400% between 1986 and 1995, giving rise to the joke that the crane was Thailand's national bird. Naturally, rents plummeted as vacancy rates soared. Likewise, in other industries: as overcapacity became the norm, product prices plunged. Corporate profit growth slowed and then turned negative.

Thailand's bubble economy hovered uncertainly through the long, unprofitable months of 1996. By the end of that year, the stock-market index had fallen below the 1,000 level for the first time since 1993 and it was clear that much worse was in store.

Finally, with a prick heard around the world, Thailand's bubble economy met its inevitable fate on July 2, 1997, when currency traders forced the devaluation of the Thai baht, ending its quasi-peg to the U.S. dollar that had existed for more than a decade. Subsequently, the baht lost more than 50% of its value against the dollar, and the Thai stock market fell by approximately 95% (in dollar terms) from its all-time high reached in late 1993.

Just as in the case of Japan, excessive inflows of foreign capital caused an expansion of reserve assets and commercial bank deposits that permitted an acceleration in lending. In both instances, bubble economies formed and then popped when overcapacity caused prices and profits to contract. Even today, industrial capacity utilization is less than 55%, and the vacancy rate in the property market in Bangkok exceeds 30%.

The extraordinary build-up in international reserves of the other crisis-affected countries from the mid-1980s is sufficient to demonstrate that the same pattern of capital inflows leading to excessive monetary expansion and economic overheating occurred across the region and was responsible for one of the greatest economic boom-and-bust cycles of the 20th century (see Figure 2.18).

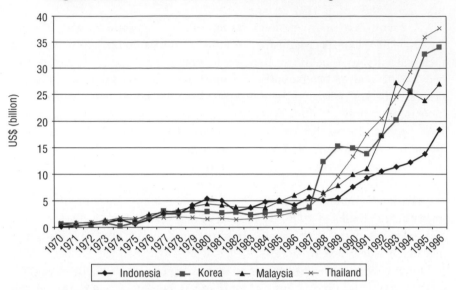

Figure 2.18   Bubble fuel: Total reserves minus gold, 1970–96

Source: IMF, *International Financial Statistics*.

Chapter 3

The New Paradigm Bubble

The functioning of the international monetary system was thus reduced to a childish game in which, after each round, the winners return their marbles to the losers.

— Jacques Rueff, 1961[1]

In 1961, the brilliant French economist, Jacques Rueff, published a prophetic article in *Fortune* in which he warned that U.S. balance of payments deficits threatened to bring down the international monetary system. Ten years later, President Nixon suspended the convertibility of U.S. dollars into gold. The Bretton Woods system had been destroyed by the U.S. balance of payments deficits, just as Rueff had predicted.

Rueff used the analogy of a game of marbles to demonstrate the problems caused by the deficits. He wrote that the international monetary system was being reduced to a game of marbles "in which, after each round, the winners return their marbles to the losers." Or,

> More specifically, the process works this way. When the U.S. has an unfavorable balance with another country (let us take as an example France), it settles up in dollars. The Frenchmen who receive these dollars sell them to the central bank, the Banque de France, taking their own national money, francs, in exchange. The Banque de France, in effect, creates these francs against the dollars. But then it turns around and invests the dollars back in the U.S. Thus the very same dollars expand the credit system of France, while still underpinning the credit system in the U.S.[2]

Chapter 2 demonstrated how the economies of Japan and the Asia Crisis countries underwent dramatic boom-and-bust cycles as their balance of payments surpluses caused rapid expansion within their credit systems. This chapter will show how those same surpluses have boomeranged back to the United States and caused economic overheating and asset price bubbles in that country as "the winners return their marbles to the losers."

THE BOOMERANG CURRENCY

Who said you can't have your cake and eat it too? The United States does. Each hour now, the U.S. buys US$50 million more in goods and services from the rest of the world than it sells to the rest of the world. The U.S. current account deficit was US$130 billion during the second quarter of 2002. It appears very likely to exceed US$500 billion for the full year. Moreover, given current exchange rates, there is every reason to believe that it will continue expanding from these levels. What does the United States exchange for this deficit? Essentially, paper – paper dollars and other U.S. dollar-denominated assets. It certainly could not pay with gold. Its gold reserves would have been depleted long ago had the U.S. settled its trade deficits with gold. What's even more remarkable, because the United States is the issuer of the world's preferred reserve currency, those dollars must buy U.S. dollar-denominated assets if they are to earn a positive rate of return. If the central banks around the world that have built up hordes of paper dollars as a result of their country's trade or financial account surpluses just stick that currency in a bank vault, it won't earn anything. On the other hand, when those central bankers buy U.S. Treasury bonds, Fannie Maes, U.S. corporate bonds, or even stocks, they earn interest income on their dollars. The only alternative to locking the dollars away in a vault or to buying U.S. dollar-denominated assets would be to exchange those dollars for their own currency. That would have the effect of driving up the value of their domestic currency, which, in turn, would make their country's exports less competitive and put an end to their country's balance of payments surplus, an unattractive alternative that is almost always avoided.

Once again, the U.S. buys a lot more from the rest of the world than it sells abroad. It pays with paper dollars. Then it gets those dollars back as its trading partners invest their dollars in U.S. dollar-denominated assets in order to earn a return on that paper. There's more. The amounts involved keep getting bigger every year. The larger the U.S. current account deficit becomes, the larger the amount of U.S. dollars that wash back into the United States through its financial account surplus. Figure 3.1 shows how it looks as a breakdown of the balance of payments.

As those dollars returned to the United States, they have helped drive up stock prices and property prices and helped push down interest rates. However advantageous this arrangement has been thus far, there are a number of very serious problems associated with it. First of all, those countries that accumulate large surpluses develop bubble economies that inevitably pop, leaving their banking sector in tatters and their government deeply in debt. Second, as the surplus countries have used their dollars to

Figure 3.1 United States: Breakdown of the balance of payments, 1984–2000

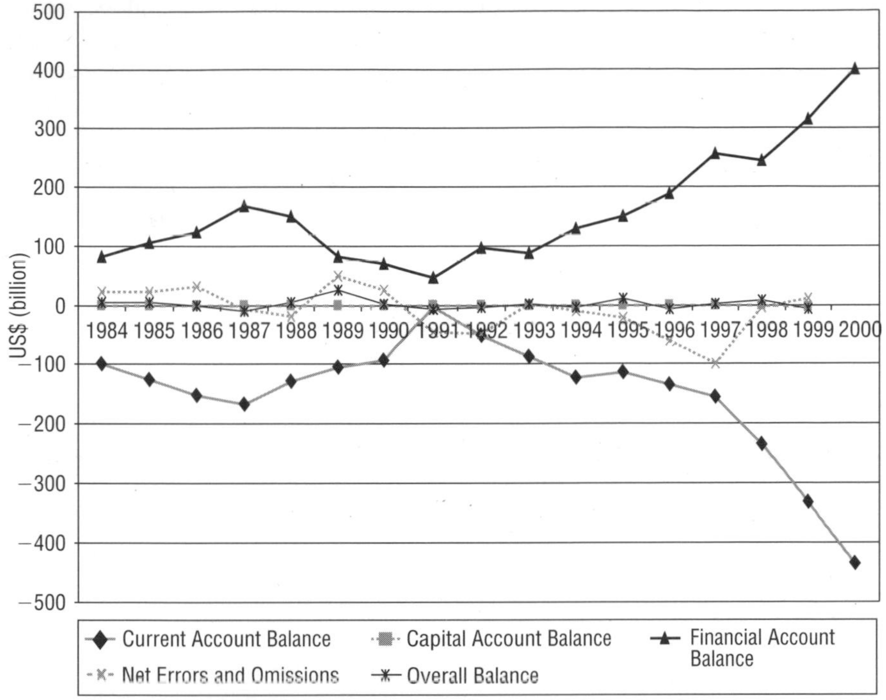

Source: IMF, *International Financial Statistics*.

acquire U.S. dollar-denominated assets, it has resulted in capital misallocation, severe asset price bubbles, and economic overheating in the United States that must also end in bankruptcies, deflation, and financial sector distress. Finally, it is completely unsustainable. The United States cannot continue to go into debt to the tune of 4–5% of its GDP each year (as it did in 2000 and 2001) indefinitely. At some point, the rest of the world will no longer be willing to accept 50 million paper dollars an hour in exchange for their products. Then, with the U.S. no longer able to act as the world's "engine of growth," a terrible economic readjustment process will ensue. At the time of writing, with corporate bankruptcies in the United States setting new records, with share prices swooning, and the dollar under pressure, it appears that this readjustment will occur sooner rather than later. In fact, in light of the horrific failures at Enron and WorldCom, it may not be an exaggeration to say that the U.S. economy has begun to choke on its own debt.

Already, most of the countries that have built up large foreign exchange reserves through trade or financial account surpluses have experienced extraordinary boom-and-bust cycles and are now left with the deflationary consequences. That process was described in the last two chapters. Also, dangerous asset bubbles have built up in the United States. Nasdaq in early 2000 was just as absurdly overvalued as the Thai stock market was in the mid-1990s. The New Paradigm asset misallocation verged on the insane – the criminally insane. Such bubbles can only inflate so far before their inherent folly becomes manifest and they are cut off from additional credit. Then, boom turns to bust. The recession that began in the United States in 2001 was as inevitable as night following day. The recovery in early 2002 was nothing more than a dead cat bounce.

Chapter 2 showed how current account and financial account surpluses caused the bubble economies in Japan and the other crisis-affected countries in Asia. This chapter will demonstrate how the U.S. financial account surpluses (which are actually only a function of the U.S. current account deficits) (see Figure 3.2) have caused economic overheating and severe asset price inflation in the United States through a process of credit creation.

The cumulative U.S. financial account surplus has exceeded US$3 trillion since 1983. That is a very large sum. That inflow has made it easier for the U.S. government to finance its debt and for U.S. corporations and government agencies such as Fannie Mae and Freddie Mac to sell their bonds. The *Flow of Funds* statement published by the Federal Reserve provides details on how those capital inflows have been invested in the

Figure 3.2 United States: Current account versus financial account, 1969–98

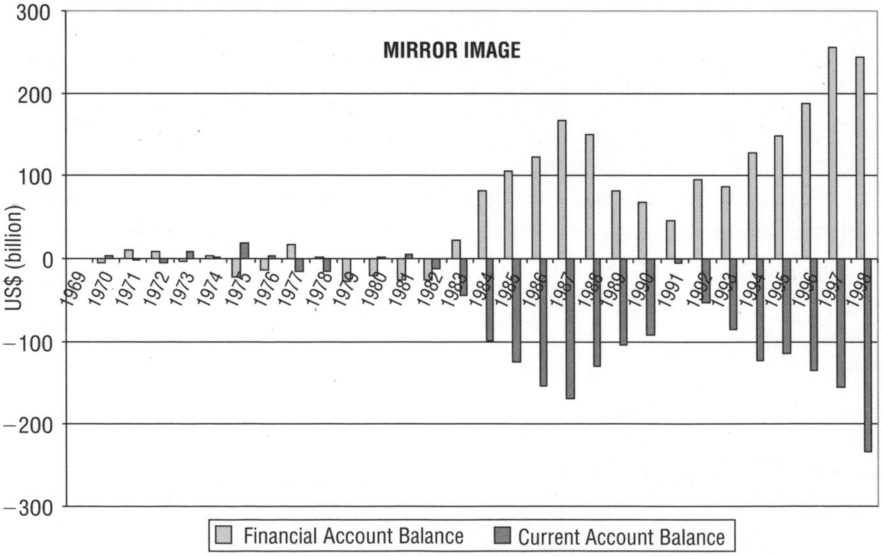

Source: IMF, *International Financial Statistics*.

United States. The data from 1995 to 2000 are sufficient to demonstrate how the U.S. economy has been affected. Table 3.1 shows the rest of the world's net acquisitions and increase in liabilities in the United States. The difference between the two represents the rest of the world's net financial investment in the United States. This figure is closely related to the U.S. financial account surplus.

The breakdown of the net acquisition of financial assets (see Table 3.2) reveals a sharp rise in U.S. corporate equities and direct foreign investment into the United States, and a relatively stable level of investment in credit market instruments.

The breakdown of credit market instruments (see Table 3.3) reveals a steady decline in U.S. government securities and a steady rise in investments in U.S. corporate bonds.

Table 3.1   The rest of the world's net foreign investments in the United States, 1995–2000 (US$ billion)

	1995	1996	1997	1998	1999	2000
Net acquisitions of financial assets	446.3	556.7	649.8	474.3	783.2	940.5
Net increase in liabilities	332.6	383.9	377.8	328.8	410.0	496.5
Net financial investment	113.7	172.8	272.0	145.5	373.2	444.0

Source: Federal Reserve Board, *Flow of Funds*.

Table 3.2   The rest of the world's breakdown of net acquisitions of financial assets, 1995–2000 (US$ billion)

	1995	1996	1997	1998	1999	2000
Credit market instrument	273.9	414.4	311.3	254.2	206.8	270.3
U.S. corporate equities	16.6	11.1	67.8	42.0	112.3	193.8
Foreign direct investment	57.8	86.5	105.6	178.2	301.0	287.7
Others	98.0	44.7	165.1	−0.1	161.1	179.7
Net acquisitions of financial assets	446.3	556.7	649.8	474.3	783.2	940.5

Source: Federal Reserve Board, *Flow of Funds*.

Table 3.3 Breakdown of credit market instruments acquired by foreign investors, 1995–2000 (US$ billion)

	1995	1996	1997	1998	1999	2000
U.S. government securities	197.2	312.4	189.6	95.4	83.8	89.7
U.S. corporate bonds	58.1	83.7	84.6	122.2	160.8	183.1
Others	18.6	18.3	37.1	36.6	−35.8	6.5
Total credit market instruments	273.9	414.4	311.3	254.2	206.8	279.3

Source: Federal Reserve Board, *Flow of Funds*.

Finally, the breakdown of U.S. government securities (see Table 3.4) shows that foreign investors have not only reduced their holding of U.S. Treasury bonds, but have even become net sellers, a trend that resulted from the government budget achieving a surplus in 1997 and the subsequent retirement of a portion of the Treasury bonds outstanding. At the same time, foreign investors sharply expanded their holding of government agency bonds, such as Fannie Maes and Freddie Macs.

Table 3.4 U.S. government securities acquired by foreign investors by type, 1995–2000 (US$ billion)

	1995	1996	1997	1998	1999	2000
Treasury bonds	168.5	270.7	139.7	38.7	−8.3	−63.0
Agency debt	28.7	41.7	49.8	56.7	92.2	152.7
Total	197.2	312.4	189.5	95.4	83.9	89.7

Source: Federal Reserve Board, *Flow of Funds*.

What all of the above tells us is that the rest of the world took its current account surplus and bought increasing amounts of U.S. stocks, corporate bonds, and agency debt, adding up to US$444 billion, US$693 billion, and US$422 billion, respectively, between 1995 and 2000. Those investments in stocks helped create the Nasdaq bubble. The investments in corporate bonds facilitated the misallocation of capital that is now laying low the dot.coms and the telecommunication companies, among others. And the investments in agency debt have helped fuel the boom in U.S. property prices that has allowed the U.S. consumer to extract additional equity through refinancing his home in order to keep spending more than he earns.

The impacts that these investments have had on the U.S. economy have been considerable in and of themselves. However, these inflows have also impacted the economy in a second and even more powerful way. They have entered the U.S. banking system as deposits and have acted as high-powered money, setting off the surge of credit creation that was the root cause of the great end of the millennium boom in the United States (see Figure 3.3).

This is not to suggest that those funds went directly on deposit when entering the United States. Nonetheless, regardless of what type of asset was initially purchased with those funds, eventually, most of that capital worked its way into American banks. For example, if the capital inflows were used to buy government bonds, the government spent the proceeds on goods and services, and the providers of those services deposited the payments they received from the government into their bank accounts. The same is true regardless of whether the funds coming into the country were used to buy corporate bonds, stocks, or any other kind of asset. Unless the money was hidden under a mattress or destroyed, most of it would have entered the banking system as deposits; and deposits make up most of the money supply.

When funds from abroad enter a banking system as deposits, they are not re-lent only once. The original amount that is lent will be redeposited and then re-lent and redeposited numerous times. This process of credit creation is only limited by the banks' need to maintain sufficient capital adequacy and prudential reserves to satisfy bank regulators. In this sense, the

Figure 3.3 United States: What is the relationship between money supply growth and the surplus on the financial account, 1984–2001?

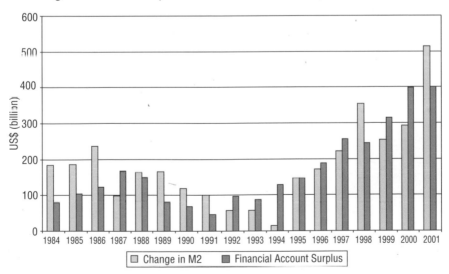

Source: IMF, *International Financial Statistics*.

foreign inflows act as high-powered money, just as if they had been created by the open market operations of the central bank. Therefore, the US$3 trillion in capital inflows after 1983 did much more than finance an additional US$3 trillion worth of debt. Those inflows were deposited, lent out, redeposited and re-lent multiple times. In that way, they caused the U.S. money supply to expand, fueling the bubble economy that emerged in the United States in the second half of the 1990s (see Figure 3.4).

In 1980, total credit market assets in the United States amounted to US$4.7 trillion. By the third quarter of 2001, that figure had risen by more than 500% to US$28.9 trillion (see Figure 3.5).

Over this period, credit market assets – that is, debt – grew at a much faster rate than the U.S. economy. Debt increased by 510%, while the GDP grew by only 246%. This difference is all the more striking when it is recognized that the GDP growth itself was in large part fueled by the expansion of debt (see Figure 3.6).

Credit could not have expanded this rapidly in absolute terms or relative to GDP had the foreign capital inflows not driven up the money supply as it entered the banking system. Taking one step back, the foreign capital inflows would not have existed had they not been created by the U.S. current account deficit. Finally, recall that such large current account deficits would

Figure 3.4 United States: Money supply growth versus the financial account surplus, 1984–2001

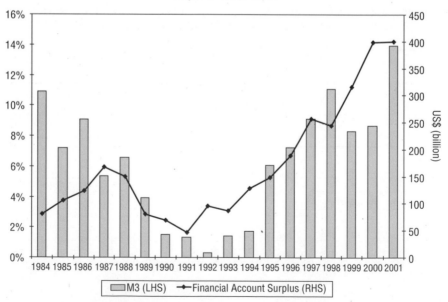

Source: IMF, *International Financial Statistics*.

Figure 3.5   United States: Total credit market assets, 1980–2001 (Q3)

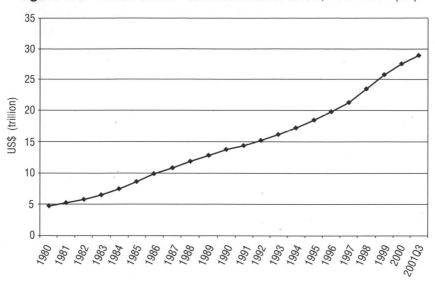

Source: Federal Reserve Board, *Flow of Funds*.

Figure 3.6   United States: Total credit market debt versus GDP,
1980–2001 (Q3)

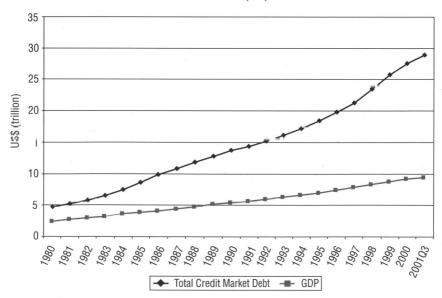

Source: Federal Reserve Board, *Flow of Funds*.

have been impossible under the classical gold standard or even the Bretton Woods system, because they would have drained the United States of its gold reserves, causing a contraction of the monetary base and throwing the country into a severe economic slump.

Once the restraints imposed by the rules of the gold standard were thrown off once and for all in 1973, paper replaced gold as the foundation of the world's monetary system. However, because one country, the United States, found itself in the fortunate position to call into existence unlimited amounts of paper dollars (or dollar-denominated debt instruments) and exchange them for the goods and services of other countries, a new international reserve currency (dollars) began flooding into the banking systems of all its major trading partners. That ignited an explosion of credit, not only in the countries with trade surpluses with the United States, but also in the United States itself as the dollars earned by its trading partners were reinvested in U.S. dollar-denominated assets in the United States and, ultimately, deposited into the U.S. banking systems. While many diagrams have been employed thus far to demonstrate the development of the global credit bubble that has brought about the present extreme disequilibrium in the world economy, none sums it up more strikingly than Figure 3.7, which shows the increase in U.S. currency held by the public.

Figure 3.7 Currency held by the public, 1890–2000

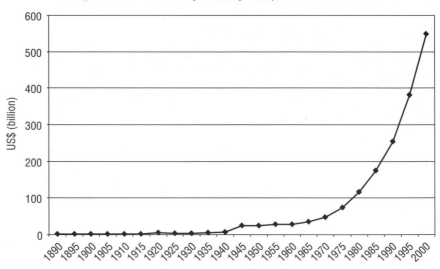

Sources: U.S. Department of Commerce, Bureau of the Census, *Historical Statistics of the United States: Colonial Times to 1970*; IMF, *International Financial Statistics.*

Because dollars have replaced gold as the new international reserve asset, Figure 3.7 helps to illustrate the near exponential explosion of the global money supply since the Bretton Woods system broke down. Those crisp green pieces of paper have acted as high-powered money as they entered the world's banking systems – just as gold would have. They have unleashed an unparalleled increase in credit around the world. That credit has blown the global economy into a bubble. Bubbles pop. Part Two examines the reasons bubbles pop. First, however, Chapter 4 will demonstrate that the first global bubble of the 20th century came about for the same reasons as the final one.

REFERENCES

1   Jacques Rueff, *Fortune*, July 1961, p. 127.
2   Ibid., p. 262.

Chapter 4

The Great American Bubble (of the 1920s)

A satisfactory theory of the boom explains the depression.
In the crisis what has been sown during the boom has to be reaped.

— Wilhelm Roepke, 1936[1]

The events described in the first three chapters of this book — namely, the collapse of an international monetary system based on gold, followed by surging trade imbalances that resulted in rapid credit expansion, an investment and stock-market boom, overcapacity, asset bubbles, panic, collapse, and deflation – have occurred once before. The collapse of the classical gold standard in 1914 set off the same chain of events. Huge trade imbalances fueled the surge in credit creation responsible for the "Roaring Twenties" … and the Great Depression that inevitably followed. This other great American bubble is the subject of this chapter.

> ## WHY THE TWENTIES ROARED

When World War I erupted in 1914, the belligerent nations in Europe terminated their commitment to convert their currencies into gold at a fixed rate, thereby destroying the international gold standard that had been the financial cornerstone of the world economy since the end of the Napoleonic Wars. Procuring the materials needed to conduct total war required government spending and trade deficits on a scale that would have been impossible under a gold standard regime, where money supply and credit are determined by the level of gold reserves. As gold left Europe to pay for material imports, credit contraction would have taken place there to the extent that economic collapse would have been unavoidable and the conduct of war impossible. Consequently, the gold standard had to give way to a monetary standard based on government credit. Table 4.1 shows the explosion in government spending that took place in the United Kingdom, France, Germany, and, after it entered the war in 1917, the United States.

Table 4.1 Total central government expenditure, 1900–32

	United States (US$ mn)	United Kingdom (Pounds mn)	Germany (Marks mn)	France (Francs mn)
1900	521	193	2,197	3,747
1901	525	205	2,324	3,756
1902	485	194	2,321	3,699
1903	517	155	2,357	3,597
1904	584	150	2,068	3,639
1905	567	147	2,195	3,707
1906	570	144	2,392	3,852
1907	579	143	2,810	3,880
1908	659	145	2,683	4,021
1909	694	157	3,266	4,186
1910	694	168	3,024	4,322
1911	691	174	2,897	4,548
1912	690	184	2,893	4,743
1913	715	192	3,521	5,067
1914	726	559	9,651	40,065
1915	746	1,559	26,689	20,925
1916	713	2,198	28,780	28,113
1917	1,954	2,696	53,261	35,320
1918	12,677	2,579	45,514	41,897
1919	18,493	1,666	54,867	39,970
1920	6,358	1,188	145,255	39,644
1921	5,062	1,070	298,766	32,848
1922	3,289	812	NA	45,188
1923	3,140	749	NA	38,293
1924	2,908	751	5,027	42,511
1925	2,924	776	5,683	36,275
1926	2,930	782	6,616	41,976
1927	2,857	774	7,168	45,869
1928	2,961	761	8,517	44,248
1929	3,127	782	8,187	59,335
1930	3,320	814	8,392	55,712
1931	3,577	819	6,995	53,428
1932	4,659	833	5,965	40,666

Source: *International Historical Statistics* (Palgrave Macmillan): for the U.S.: "The Americas," p. 656; for the U.K., France and Germany, pp. 799, 801. The figures for Germany in 1921 are not comparable with those of earlier years. For France, the figure for 1929 is for 15 months. The figure for 1932 is for nine months.

The importance of the United States' role as a source of war materials can be seen in its ballooning trade surplus during the war years, as well as its rising gold reserves during this period (see Table 4.2).

Table 4.2 United States: When European gold flowed to America, 1910–29

	Visible trade balance	Gold component of high-powered money inside and outside the Treasury	
	(US$ mn)	(US$ mn)	(% change)
1910	386	1,636	0
1911	652	1,753	7
1912	666	1,818	4
1913	771	1,871	3
1914	415	1,891	1
1915	1,873	2,300	22
1916	3,137	2,800	22
1917	3,392	3,100	11
1918	3,329	3,100	0
1919	4,896	3,050	−2
1920	3,097	3,100	2
1921	2,014	3,700	19
1922	745	4,000	8
1923	400	4,200	5
1924	1,057	4,350	4
1925	720	4,300	−1
1926	422	4,400	2
1927	742	4,350	−1
1928	1,090	4,200	−3
1929	884	4,300	2

Sources: Column 1: *International Historical Statistics* (Palgrave Macmillan), "The Americas," pp. 788–9. Columns 2 and 3: Milton Friedman and Anna Jacobson Schwartz, *A Monetary History of the United States, 1867–1960*: 1910–14: p. 179; 1915–21: p. 211; 1922–29: p. 282.

Between 1914, when the war began, and 1917, when the United States became an active participant, U.S. gold reserves rose 64% as Europe exchanged its gold for American goods. Once the United States entered the war, however, it began to accept government debt from its allies as payment for war materials, at which point gold inflows into the country ceased despite a continued expansion of the U.S. trade surplus. Once the war had ended, gold again began to flow into the United States, since the American trade surplus remained high and as the United States' allies began to repay their war debts.

From the information presented thus far, it is clear that World War I and the collapse of the gold standard resulted in a surge of gold reserves in the United States and an enormous expansion of public debt in Europe. It is important to emphasize that U.S. gold reserves could not have increased so significantly during these years had the European nations not abandoned the gold standard, just as the worldwide explosion of central bank reserves over the last three decades could not have occurred had Bretton Woods not collapsed.

Predictably, rapid credit growth in the United States accompanied the surge in U.S. gold reserves (see Table 4.3).

Table 4.3 United States: The relationship between gold, the money supply, and GDP, 1913–32

	Gold reserves (% change)	All commercial bank loans (% change)	Money supply (d) (% change)	Velocity (e) (X)	GNP (% change)
1913	3	4.9	3	NA	0.9
1914	1	4.7	3	NA	−4.4
1915	22	3.0	16	NA	−0.8
1916	22	16.7	16	NA	7.9
1917	11	15.5	17	NA	0.7
1918	0	10.8	13	NA	12.3
1919	−2	10.7	13	35.0	−3.6
1920	2	25.4	−1	35.4	−4.4
1921	19	−7.7	−11	32.6	−8.7
1922	8	−5.3	11	34.2	15.8
1923	5	9.6	0	34.1	12.1
1924	4	3.7	6	34.4	−0.2
1925	−1	6.7	7	36.3	8.4
1926	2	6.3	−2	37.7	5.9
1927	−1	2.5	1	41.0	−0.1
1928	−3	4.9	3	46.8	0.6
1929	2	4.6	0	53.6	6.7
1930	NA	−3.0	−6	40.4	−9.3
1931	NA	16.3	−12	33.2	−8.6
1932	NA	−24.9	NA	27.3	−13.4

Notes: (d): Currency plus demand deposit at commercial banks. (e): Annual turnover rate of demand deposits at all commercial banks.
Sources: Column 1: same as column 3 in Table 4.2. Column 2: U.S. Department of Commerce, *Historical Statistics of the United States*, p. 1021. Column 3: Milton Friedman and Anna Jacobson Schwartz, *A Monetary History of the United States, 1867–1960*, Appendix A, pp. 707–13. Column 4: *Historical Statistics of the United States*, p. 1034. Column 5: *International Historical Statistics* (Palgrave Macmillan), "The Americas," p. 753.

In attempting to discover the causes of the Great Depression, most studies on the subject limit their analysis to events occurring during the 1920s. In doing so, they ignore the doubling of the credit base that occurred between 1914 and 1920 and the impact this expansion of credit had on the country's industrial production. During those seven years, the value of the output of industrial machinery and equipment rose by 205% and the value of the output of all producer durables increased by 257%. It was this surge in industrial capacity during those years that was primarily responsible for bringing about a situation of general oversupply by 1926, when wholesale prices in the United States began to decline (see Table 4.4).

Table 4.4 United States: Credit and industrial production, 1910–32 (percent change)

	All commercial bank loans	Industrial production index	Total producer durables	Industrial machinery and equipment	Wholesale price index	S&P industrials stock-market index
1910	NA	3.8	22.6	14.6	4.1	0.6
1911	NA	5.5	-11.6	-6.8	-7.8	-4.0
1912	NA	20.6	21.3	8.4	6.5	7.5
1913	4.9	4.8	11.8	5.0	1.0	-12.0
1914	4.7	-5.1	-19.1	-15.3	-2.4	-1.3
1915	3.0	17.5	6.3	16.7	1.5	16.0
1916	16.7	18.9	60.9	68.7	23.0	26.8
1917	15.5	-1.1	50.0	49.9	37.4	-7.1
1918	10.8	-1.1	44.1	16.1	11.7	-9.4
1919	10.7	-12.8	-1.6	-8.6	5.5	28.0
1920	25.4	9.3	-4.8	14.1	11.4	-8.8
1921	-7.7	-19.5	-44.3	-43.5	-36.8	-22.0
1922	-5.3	27.3	0.8	17.6	-0.9	25.2
1923	9.6	13.1	46.3	-39.3	4.0	3.0
1924	3.7	-4.2	-10.2	-13.7	-2.5	4.4
1925	6.7	11.0	7.8	14.0	5.5	27.2
1926	6.3	5.9	9.7	8.1	-3.4	15.5
1927	2.5	1.0	-7.4	-8.2	-4.6	24.8
1928	4.9	2.8	7.9	11.4	1.4	35.0
1929	4.6	11.7	20.7	22.7	-1.4	26.2
1930	-3.0	-14.5	-23.1	-27.7	-9.3	-23.1
1931	-16.3	-16.0	-39.3	-35.7	-15.5	-36.0
1932	-24.9	-24.7	-46.8	-43.9	-11.2	-48.9

Sources: Column 1: *Historical Statistics of the United States*, p. 1021. Column 2: *International Historical Statistics* (Palgrave Macmillan), "The Americas," p. 302. Columns 3 and 4: U.S. Department of Commerce, *Historical Statistics of the United States*, p. 701. Column 5: ibid., p. 200. Column 6: ibid., p. 1004.

Beginning in 1921, the Federal Reserve system began to control the money supply and credit growth through open market operations. In that year, it sold large amounts of government debt and commercial bills to counter the rise in liquidity being caused by a new influx of gold into the country. Consequently, despite a 19% increase in gold reserves that year, credit actually contracted by 8%, throwing the country into a sharp, although brief, recession. The industrial production index fell by 25% in 1921 and gross national product (GNP) declined by 8.7%. Backpedaling, the Fed injected liquidity into the economy in 1922, producing a quick recovery.

After these initial teething problems, the Federal Reserve system was able to achieve steady and moderate credit growth, averaging 4.8% annually between 1924 and 1929; and in this respect shares no responsibility for the asset bubble that was forming on Wall Street. However, the damage had already been done during the war years when the domestic credit supply had ballooned. During the second half of the 1920s, credit expanded at a moderate rate, but on the back of a greatly inflated credit base. When the real economy was no longer able to profitably invest the available liquidity in new plant and equipment due to overcapacity and falling prices, increasing amounts of money were shifted into the stock market. The bull market gained momentum just as falling wholesale prices began to cut into corporate profits. The bubble burst when profit growth was unable to keep pace with rapidly rising share prices. (The reader will certainly recognize the similarity between the situation then and the situation today.) Share prices plunged, credit contracted, bankruptcies proliferated, and a banking crisis developed.

CONCLUSION

The events leading up to the Great Depression were the same as those that created Japan's bubble economy, the Asia Crisis, and the New Paradigm bubble in America. When the discipline inherent in the gold standard and in the Bretton Woods system ceased to exist, trade imbalances produced an expansion of international liquidity. In turn, surging liquidity permitted credit expansion that resulted in over-investment, overcapacity, asset price bubbles, and deflation. The pattern is very clear.

Once it is recognized that the source of these economic bubbles has been excessive credit creation brought about by global current account imbalances, rather than "crony capitalism" or "infectious greed," effective measures could be taken by the international community to combat the crisis and prevent the recurrence of bubble economies in the future. Recommendations as to the measures required, and how they could be implemented, are discussed in Part Four.

REFERENCE

1   Wilhelm Roepke, *Crisis and Cycles* (London: William Hodge and Company, Limited, 1936).

PART TWO

Flaws in the Dollar Standard

The first part of this book described how the international monetary system that evolved out of the collapse of the Bretton Woods system has brought about extraordinary disequilibrium in the global economy. Part Two will explain why the unwinding of the economic imbalances at the core of that disequilibrium is inevitable.

There are three flaws inherent in the international monetary system as it now functions. The first is that it has brought about a situation where the health of the global economy depends on the United States going steadily deeper into debt to the rest of the world. That is a prerequisite that the United States will not be able to fulfil indefinitely. The second flaw is that the system creates asset price bubbles in the countries with balance of payments surpluses that wreck the banking sector and government finances of those countries when they pop. The third flaw is that it generates deflationary pressures that will continue to undermine corporate profitability so long as the trade imbalances at the core of the system continue to flood the world with excessive credit creation.

Over the last 30 years, the United States has been transformed by its balance of payments deficits from the world's largest creditor into the world's most heavily indebted nation. At the end of 2001, the net indebtedness of the United States to the rest of the world amounted to US$2.3 trillion, or approximately 23% of U.S. GDP. The dollar standard has incentivized countries with balance of payments surpluses to reinvest their dollar surpluses in U.S. dollar-denominated assets. Those surpluses are expected to approach US$500 billion, or 5% of U.S. GDP, in 2002. Now, however, heavily indebted corporations and individuals in the United States are reaching the limit of their ability to service their debt, and bankruptcies are on the rise. Soon individuals will have to retrench and pay down their debt, while corporations will be unable to issue and service new credit instruments in sufficient amounts to enable the surplus countries to reinvest all of their dollar surpluses in dollar-denominated assets – at least not those issued by the private sector. Only the U.S. government, which has recently begun to run large budget deficits again, will have the debt servicing capacity to meet that need over the next few years. There are limits, however, to even the U.S. government's ability to incur debt.

The U.S. current account deficit is approaching 5% of GDP and accelerating. It is only a matter of time before it will become impossible for the United States to continue increasing its indebtedness to the rest of the world at the rate of 5% of GDP per year. At that point, the countries with balance of payments surpluses will be forced to convert their dollar surpluses into their own currencies, causing a sharp appreciation in their currencies and a sharp decline in the value of the dollar. That shift will help restore equilibrium to the U.S. balance of payments, but also it will throw the major exporting nations into recession as their exports to the United States collapse. This predicament is described in Chapters 5 and 6.

A second flaw of the dollar standard is that it causes unsustainable asset price bubbles, both in the countries with large balance of payments surpluses and in the United States, the principal deficit country. Asset price bubbles, like all bubbles, are ephemeral by nature. When they pop, they tend to cause systemic banking crises that require costly government rescue packages for the financial sector. The fiscal health of the governments of Japan and the Asia Crisis countries has been substantially impaired by the (less than entirely successful) attempts of those governments to stabilize their banking systems following the collapse of asset bubbles in those countries. Neither Japan nor any of the Asia Crisis countries could afford to bail out the depositors of their banks a second time. However, so long as those countries continue to generate large balance of payments surpluses, the risk of a new round of hyperinflation in asset prices cannot be ruled out. A second round of asset bubbles in Asia would inevitably end in fiscal crisis in a number of countries. Furthermore, the possibility of a costly financial sector crisis in the United States will also continue to increase so long as its current account deficits continue to boomerang back into that country as foreign capital inflows, feeding the asset price bubbles there. Chapter 7 addresses these issues.

The third flaw in the international monetary system is that it generates deflation. As described in Part One, enormous trade imbalances have facilitated a worldwide explosion of credit. Excessive credit expansion has resulted in over-investment, excess capacity, and falling product prices in almost every industry. Falling prices are undermining corporate profitability and resulting in widespread corporate distress. So long as this system continues to flood the world with liquidity, corporate distress can only intensify. Credit-induced over-investment is compounding the downward pressure on prices brought about by the precipitous relocation of the world's manufacturing facilities to very-low-wage countries over the last 20 years. Chapter 8 analyzes why deflation has become a serious threat again for the first time since the Great Depression.

The outlook for the global economy is profoundly disturbing. Until the dollar adjusts sharply lower, asset price bubbles and deflation will continue to undermine corporate profitability, banking systems, and government finances. When the dollar does fall, as it inevitably must, the global economic slump will intensify as the major exporting nations fall deeper into recession and the overheated U.S. economy deflates.

This unfortunate state of affairs has arisen because of the international monetary system's most serious defect: the dollar standard lacks an adjustment mechanism to prevent persistent trade imbalances. Balance of payments deficits of an unprecedented magnitude have resulted in credit-induced economic overheating on a global scale. The foundations for sustainable economic growth will not be restored until this flaw is corrected and the U.S. trade deficit ceases to flood the world with U.S. dollar liquidity. That will require that the dollar standard be replaced by a new international monetary system that does not generate, or even tolerate, rampant credit creation.

Chapter 5

The New Paradigm Recession

A sound banker, alas, is not one who foresees danger and avoids it, but one who, when he is ruined, is ruined in a conventional and orthodox way along with his fellows, so that no one can really blame him.

— John Maynard Keynes

INTRODUCTION

For the last 20 years, the world's engine of economic growth has been fueled by credit. In 1980, the ratio of total debt to GDP in the United States was 169%. By early 2002, that ratio had almost doubled to 292%. American consumers and businesses took the credit they were offered and spent it. Strong consumer spending and brisk business investment fueled the U.S. economy and, through its current account deficits, the U.S. economy powered the world.

Now, however, the engine of global growth is flooded and beginning to stall. Too much credit has been extended that can't be repaid. Businesses have badly misallocated capital, and consumers have grown accustomed to living beyond their means. Bankruptcies are soaring as share prices plunge. The U.S. economy is coming in for a hard landing … perhaps even a crash landing. This chapter explains why.

GIVING CREDIT WHERE CREDIT ISN'T DUE

Sometimes economic growth causes loan growth, but at other times, it is credit growth that spurs economic growth. Generally, at the beginning of economic upswings, expanding economic growth generates credit growth. However, in the later stages of the business cycle, often it is credit growth that drives the economic growth, by facilitating over-investment and profligate consumption. The business cycle turns down and recession begins when that credit cannot be repaid.

In the United States, credit expansion has played a leading, perhaps *the* leading, role in the country's strong economic growth and booming stock markets over the last 20 years. As Figure 5.1 illustrates, the periods of strongest economic expansion (not to mention stock market excesses), the

Figure 5.1 Credit-fueled expansion: The ratio of debt to GDP, 1969–2002 (Q1)

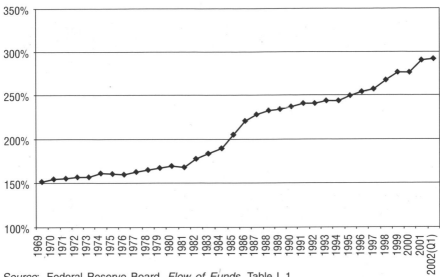

Source: Federal Reserve Board, *Flow of Funds*, Table L.1.

mid-1980s and from 1995 onward, corresponded to sharp increases in the ratio of the country's total debt to GDP.

Now, however, collapsing corporate profitability and record-breaking bankruptcies at both the corporate and the individual level are signaling the end of the longest economic boom on record. It is the nature of the business cycle – or the credit cycle, as it is sometimes referred to – that economic booms are followed by economic bust; and, generally, the bigger the boom, the bigger the subsequent bust.

At the time of writing, July 2002, the economy had bounced back in the first quarter of 2002 from a shallow recession in 2001 thanks to a very rapid reduction in interest rates to historically low levels. That reprieve has given rise to the hope that the worst has passed. Unfortunately, nothing could be further from the truth. The entire situation is reminiscent of the exchange between Julius Caesar and the soothsayer who had warned Caesar to "beware the Ides of March." When that day arrived, proud Caesar, on his way to the senate, met the soothsayer and mockingly pointed out that the Ides had arrived and that all was still well despite the predictions of doom. The soothsayer responded, "Yes, the Ides has arrived, but it has not yet passed." Caesar was hacked to death by his colleagues later that day.

So it is in the United States. The day of economic reckoning has arrived. Ill omens and signs of looming disaster are glaringly obvious. And yet, the country continues to wear a brave face and to hope for the best. Just as well. Nothing can be done to prevent the economic downturn now, for, as Lionel

Robbins wrote in his 1934 book, *The Great Depression*, "It is agreed that to prevent the depression the only effective method is to prevent the boom."[1] Sadly, it is way too late for that.

Irrational exuberance and infectious greed have held sway for too long. The "boom" has been most apparent in share prices. The Dow Jones Industrial Average first broke above the 1,000 level in 1972. However, by late 1974, the index had fallen 40% from that peak. It was not until almost 1983 that the Dow was able to break through and remain above the 1,000 index level (see Figure 5.2). Not coincidentally, 1983 was also the year that the extraordinary and unprecedented deterioration of the U.S. current account deficit began. The Dow's sustained rise above 1,000 was the milestone that marked the beginning of the Great End-of-the-Century Stock Market bubble.

Between the beginning of 1983 and the end of the decade, the Dow rose 163%. Then, from 1990 to 2000, it rose a further 320% to 11,500. Within 17 years, the stock market soared more than 1,000%. It was a boom not unlike the one that put the roar in the Roaring Twenties (see Figure 5.3).

THE BUSINESS CYCLE

The U.S. economy, like every economy, is comprised of personal consumption expenditure, private investment, government spending, and net exports (see Figure 5.4).

Figure 5.2   The Dow Jones Industrial Average, 1969–2002 (monthly averages)

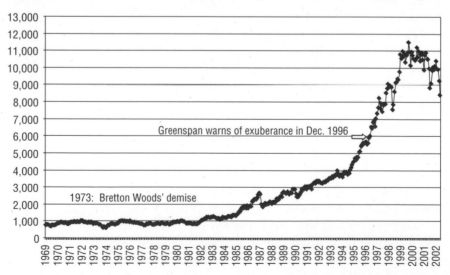

Source: Economagic.

Figure 5.3 Dow Jones Industrial Average, 1910–40 (monthly close)

Source: Economagic.

Figure 5.4 United States: Sector contributions to 2001 GDP (based on end demand)

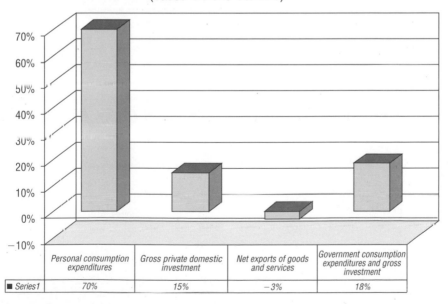

Source: Bureau of Economic Analysis.

In 2001, personal consumption expenditure accounted for 70% of final demand in the economy. Private investment accounted for 15% and government spending contributed 18%. Net exports of goods and services detracted 3% from GDP because imports into the United States exceeded U.S. exports abroad.

The Business Sector (and Private Investment)

It has long been understood (although, from time to time, temporarily forgotten) that industrial economies expand in a cyclical manner. Private investment typically acts as the driving force in the business cycle. When businesses expand, jobs are created and personal consumption rises. When businesses rein in their investment, jobs are cut and personal consumption slows. Personal consumption makes up the largest share of end demand in all major economies, but private investment drives the cycle. It can be seen in Figure 5.5 that private investment rises more than consumption during periods of strong economic expansion and contracts more during slumps. Table 5.1 provides a breakdown of U.S. GDP in 2001.

Figure 5.5 United States: Real GDP, private investment, and personal consumption, 1955–2001

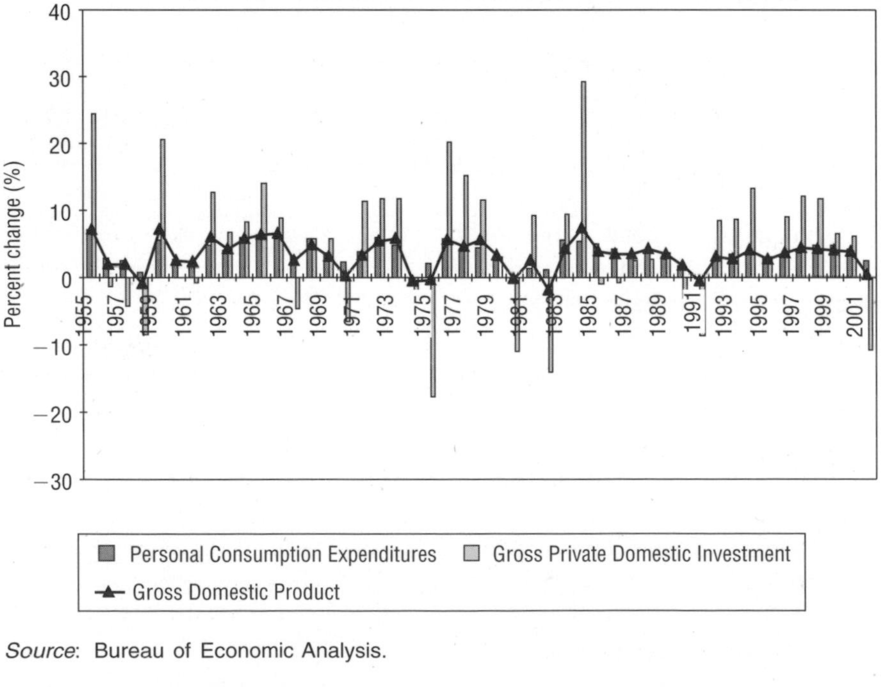

Personal Consumption Expenditures Gross Private Domestic Investment
Gross Domestic Product

Source: Bureau of Economic Analysis.

Table 5.1 United States: Breakdown of GDP, 2001

	US dollar (billion) 2001	Percent change (%) 2001
Gross domestic product	10,082	0.3
Personal consumption expenditures	6,987	2.5
Durable goods	836	6.0
Nondurable goods	2,041	2.0
Services	4,110	2.0
Gross private domestic investment	1,586	−10.7
Fixed investment	1,646	−3.8
Nonresidential	1,202	−5.2
Structures	325	−1.7
Equipment and software	877	−6.4
Residential	445	0.3
Change in private inventories	−60	−194.5
Net exports of goods and services	−349	4.3
Exports	1,034	−5.4
Goods	734	−5.9
Services	301	−4.0
Imports	1,383	−2.9
Goods	1,167	−3.3
Services	216	−0.5
Government consumption expenditures and gross investment	1,858	3.7
Federal	628	4.8
National defense	400	5.0
Nondefense	228	4.5
State and local	1,230	3.1

Source: Bureau of Economic Analysis.

During the second half of the 1990s, the growth rate of private investment accelerated (see Figure 5.6). The stock market boom inflated stock market capitalizations, making it easy for corporations to raise money cheaply by selling shares. The widening U.S. current account deficit also meant that the rest of the world had large dollar surpluses, substantial portions of which they were willing to invest in U.S. corporate bonds.

During those years, private investment came to account for a larger portion of GDP than normal. The increase in the share accounted for by private investment in equipment and software was particularly pronounced, as dot.coms and telcos burned through cash as if there were no tomorrow – and, of course, as it turned out, for many of them there wasn't (see Figure 5.7).

Figure 5.6 United States: The annual average increase in private investment, 1955–99

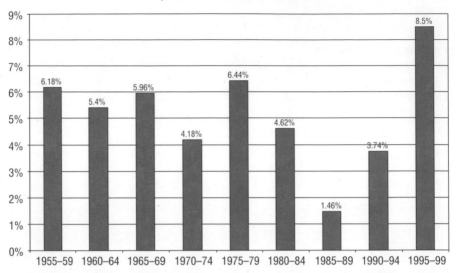

Source: Bureau of Economic Analysis.

Figure 5.7 United States: Investment in equipment and software as percent of GDP, 1970–2001

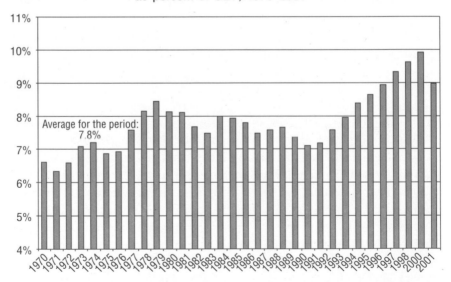

Source: Bureau of Economic Analysis.

The extraordinary economic growth and stock market boom of the second half of the 1990s gave rise to the belief that a "New Paradigm" had made the business cycle obsolete. Faith in economic miracles rarely lasts very long, however. The New Paradigm bubble began deflating rapidly in the spring of 2000 and the United States was once again in recession the following year. Corporate profitability began to suffer (see Figure 5.8).

Very quickly it became obvious that corporate America had made some tremendous mistakes during the bubble era; and, in 2002, the public learned that many of the largest corporations had resorted to fraud in an attempt to cover them up. Scandal followed scandal. In quick succession, Enron Corporation, Global Crossing, and WorldCom filed for bankruptcy, with combined assets of US$196 billion, an amount considerably larger than all the assets of the 10 largest companies to file for bankruptcy during the 1980s and 1990s combined (see Table 5.2). When Arthur Andersen, one of the "Big Four" accounting firms, disintegrated after it was found guilty of obstructing justice by destroying documents in order to cover up malpractices at Enron, faith in the entire system was shaken to the core. Stock markets plunged sharply during the summer of scandal.

Figure 5.8 United States: Corporate profits after tax, 1990–2001 (percent change from previous year)

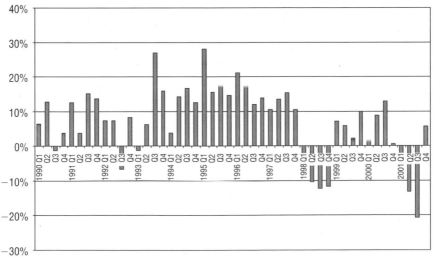

Source: Federal Reserve Economic Data: St. Louis Fed.

Table 5.2 The largest bankruptcies in the United States, 1980 to the present

Company	Bankruptcy date	Total assets pre-bankruptcy (US$ billion)
1 WorldCom	July 21, 2002	107.0
2 Enron Corp.	December 2, 2001	63.4
3 Texaco, Inc.	April 12, 1987	35.9
4 Financial Corp. of America	September 9, 1988	33.9
5 Global Crossing	January 28, 2002	25.5
6 Pacific Gas & Electric Co.	April 6, 2001	21.5
7 Mcorp	March 31, 1989	20.2
8 Kmart Corp.	January 22, 2002	17.0
9 NTL, Inc.	May 8, 2002	16.8
10 First Executive Corp.	May 13, 1991	15.2
11 Gibraltar Financial Corp.	February 8, 1990	15.0
12 FINOVA Group, Inc.	March 7, 2001	14.0
13 HomeFed Corp.	October 22, 1992	13.9
14 Southeast Banking Corporation	September 20, 1991	13.4
15 Reliance Group Holdings, Inc.	June 12, 2001	12.6
16 Imperial Corp. of America	February 28, 1990	12.3
17 Federal-Mogul Corp.	October 1, 2001	10.2
18 First City Bancorp of Texas	October 31, 1992	9.9
19 First Capital Holdings	May 30, 1991	9.7
20 Baldwin-United	September 26, 1983	9.4

Source: BankruptcyData.com.

Financial difficulties were not confined only to a few large companies, either. Beginning in 1999, credit quality began to worsen all across the corporate sector and problems accelerated quickly thereafter (see Figures 5.9 and 5.10).

When the creditworthiness of the corporate sector began visibly to worsen, credit extension to the sector finally began to slow down. Business debt, which had increased by 12% in both 1998 and 1999, expanded at only a 2% annualized rate in the first quarter of 2002.

Facing glutted markets and falling product prices on the one hand and a drastically reduced access to credit on the other, corporations began to invest less and private investment plunged in 2001 (see Figure 5.11).

Hit hard by the troubles of its own making, the corporate sector was quick to fire workers. Between October 2000 and June 2002, the number of unemployed U.S. workers rose by 2.9 million to 8.4 million, an increase of 52%. The unemployment rate jumped from 3.9% to 5.9% (see Figure 5.12).

Figure 5.9 United States: Total adversely rated syndicated loans, 1991–2002

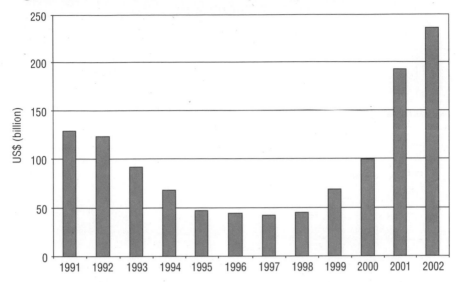

Source: *The Shared National Credit Review.*

Figure 5.10 United States: Syndicated loans adversely rated as a percentage of total committed, 1991–2002

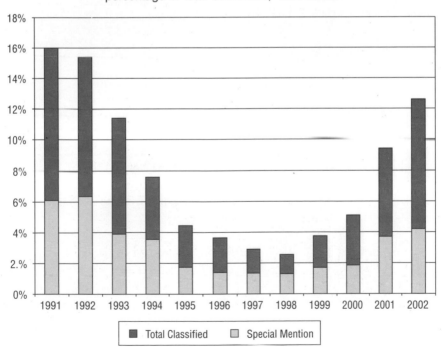

Source: *The Shared National Credit Review.*

Figure 5.11 United States: Real GDP, private investment, and private consumption, 1988–2001

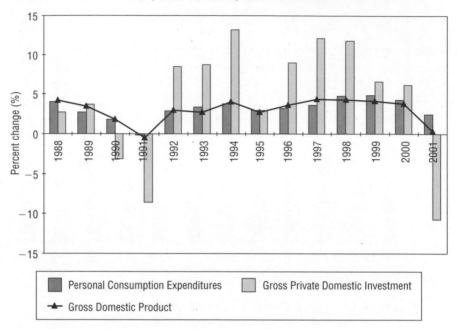

Source: Bureau of Economic Analysis.

Figure 5.12 United States: Unemployment rate, 1948–2002

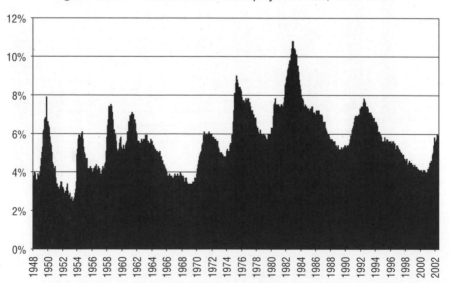

Source: Federal Reserve Economic Data: St. Louis Fed.

Falling investment and rising unemployment is the normal pattern when the business cycle begins to turn down. Personal consumption expenditure should have begun slowing sharply as well. Surprisingly, however, consumption remained robust despite rising joblessness and collapsing stock market wealth. This extraordinary divergence between the change in private investment and the change in personal consumption was due to trends in the credit market.

The increase in business debt slowed to only 2% on an annualized basis in the first quarter of 2002. Cut off from new credit to refinance the old, many companies began going under. Credit to consumers continued to flow freely, however (see Figure 5.13).

For the time being, sharply rising consumer indebtedness is continuing to fuel consumption in the United States. Consumption is supporting the U.S. economy and, by extension, the global economy. However, consumers are beginning to have a very hard time servicing their debt. You can't get blood out of a stone, as they say. When new consumer credit is cut off, the game is up. Without new loans to help repay the old ones, the house of cards in the consumer lending business will come crashing down. The New Paradigm recession will then begin in earnest.

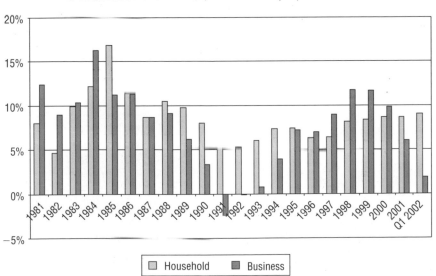

Figure 5.13 United States: Percent change in household and business-sector debt, 1981–2002 (Q2) annualized

Source: Federal Reserve Board, *Flow of Funds*.

The Household Sector (and Personal Consumption Expenditure)

American consumers are on a buying binge – a long one. Since 1980, household debt has risen from 50% of GDP to 78%. Even over the last two years, in spite of everything that has gone wrong, consumer spending has held up remarkably well. Their creditors have encouraged them. Borrowing has never been easier or cheaper. Mortgage financing and consumer credit have been flowing freely (see Figure 5.14). As one bank chairman recently put it, "You'd have to be an insolvent arsonist not to get a loan right now."

The question, of course, is how much more debt can the American consumer handle? Almost every indicator suggests that they are over-indebted relative to their income and their earning prospects. They are also filing for bankruptcy in record numbers.

Debt cannot continue to expand more rapidly than income indefinitely – neither at the household level nor at the national level. In the United States, the rate of increase in personal income has slumped precipitously over the last two years, but the increase in consumer debt has not slowed. By the end of 2001, the annual increase in personal income had decreased to 2.5%, the slowest pace in 40 years, while household debt continued to rise by more than 8% for the fourth year in a row (see Figure 5.15).

Figure 5.14   United States: An increasingly indebted society: Mortgages and consumer credit as a percentage of GDP, 1980–2001

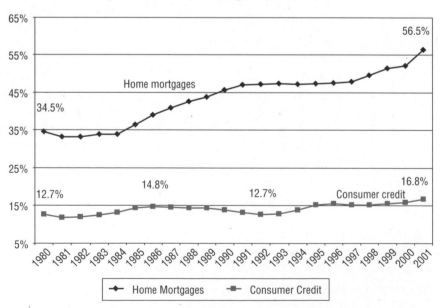

Source: Federal Reserve Board, *Flow of Funds*.

Figure 5.15 United States: Personal income, 1960–2002
(percent change from previous year)

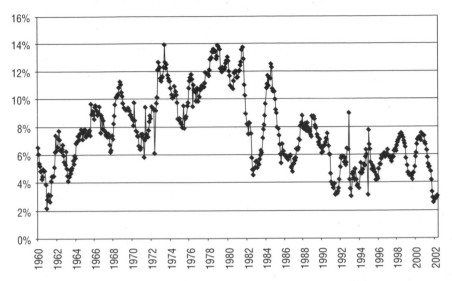

Source: Federal Reserve Economic Data: St. Louis Fed.

The trend in wages and salaries tells the same story. The rate of increase in wages has plummeted in the United States since mid-2000, and is now on par with that corresponding with the recession in the early 1990s. Moreover, in the near term, with unemployment rising and corporate distress intensifying, wages seem more likely to begin falling in absolute terms, rather than rebounding (see Figure 5.16).

Nor will the American consumer simply be able to cut back on the amount set aside as savings each month in order to continue shopping. The personal savings rate in the United States fell to its lowest recorded level during the final days of the New Paradigm bubble in 2000 and 2001, when, during seven out of 24 months, Americans saved less than 1% of their income (see Figure 5.17). For a point of comparison, consider that the average savings rate between 1959 and 1998 was 8.4%. This unprecedented paucity of savings strongly suggests that U.S. consumers will soon be forced to tighten their belts, reduce their borrowing, and cut back on their spending.

The consumer's distress is apparent in the surge in bankruptcy filings (see Figure 5.18). The correlation between the rising amount that consumers spend to service their debt and the rise in bankruptcies is no coincidence. The most alarming aspect of the sharp rise in the consumer's debt service burden is that it is occurring at a time when interest rates have never been lower. At the time of writing, the Federal Funds rate is 1.75%. Should

Figure 5.16   United States: Wages and salaries, 1947–2001
(percent change year on year)

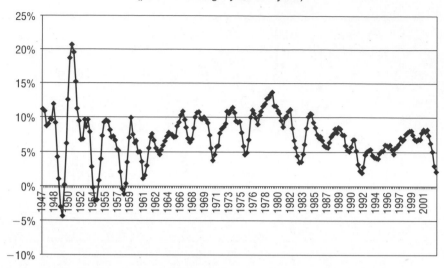

Source: Federal Reserve Economic Data: St. Louis Fed.

Figure 5.17   United States: Personal savings rate, 1959–2001

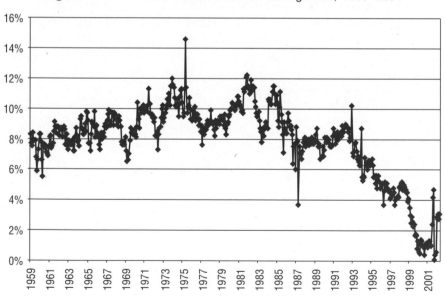

Source: Federal Reserve Economic Data: St. Louis Fed.

Figure 5.18   United States: Influence of total consumer debt
on bankruptcy filing trends by year, 1980–2001

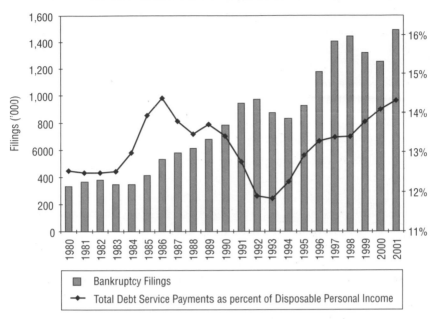

Sources: ABI World: www.abiworld.org/stats/1980annual.html, October 26, 2002; Federal
Reserve Economic Data: St. Louis Fed.

interest rates begin to go up, a still larger portion of disposable income
would have to be set aside as interest payments. Higher interest rates would
inevitably push still more households into bankruptcy.

In light of all of the above, there can be little doubt that the American
consumer is overextended financially. So long as subprime lenders keep the
credit flowing in growing amounts, new loans can be drawn upon to repay
the principal and interest on the old ones, with some left over for a trip to
the mall. And, so long as mortgage providers continue to push out new
mortgage loans and Fannie Mae continues to buy them, property prices will
continue to rise. Unfortunately, with personal income depressed and
unemployment rising, it won't take long for the property market to become
unaffordable to many, and then for most. Every Ponzi scheme ends in crisis.
The Great End-of-the-Century Consumer Credit bubble will be no different.

When the consumer folds and begins to rein in his debt, there will be
ramifications throughout the debt market. Hardest hit will be the financial
sector. The federally related mortgage pools, government-sponsored
enterprises (GSEs), issuers of asset-backed securities, and commercial banks
all depend on the expansion of consumer credit for their growth. Rising

consumer bankruptcies are signaling that the extraordinary credit-induced spending spree in the United States will soon come to an end. Problems that were manageable when new credit was easily available will become crises as consumer credit growth slows. Distraught creditors will turn off the credit taps and a new "credit crunch" will begin.

The Government Sector

There are two positive observations that can be made about the fiscal condition of the U.S. government. The first is that, as a percentage of GDP, government debt is not as high as it was in the mid-1990s. The second is that, despite the government's heavy indebtedness, it would be very surprising if it encountered much difficulty in raising trillions of dollars more debt if it chose to do so. This latter point is very important, not only because the government's finances have once again begun to deteriorate badly, but even more so because the government will be forced to run much larger budget deficits in the years immediately ahead if the current recession is not to become something much worse.

The federal government's total debt is US$6 trillion, or roughly 58% of GDP (see Figure 5.19). In absolute terms, it has never been higher. It has increased every year without interruption since 1956. However, as a percentage of GDP, it is well below its peak level set in 1995 when it hit 67% of GDP.

Figure 5.19   Total U.S. federal government debt, 1954–2002 (March)

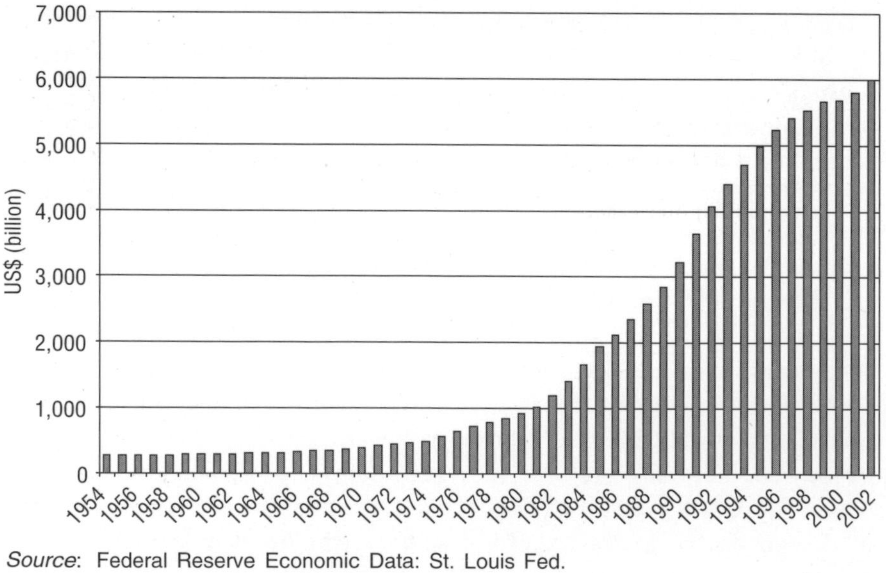

Source: Federal Reserve Economic Data: St. Louis Fed.

Approximately 57% of the government's total debt, or US$3.4 trillion, is held by the public (see Table 5.3). The rest, US$2.6 trillion, is held in the government accounts listed in Table 5.3.

The public has been led to believe that the government achieved a budget surplus from 1998 to 2001. That is not really the complete truth. The government has been counting a large part of the contributions paid into Social Security and some of the contributions paid into the pension plans of government employees as government revenues – without counting the government's obligations to pay benefits in the future as government liabilities.

At present, Social Security and the government employee pension plans receive more in contributions than they pay out in benefits, generating a surplus. The government includes that surplus as part of government revenues. By doing so, it made the government's budget appear to be in surplus from 1998 to 2001.

That is not all. The government has been spending part of the current surpluses of Social Security and the government pension plans on other things. The amounts involved are huge, totaling almost US$1 trillion over

Table 5.3 United States: Public debt held in government accounts, March 2002 (US$ million)

	March-02	
Airport and Airway Trust Fund	13,500	0.5%
Bank Insurance Fund	29,328	1.1%
Employees Life Insurance Fund	24,306	0.9%
Exchange Stabilization Fund	0,813	0.4%
Federal Disability Insurance Trust Fund	144,686	5.6%
Federal Employees Retirement Funds	541,352	20.9%
Federal Hospital Insurance Trust Fund	214,168	8.3%
Federal Housing Administration	20,244	0.8%
Federal Old-Age and Survivors Insurance Trust Fund	1,096,981	42.4%
Federal Savings and Loan Corporation, Resolution Fund	2,719	0.1%
Federal Supplementary Medical Insurance Trust Fund	42,788	1.7%
Highway Trust Fund	19,969	0.8%
National Service Life Insurance Fund	11,561	0.4%
Railroad Retirement Account	25,023	1.0%
Unemployment Trust Fund	75,874	2.9%
Others	317,353	12.3%
Total	2,589,665	100.1%

Source: U.S. Department of the Treasury, Treasury Bulletin, Table FD3 Government Account Series.

the past five years alone. When the government spends the current surpluses of those retirement plans, it gives them non-marketable government IOUs in exchange. It is those IOUs that comprise most of the debt securities held in the government accounts listed above.

In other words, the government has spent most of the Social Security Trust Fund. Social Security is an unfunded pension scheme. Some of the government employee pension plans are also, at least partially, unfunded. It is illegal for a private company to have unfunded pension plans. It is not illegal for the government to do so, however. Nor is it illegal for government officials to tell the public that there is a large budget surplus, without explaining how that is possible when the government's debt continues to rise year after year.

Of course, Social Security's problems go deeper than that. Because of unfavorable demographic trends, within 20 years, annual payments into the Social Security system will be insufficient to meet the benefits then due to be paid to retirees. So, the system that is currently generating a surplus, which the government spends on other things, will soon begin to generate very large deficits that will add to the government's liabilities at that time. It is no surprise that the general public recognizes there is a crisis within the Social Security system. They just don't yet realize that the Social Security surplus was appropriated to make it appear that the government achieved a budget surplus from 1998 to 2001.

The purpose of the preceding discussion was to explain the true state of the U.S. government's financial position – not to suggest that problems with the Social Security system will result in a near-term fiscal disaster. With any luck, the insolvency of the Social Security system will play a leading role in some future economic crisis, rather than in the current one. Figure 5.20 presents the trends in both total government debt and in that portion of government debt held by the public. The difference between the two is the amount of government debt held in government accounts, such as the Federal Old-Age and Survivors Insurance Trust Fund, which was created under the Social Security Act.

For the sake of simplicity, the rest of this section will focus primarily on only that part of the government debt that is held by the public. This will minimize confusion, since that is the way the government generally has presented its debt and its budgets to the public.

Between 1980 and 1997, government budget deficits ran out of control. Over that period, government debt held by the public increased by US$3.1 trillion; as a percentage of GDP, it increased from 33% to 65%.

However, beginning in 1998, the U.S. government not only balanced its budget, but actually achieved a budget surplus (of a type, see above) over four straight years (see Figure 5.21). Two tax increases, the first during the

Figure 5.20 U.S. federal government debt as a percentage of GDP (both total debt and debt held by the public), 1980–2002 (Q1)

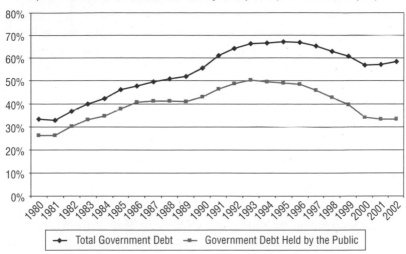

Source: Federal Reserve Economic Data: St. Louis Fed.

Bush administration and the second during Clinton's, played an important role in enabling the government to re-establish a more responsible financial position. Equally important, however, were the inflated tax revenues

Figure 5.21 The U.S. government's budget has fallen back into deficit, 1980–2003F

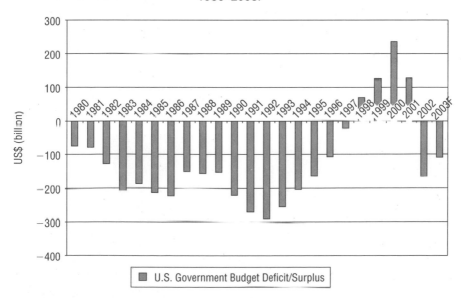

Source: Office of Management and Budget, The Executive Office of the President.

generated by the overheated economy. In particular, capital gains taxes surged as the stock market blew into an enormous bubble.

Extrapolating those trends indefinitely into the future, politicians and political functionaries published absurd projections showing that government revenues would continue to be so strong over the next decade that the entire US$3.8 trillion in government debt held by the public would be paid off by 2010. The second Bush administration went so far as to enact a large, multi-year tax cut in 2001, just as much of the government's bubble-inflated tax revenues began to disappear. When the stock market crashed, the capital gains that had generated so much tax revenue quickly turned into capital gains losses that could be used to offset other taxes owed to the government.

Very suddenly, projections that had shown endless budget surpluses were revised to show multi-year deficits. The budget surplus in fiscal year 2001 came to US$127 billion. For fiscal year 2002, a deficit of US$165 billion is now expected, according to the Office of Management and Budget. This turnaround represents a deterioration of US$290 billion from one year to the next.

Looking ahead, as the recession worsens, a very sharp blowout in the government's budget deficit should be anticipated, as tax revenues continue to fall and as expenditure programs designed to stimulate the economy are launched. It is quite likely that by 2004, if not sooner, the budget deficit will exceed the record of US$290 billion set in 1992.

The good news is that the government can afford to go deeper into debt. In fact, large-scale deficit spending by the government may well be absolutely necessary over the next five years to prevent a severe recession from becoming a depression. Government spending accounts for only 18% of the end demand in the economy, compared with 15% for private investment and 70% for personal consumption. Nonetheless, aggressive deficit spending can support the economy and generate badly needed jobs at a time when the other sectors of the economy are contracting. Furthermore, the sale of large amounts of U.S. Treasury bonds will supply secure debt instruments that the United States' trading partners will require if they are to reinvest their dollar surpluses into dollar-denominated assets in the years immediately ahead, a subject that is elaborated on in the following chapter.

The U.S. government would have little trouble financing a US$500 billion annual budget deficit each year between 2002 and 2005, as an addition of US$2 trillion in debt would only increase its debt held by the public to approximately 50% of GDP by the end of that period, even though total government debt would increase to almost 75% of GDP. Compare that with the Japanese government's debt which, during 12 years of post-bubble economic difficulties, has ballooned to approximately 140% of GDP without (yet) provoking a crisis.

In 2001, the federal government paid US$359.5 billion in interest expense on its total debt of around US$5.8 trillion, implying an average rate of interest near 6.2% (see Figure 5.22). Should total federal debt jump to US$8 trillion by the end of 2005, the government's interest expense would increase to just under US$500 billion annually, equivalent to roughly 4.5% of GDP, assuming the rate of interest it pays on its debt remains at the same level and an annual increase in GDP of 2% a year. In 1991, the government's interest expense was higher than that, reaching the equivalent of 4.8% of GDP. Therefore, there is little reason to fear that the government could not service the interest payments on US$8 trillion in debt in 2005.

The ability of the government to spend generously may be the only factor that keeps the U.S. economy from falling completely into crisis between now and then, as the heavily indebted corporate and household sectors are forced to retrench and all the excesses of the New Paradigm era are unwound. There are risks, however, that the government's finances could deteriorate much more drastically than anticipated in the preceding paragraphs.

Systemic banking crises typically accompany the implosion of economic bubbles. The Japanese government and the governments of the Asia Crisis countries were required to go deeply into debt to salvage their banks when their economic bubbles ended in crises. During the Great Depression, a third of all U.S. banks failed. The economic excesses in the United States during the second half of the 1990s were unprecedented. Extraordinary financial leverage was built up as unimaginably large amounts of derivatives and

Figure 5.22 U.S. government interest expense on total debt, 1988–2001

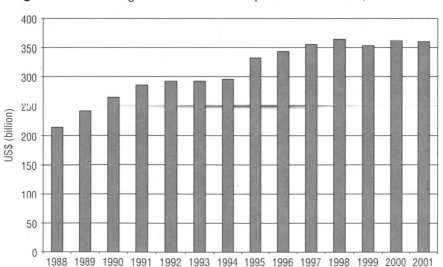

Source: U.S. Department of the Treasury, Bureau of the Public Debt.

other credit-related instruments were put into place for the first time. The possibility cannot be ruled out that the unwinding of that leverage will bring down a significant portion of the U.S. banking sector. In such a scenario, "bad case" becomes "worst case" very quickly.

Similarly, should the government-sponsored enterprises, such as Fannie Mae and Freddie Mac, come unglued under the enormous debt they built up during the 1990s, the government might also decide to come to the rescue of their creditors even though it does not formally guarantee the GSE debt. At the end of 2001, the debt of GSEs amounted to US$2.25 trillion.

Either scenario could cost the government hundreds of billions, if not trillions, of dollars. But still yet, the financial clout of the U.S. government is such that it could raise sufficient credit to resolve any conventional financial-sector crisis and, simultaneously, stimulate the economy through large-scale spending programs. Only one, very worst-case scenario could truly break the bank: a systemic meltdown of the US$150 trillion derivatives market. The derivatives market has grown from roughly US$10 trillion in 1990 to US$150 trillion today, a size approximately five times larger than the annual economic output of the entire world. It is an industry in itself, and one shrouded in mystery. It could prove to be the global economy's Achilles' heel. Any systemic meltdown of the derivatives market could be too costly for even the U.S. government to fix.

To summarize, then, with debt equivalent to 60% of GDP and huge unfunded contingent liabilities for the Social Security system, the U.S. government's financial position is not good. However, it is not so bad that it will block the government from aggressively increasing its deficit spending in the years immediately ahead in an attempt to prevent the economy from collapsing into depression. The ability of the United States to fund large-scale Keynesian stimulus programs holds out the greatest hope that this recession will not spiral into crisis. In all probability, U.S. government deficit spending will come to the rescue of the global economy.

The U.S. government can be relied on to spend enough to stave off economic collapse. During the midst of the Great Depression, Franklin Roosevelt told his nation, "We have nothing to fear, but fear itself." Today, the only reason to fear is *not* fear itself. It is the possibility that a derivatives market meltdown could cause a global systemic banking collapse that no government could afford to repair.

CONCLUSION

The aim of this chapter has been to demonstrate, first, that the business and household sectors in the United States are overly indebted; second, that the inability of those sectors to increase their indebtedness further makes an economic slump in the United States inevitable; and, finally, that deficit spending by the government should prevent the recession from becoming a depression, despite the extraordinary excesses that have occurred in America in the 1980s and 1990s. The impact that the intensifying U.S. recession will have on the rest of the world is taken up in Part Three. First, Chapter 6 will describe why the unwinding of the New Paradigm excesses must drive the dollar sharply lower.

REFERENCE

1   Lionel Robins, *The Great Depression* (New York: The Macmillan Company, 1934).

Chapter 6

The Fate of the Dollar: Half a Trillion Reasons Why the Dollar Must Collapse

The function of the Federal Reserve System is to foster a flow of credit and money that will facilitate orderly economic growth, a stable dollar, and long-run balance in our international payments.

— *The Federal Reserve System*, 50th Anniversary Edition, 1963[1]

INTRODUCTION

Until recently, the economy of the United States was the one bright spot in a very troubled global economy. Most of the United States' major trading partners are either in economic crisis, attempting to recover from crisis, or verging on crisis. Europe is the only exception. Japan, the Asia Crisis countries, and Mexico are all very fragile, and China has a bubble economy just waiting to pop. All of those countries, along with many others, have large and growing current account surpluses with the United States. Their economies have grown dependent on their surpluses with the United States. Economic disaster looms should their exports to the U.S. begin to decline. Consequently, the possibility of an appreciation of their currencies against the dollar represents a grave threat to their prosperity.

For that reason, the surplus nations must buy U.S. dollar-denominated assets with the dollars they earn from their current account surpluses with the United States. The alternative of converting those dollars into their own currencies would cause their currencies to appreciate, their exports to decline, and their economies to collapse into crisis.

This dilemma explains why the surplus nations have accumulated such large U.S. dollar foreign exchange reserves over the last 20 years. Their acquisition of trillions of dollars of U.S. dollar-denominated assets also helps explain the stock market boom, the rapid expansion of debt, and the low savings rate in the United States over that period. Now, however, their dilemma is becoming more acute. The U.S. economy has been blown into a bubble because of excess credit expansion. Neither the business sector nor the consumer sector can afford to take on any more debt. In fact, both will soon be compelled to reduce their indebtedness. Similarly, the over-inflated equities market is beginning to crash. Under these circumstances, in which U.S. dollar assets will the surplus nations invest their US$500 billion current account surpluses, not only this year, but every year into the future so long as the U.S. current account deficit persists? Those countries will not continue to put half a trillion dollars into U.S. assets every year if they are certain they are going to lose much of it. This chapter will describe why it is becoming increasingly difficult to find so many new, secure investments in the United States. The impossibility of doing so for much longer makes a plunge in the value of the U.S. dollar inevitable.

This chapter will begin by taking another look at the United States' rapidly increasing net indebtedness to the rest of the world. Then, it will examine, in turn, the major categories of U.S. investment alternatives available to the surplus nations: debt, equity, and direct investment. The US$30 trillion U.S. credit market will be analyzed in considerable detail. Trends in individual debt, financial sector debt, non-financial corporate debt, and U.S. government debt will be analyzed in order to assess the creditworthiness of each of those sectors. It will be shown that only the U.S. government will have the debt servicing capacity to issue the amounts of debt that will be needed if the surplus nations are to recycle their dollar surpluses. However, the magnitude of the U.S. current account deficit is such that not even the U.S. government will be able to issue enough debt to absorb it indefinitely.

The alternative investment categories – equities and direct investment – are described next. Equities are shown not only to be overvalued, but also suspect due to the accounting scandals that have undermined trust in corporate America in general and Wall Street in particular. Direct investment remains an alternative, but an illiquid one, not suitable for many of the surplus nations.

The wave of defaults on corporate debt and the 50% plunge in the S&P from its peak underline the risks the rest of the world faces in making further investments in dollar-denominated assets. As the surplus nations realize that large parts of the U.S. economy are no longer creditworthy, they will stop throwing good money after bad and, instead, reluctantly convert their dollars into something less certain of producing a loss, whether that be their own currencies, gold, or some other non-U.S. dollar-denominated assets. Then the collapse of the dollar will begin. Part Three will describe the impact that a plunging dollar will have on the global economy.

FINANCING THE U.S. CURRENT ACCOUNT GAP: HALF A TRILLION DOLLARS A YEAR REQUIRED

It is useful to begin by taking another look at the trend in the U.S. current account balance over the last two decades (see Figure 6.1).

This string of record-breaking deficits began in the early 1980s, peaking at US$161 billion in 1987. The current account deficit shrank as the dollar weakened during the late 1980s, with the account briefly returning to a balanced position in 1991. From 1992, however, the deficit began to widen again, growing steadily worse as the currencies of one country after another weakened relative to the dollar. The peso was devalued in 1994 and the Chinese Renminbi the following year (see Figure 6.2). The yen peaked in 1995 and then fell back sharply. In 1997, a severe round of currency instability began as the Asia Crisis erupted. Surprisingly, even the euro proved to be weak relative to the dollar after its launch at the end of the decade (see Figure 6.3).

Naturally, the U.S. trade deficit widened with each of these countries as their currencies plunged (see Figure 6.4).

By 2000, the United States' current account deficit had grown to US$410 billion, or more than 4% of U.S. GDP. The following year, there was a slight improvement as the overheated economy dipped into a shallow recession. In 2002, the deficit is expected to establish a new record of disequilibrium at almost 5% of GDP. To put that into perspective, the U.S.

Figure 6.1 United States: Balance on the current account, 1980–2001

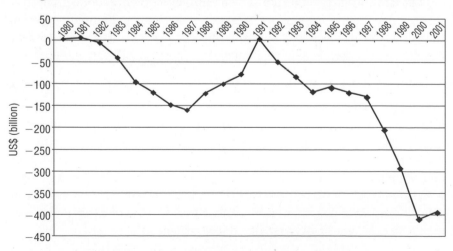

Source: U.S. Department of Commerce, Bureau of Economic Analysis.

Figure 6.2 The violent depreciation of the Chinese yuan, Mexican peso, and Thai baht against the U.S. dollar, 1990–2002

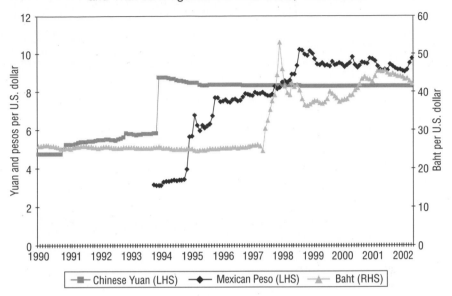

Source: Federal Reserve Economic Data: St. Louis Fed.

Figure 6.3 Weakness in the yen and euro, 1995–2002

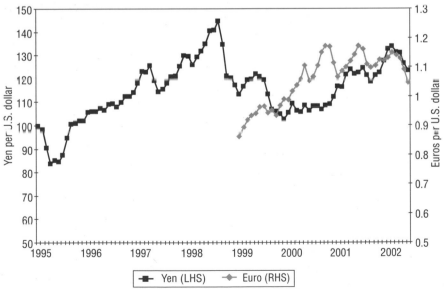

Source: Federal Reserve Economic Data: St. Louis Fed.

Figure 6.4   Giant sucking sound? The U.S. trade deficit widens with each
country as their currencies depreciated, 1990–2001

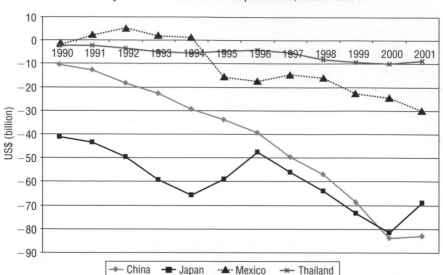

Source: U.S. Census Bureau, Foreign Trade Division.

current account deficit, at US$500 billion, will be the equivalent of 1.5% of global GDP.

To finance this extraordinary current account deficit, it has been necessary for the United States to attract approximately US$3 trillion of foreign investment into the country since 1980. This is reflected in the symmetry between the country's current account deficit and its financial account surplus (see Figure 6.5).

As a result of its current account deficit, the United States, which up until the early 1980s had been an important source of credit to the rest of the world, is now more deeply in debt to the rest of the world than any other country ever has been. Its transformation from creditor to debtor is illustrated in Figure 6.6, which shows the change in the net international investment position of the United States from 1982 to 2001.

The net international investment position of the United States is a snapshot of the amount that country owes to the rest of the world, or, in other words, the value of all U.S. assets abroad less the amount of U.S. assets owned by the rest of the world.

The net investment position of the United States has deteriorated more or less in line with the U.S. current account deficit because the United States has had to finance that deficit by selling U.S. dollar-denominated assets of one kind or another – stocks, bonds, property, paper dollars, etc. – to its

Figure 6.5 United States: Mirror image: Current account versus financial account, 1969–98

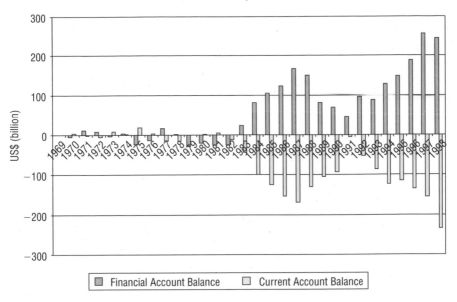

Source: IMF, *International Financial Statistics Yearbook 2001*.

Figure 6.6 United States: Net international investment position, 1982–2001 (at market costs)

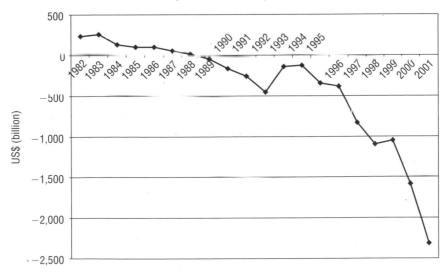

Source: U.S. Department of Commerce, Bureau of Economic Analysis.

trading partners in exchange for their goods and services. At the end of 2001, the net international investment position of the United States was – US$2.3 trillion, an amount equivalent to 22.6% of GDP. In 2001 alone, the United States' external debt as a percentage of GDP rose 6.6 percentage points, from 16.0% to 22.6%. Over the next five years, if the U.S. current account deficits persist at a level equivalent to 5% of GDP per annum, the net indebtedness of the United States to the rest of the world will increase to the equivalent of 50% of U.S. GDP by 2006 (see Figure 6.7).

The blowout in the current account deficit, particularly since 1997, has meant that the foreign share of the ownership of U.S. assets has already risen very sharply. For example, the foreign ownership of U.S. equities increased from less than 7% in 1997 to more than 11% at the end of 2001,[2] while the foreign holdings of privately held U.S. Treasuries jumped from 20% in 1994 to 40% in 2001.[3]

Those large foreign capital inflows had a significant impact on the U.S. economy. For instance, it should be easily understood from the preceding figures that share prices in the United States would have risen less – and Treasury bond yields would have fallen less – in the late 1990s in the absence of such large foreign purchases.

Because the private sector in the United States is now over-leveraged, it will become increasingly difficult for the surplus nations to find sufficient amounts of new investment vehicles in which to park their dollar surpluses.

Figure 6.7 U.S. credit market assets owned by the rest of the world, 1980–2002 (Q1)

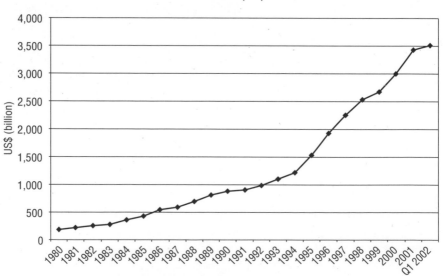

Source: Federal Reserve Board, *Flow of Funds*.

When they become unwilling to finance the United States' extraordinary current account deficit, the dollar will collapse and the United States will no longer be able to buy US$500 billion more in goods and services from the rest of the world than it sells each year.

THE INVESTMENT ALTERNATIVES

The surplus nations must buy U.S. dollar-denominated assets with their dollar surpluses if they are to avoid converting those dollars into their own currencies and killing the goose that laid the golden egg. There are three broad categories of U.S. dollar-denominated assets they have to choose from: credit market (that is, debt) instruments, U.S. corporate equities, and foreign direct investment. Table 6.1 shows where the surplus nations have chosen to invest their dollars each year from 1996.

The table provides a breakdown of the net acquisitions of financial assets by the rest of the world, a figure that amounted to US$791.1 billion in 2001. The net amount of their acquisitions is offset by their net increase in liabilities (US$337.9 billion in 2001), with the result being the net financial investment by the rest of the world in the United States (US$453.1 billion in 2001). The U.S. current account deficit is included at the bottom of the table to demonstrate that the net financial investment by the rest of the world has been sufficiently large to finance the U.S. current account over this period. That, in fact, must be the case. The United States has to pay the rest of the world for their goods and services. To the extent that the U.S. imports more than it exports, it must finance the deficit by selling financial assets to its trading partners.

Over the five-year period depicted in the table, the U.S. current account deficit has increased by 3.5 times, from US$121 billion in 1996 to US$417 billion in 2001. Consequently, the net financial investment into the United States by the rest of the world has had to increase as well. This presents a good opportunity to debunk one of the most absurd ideas ever to circulate in the late 20th century.

Government officials and investment bankers frequently tell the public that the U.S. current account deficit is caused by the eagerness of the rest of the world to invest in the United States. They reason that the large U.S. financial account surpluses resulting from foreign investment in the United States necessitate the large U.S. current account deficits, given that the financial account and the current account must completely offset one another when added together.

It is hard to understand how such a ridiculous idea could be taken seriously. Americans buy more from the rest of the world than the rest of the

Table 6.1 The acquisition of U.S. financial assets by the rest of the world, 1996–2002 (Q1) (US$ billion)

	1996	1997	1998	1999	2000	2001	2002 Q1 (annualized)
Net acquisition of financial assets	556.7	649.7	474.3	782.2	941.8	791.1	480.9
Credit market instruments:							
U.S. government treasury securities	270.7	139.7	38.7	-8.3	-63.0	26.6	0.9
U.S. government agency securities	41.7	49.8	56.7	92.2	152.7	165.2	120.3
U.S. corporate bonds	83.7	84.6	122.2	160.8	183.1	230.7	194.6
Other credit market instruments	18.3	37.1	36.6	-35.8	6.5	5.6	-44.3
U.S. corporate equities	11.1	67.8	42.0	112.3	193.8	129.2	70.5
Foreign direct investment in the U.S.	86.5	105.6	178.2	301.0	287.7	157.9	165.9
Others	44.7	165.1	-0.1	160.0	181.0	75.9	-26.9
Net increase in liabilities	383.9	377.8	328.8	408.9	497.8	337.9	140.9
Net financial investment	172.8	272.0	145.5	373.2	444.0	453.1	340.0
U.S. current account deficit 2002 estimate	-120.9	-139.8	-217.5	-324.4	-444.7	-417.0	-500.0

Note: The figures for the U.S. current account deficit were subsequently revised down to US$410 billion in 2000 and US$393 billion in 2001.
Source: Federal Reserve Board, *Flow of Funds*, Table F.107.

world buys from the United States, because the rest of the world uses very low-cost labor to make goods at a much lower cost than US-based manufacturers can. This could not be more obvious. That is why the current account surpluses of Mexico, China, Thailand, and the rest of the Asia Crisis countries rose sharply following the devaluation of their currencies: their labor costs fell, making their products even more attractively priced to the U.S. consumer. Is it conceivable that American consumers buy all the foreign-made products in their homes and in their closets because other countries want to invest in the United States? Or is it because those imported products were 50% cheaper than similar goods made in the U.S.? Wage rates in Chinese factories are US$4 per day. Think about it.

In 2001, the United States ran a current account deficit of approximately US$400 billion because the rest of the world can manufacture products more cheaply than the U.S. can. Anyone who tries to persuade the public that the U.S. current account deficit is caused by the desire of foreign investors to buy U.S. assets should be laughed at if he actually believes that and be ashamed of himself if he doesn't. These deficits have resulted in tremendous disequilibrium in the global economy. The public should not be misled about their origin.

Figure 6.8 shows how the rest of the world decided to allocate their dollar surpluses between the alternative dollar-denominated investment vehicles available to them.

Figure 6.8 A breakdown of net acquisition of U.S. financial assets by the rest of the world, 2001 (US$ billion)

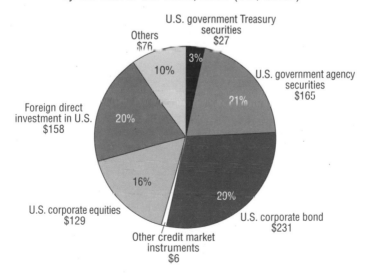

Source: Federal Reserve Board, *Flow of Funds*, Table F.107.

In 2001, the United States' trading partners divided their (net) acquisitions of U.S. financial assets between debt instruments, including U.S. corporate bonds (29%), U.S. government agency securities (21%), and U.S. government Treasury securities (3%); and foreign direct investment (20%), U.S. corporate equities (16%), and others (10%).

The rest of this chapter will analyze trends in each of these asset categories in order to assess whether there will be sufficient security in any of these vehicles, either individually or in combination, to entice the surplus nations to continue investing their annual US$500 billion surpluses in the United States.

Debt Instruments

Total credit market debt as a ratio of GDP practically doubled in the United States between 1969 and 2001, rising from 152% to 290% (see Figure 6.9). While the trend has been rising almost without interruption every year, there were two periods when the increase in debt accelerated noticeably relative to economic output – from 1982 to 1988, and again from 1996 to the present. It is no coincidence that those two periods corresponded almost exactly to the two worst episodes of deterioration in the U.S. current account deficit. As the surplus nations sought to reinvest their dollar surpluses into dollar-denominated assets, debt issuance expanded to meet that need. Share prices also rose rapidly during those periods, as the rest of the world used their trade surpluses to buy U.S. equities.

Before we take a more detailed look at the various sectors of the economy that issue debt instruments, consider the following extract from the Bond Market Association's *Research Quarterly* of August 2002, which will help put the latest trends in the debt market into perspective.

> New issue volume in the U.S. bond market totaled US$2.5 trillion for the first half of 2002, up 16.8 percent versus the US$2.1 trillion issued during the same period last year. Investors found in bonds a respite from poor equity performance, and issuers took advantage of some of the lowest interest rates in decades.
> - Commercial paper outstanding decreased 4.1 percent, to US$1.32 trillion at the end of the second quarter, down from US$1.38 trillion at the end of the first quarter. Concerns over issuer credit quality have led to a decrease in the use of commercial paper in recent quarters.
> - Issuance of mortgage-related securities totaled US$1.01 trillion in the first half of this year, up 51.6 percent from US$664.1 billion issued during the same period last year.

Figure 6.9 Debt to GDP: Total credit market debt in the United States, 1969–2002 (Q1)

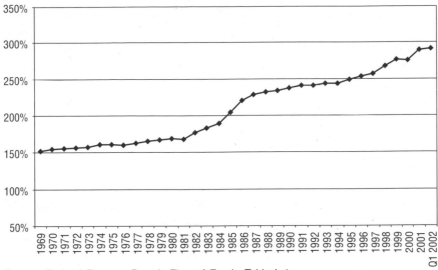

Source: Federal Reserve Board, *Flow of Funds*, Table L.1.

- Federal agencies increased long-term new issue volume during the first half of 2002, to US$453.7 billion. Short-term federal agency debt outstanding decreased 4.0 percent, to US$651.9 billion as of the end of June.
- New issues of corporate bonds totaled US$388.2 billion in the first half of 2002, with volume decreases across all sectors – investment-grade, high yield, and convertibles.
- Asset-backed issuance increased to US$237.9 billion, up 6.2 percent from the US$223.9 billion issued during the same period last year.
- Treasury gross coupon issuance increased 50.0 percent, to US$233.1 billion during the first half of 2002, compared to US$155.1 billion in the first half of 2001.
- Municipal issuance totaled a record US$194.6 billion in the first two quarters of 2002. Long-term new issues increased to US$164.6 billion and short-term issuance increased to US$30.0 billion through June.

A great deal can be learned about the U.S. economy by examining these trends in the bond market. As will be seen, this US$400 billion, 16.8% year-on-year increase in bond issuance in the 12 months up to the end of June 2002 has played the principal role in providing American consumers with the means to continue living beyond their means up until now. Over the following pages, a dissection of the U.S. credit market will show how this was done.

The Flow of Funds

The most comprehensive source of information concerning U.S. debt is published by the Board of Governors of the Federal Reserve System in the *Flow of Funds Accounts of the United States*. Those accounts provide a breakdown of all debt in the U.S. credit market, in terms of both who owes the debt and who the debt instruments are owned by. Figure 6.10 and Table 6.2 show the rise in total credit market debt from 1980 to the present and a breakdown of that debt by sector, respectively.

The largest debtors are the financial sector, the household sector, the non-financial corporate sector, and the federal government, in that order (see Figure 6.11).

The two most significant trends here are the rapid increase in financial sector debt throughout the period and the absolute decline in federal government debt at the end of the 1990s. Those trends are put into even better focus when the debt of each sector is shown as a percentage of GDP (see Figure 6.12).

As a percentage of GDP, financial sector debt skyrocketed from 20% in 1980 to 93% in early 2002. Household debt rose from 50% of GDP to 78% over the same period. The debt of the business sector rose from 52% to 69%. Even the federal government debt increased from 27% of GDP in 1980 to 32% in 2002 despite the government's uncharacteristic budget surpluses for

Figure 6.10   Total debt in the U.S. credit market, 1980–2002 (Q1)

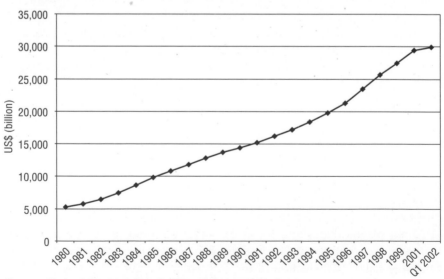

Source: Federal Reserve Board, *Flow of Funds*, Table L.1.

Table 6.2 Total credit market debt broken down by sector, 1995–2002(Q1)

Credit market debt outstanding
Billions of dollars; amounts outstanding end of period, not seasonally adjusted

	1995	1996	1997	1998	1999	2000	2001 Q1	2002 Q1	
Total credit market debt owed by:	**18439.9**	**19812.1**	**21310.2**	**23483.8**	**25700.4**	**27475.8**	**29472.9**	**29934.9**	1
Domestic nonfinancial sectors	13707.5	14441.1	15244.2	16287.1	17391.1	18272.0	19376.3	19696.1	2
Federal government	3636.7	3781.7	3804.8	3752.2	3681.0	3385.1	3379.5	3430.3	3
Nonfederal sectors	10070.0	10659.4	11439.4	12534.9	13710.2	14886.9	15996.8	16175.8	4
Household sector	4913.8	5223.9	5556.9	6011.4	6513.3	7078.3	7692.9	7800.1	5
Non-financial corporate business	2879.9	3093.0	3383.1	3776.1	4209.3	4612.3	4840.1	4866.2	6
Non-farm noncorporate business	1062.0	1129.3	1224.0	1383.7	1566.1	1736.8	1893.6	1921.4	7
Farm business	144.8	149.7	155.9	163.9	169.4	180.2	187.6	186.9	8
State and local governments	1070.2	1063.4	1119.5	1199.8	1252.1	1279.3	1382.5	1401.2	9
Rest of the world	453.7	542.2	608.0	651.5	679.6	746.7	712.9	725.6	10
Financial sectors	4278.8	4828.8	5458.0	6545.2	7629.6	8457.1	9383.8	9603.3	11
Commercial banking	250.6	263.6	309.2	382.1	449.3	509.3	562.1	565.2	12
U.S. chartered commercial banks	92.2	103.9	133.4	186.2	228.0	264.8	294.9	294.8	13
Foreign banking offices in U.S.	10.4	9.6	7.2	2.4	2.0	2.0	1.1	1.0	14
Bank holding companies	148.0	150.0	166.6	193.5	219.3	242.5	266.1	269.4	15
Savings institutions	115.0	140.5	160.3	212.4	260.4	287.7	295.1	280.4	16
Credit unions	0.4	0.4	0.6	1.1	3.4	3.4	4.9	5.5	17
Life insurance companies	0.5	1.6	1.8	2.5	32.	2.5	3.1	3.7	18
Government-sponsored enterprises	806.5	896.9	995.3	1273.6	1591.7	1825.8	2114.0	2161.8	19
Federally related mortgage pools	1570.3	1711.3	1825.8	2018.4	2292.2	2491.6	2830.1	2955.5	20
ABS issuers	712.5	863.3	1076.6	1398.0	1621.4	1829.6	2117.8	2200.1	21
Finance companies	483.9	534.5	568.3	625.5	695.7	776.9	777.0	759.1	22
Mortgage companies	16.5	20.6	16.0	17.7	17.8	17.9	18.6	18.8	23
REITs	44.6	56.5	96.1	158.8	165.1	167.8	170.2	172.1	24
Brokers and dealers	23.3	27.3	35.3	42.5	25.3	40.9	42.3	39.7	25
Funding corporations	243.6	312.4	372.6	412.6	504.0	503.7	448.5	441.3	26

Source: Federal Reserve Board, *Flow of Funds*, Table L.1.

Figure 6.11   The major components of U.S. credit market debt, 1980–2002 (Q1)

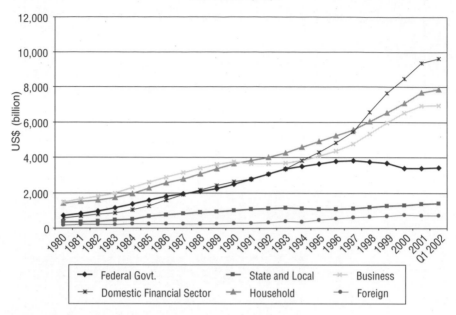

Source: Federal Reserve Board, *Flow of Funds*, Table L.1.

Figure 6.12   Sector debt as a percentage of GDP, 1980–2002 (Q1)

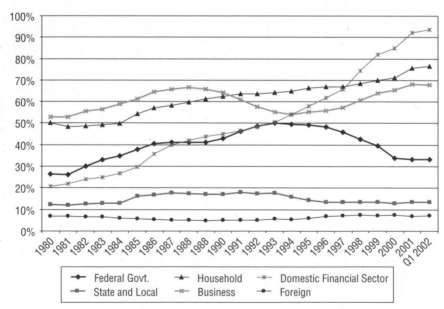

Source: Federal Reserve Board, *Flow of Funds*.

a few years at the end of the 1990s. The debt of state and local governments and of the foreign sector remained relatively constant throughout the period.

The following sections look at the trends in the indebtedness of each of the four largest sectors in order to assess their current creditworthiness.

The Financial Sector

The growth in the debt of the financial sector has been extraordinary over the last two decades. Jumping from US$578 billion in 1980 to US$9.6 trillion in early 2002, the debt of the financial sector in the United States has soared from 21% of GDP to 93%. Equally important, in terms of debt outstanding, the institutions that traditionally supplied credit – commercial banks and savings institutions – have been dwarfed by the rise of federally related mortgage pools, government-sponsored enterprises, and asset-backed securities (ABS) issuers over that period (see Figures 6.13 and 6.14). For example, in 1980, the debt of federally related mortgage pools and GSEs amounted to 4% and 6% of GDP, respectively, while the asset-backed securities market had not yet come into existence. By early 2002, the combined debt of those three groups had risen to 71% of GDP, whereas the debt of the traditional lenders had hardly changed relative to GDP.

Because the nature of the financial sector has changed so radically over the last 20 years, some description of each of the categories comprising the financial sector is necessary.

Figure 6.13 Components of financial sector debt, 1980–2002 (Q1)

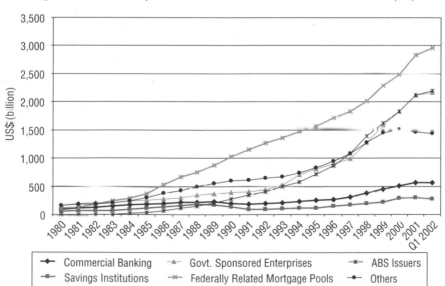

Source: Federal Reserve Board, *Flow of Funds.*

Figure 6.14   Components of financial sector debt as a percentage of GDP, 1980–2002 (Q1)

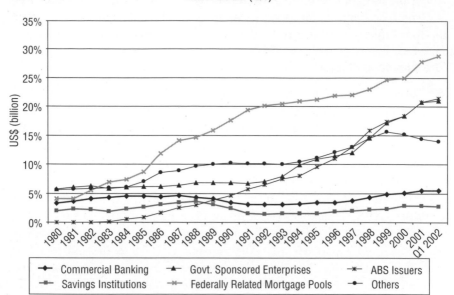

Source: Federal Reserve Board, *Flow of Funds*.

Federally Related Mortgage Pools. Pools are groups of related financial instruments, such as mortgages, combined for resale to investors on a secondary market. Federally related mortgage pools, as classified in the Flow of Funds Accounts, are pools of mortgage securities issued by the Government National Mortgage Association (Ginnie Mae), the Federal National Mortgage Association (Fannie Mae), the Federal Home Loan Mortgage Corporation (Freddie Mac), and the Farmers Home Administration.

The liabilities of federally related mortgage pools have surged from US$114 billion, or 4% of GDP, in 1980 to US$3 trillion, or 29% of GDP, in early 2002. Since the beginning of 1999 alone, their liabilities have risen by more than US$1 trillion. On the other side of their balance sheets, these organizations hold roughly an equivalent amount of residential mortgages as assets.

Although the debt of Fannie Mae and Freddie Mac is not guaranteed by the U.S. government, their bonds trade in the market with a yield that is at a very low premium to Treasury bonds. Apparently, it is generally believed that the government would not allow those institutions to default on their debt should they encounter financial difficulties. In recent years, their size and rate of growth have given rise to a series of concerns regarding these groups, ranging from worries that their government ties give them an unfair advantage relative to their competitors, to fears that their aggressive acquisition of mortgages has fueled a property bubble. Their supporters counter that these institutions have made home ownership more accessible. In any case, by acquiring mortgages, these pools have funneled very large sums into the U.S. property market and, thereby, played a role in pushing property prices higher.

The Bond Market Association's August 2002 *Research Quarterly* provided the following details:

> Mortgage-related securities issuance, which includes agency and private-label pass-throughs and CMOs (collateralized mortgage obligations), totaled US$1.01 trillion in the first half of this year, up 51.6 percent from the US$664.1 billion issued during the same period in 2001.
>
> Agency mortgage-backed securities (MBS) issuance increased to US$637.6 billion in the first half of the year, up 38.8 percent versus the US$459.5 billion issued during the first half of 2001. Fannie Mae's issuance increased to US$311.0 billion in the first half of the year, up 37.2 percent from the US$226.7 billion issued in the first half of 2001. New issue volume of Freddie Mac MBS totaled US$240.4 billion in the first two quarters of 2002, up 52.8 percent from last year's first-half volume. Issuance of Ginnie Mae MBS increased 14.2 percent in the first half of 2002, to US$86.2 billion.
>
> Issuance in the agency collateralized mortgage obligation (CMO) market increased to US$241.0 billion in the first half of 2002, more than double the US$111.5 billion issued during the first two quarters of 2001. Freddie Mac CMO new issue activity totaled US$148.7 billion, up from the US$71.9 billion issued last year during the same period. Additionally, CMO issuance volume of both Fannie Mae and Ginnie Mae increased during the first half of the year. Fannie Mae issuance increased to US$58.4 billion, up from the US$22.2 billion issued during the same period of 2001. Issuance of Ginnie Mac CMOs almost doubled to US$33.9 billion, when compared to the US$17.4 billion issued during the first half of 2002.
>
> Every asset price bubble requires credit as fuel. The preceding paragraphs make clear the origins of the credit that is fueling the U.S. property market bubble and, by extension, the consumer spending spree in the United States.

Government-sponsored Enterprises. At the end of the first quarter of 2002, the liabilities of government-sponsored enterprises amounted to US$2.2 trillion, up more than US$1.1 trillion since the end of 1997. Those liabilities are comprised primarily of GSE debt instruments.

The GSEs that are included in the Federal Reserve's *Flow of Funds Accounts* are: the Federal Home Loan Banks, the Federal National Mortgage Association (Fannie Mae), the Federal National Mortgage Association (Freddie Mac), the Farm Credit System, the Financing Corporation, the Resolution Funding Corporation, and the Student Loan Marketing Association (Sallie Mae).

Their assets are comprised of U.S. government agency securities, including those of Fannie Mae and Freddie Mac (46%), mortgages (13%), corporate and foreign bonds (6%), and loans to one another (23%). In other words, these institutions issue bonds and use most of the proceeds to make loans to or buy bonds from other GSEs.

Issuers of Asset-backed Securities. The most striking explosion of debt has been that undertaken by issuers of asset-backed securities (ABSs). The ABS market only began to develop in the early 1980s, but it has grown at a remarkable rate since then. Debt owed by issuers of ABSs surpassed that owed by commercial banks for the first time in 1990. Less than 12 years later, their debt exceeds that of commercial banks by almost four times. By early 2002, the assets and liabilities of the issuers of ABSs had grown to US$2.2 trillion. Their assets are comprised of mortgages (42%), consumer credit (27%), trade receivables (11%), agency securities (13%), and other loans and advances (7%).

ABSs are made up of a pool of assets such as mortgages, credit cards, auto loans, equipment leases, corporate loans, trade receivables, etc. Originators, such as banks and leasing companies, pool groups of loans and sell them to special-purpose vehicles (SPVs), which, in turn, issue ABSs to investors.

ABSs offer several advantages to the originators of the asset pools. First, selling those assets to SPVs reduces their risk-weighted assets and thereby frees up their capital, enabling them to originate still more loans. Next, it lowers their risks. In a worse-case scenario where the pool of assets performs very badly, the SPVs would pay the price of bankruptcy rather than the originator. Finally, the originators earn fees from originating the loans, as well as from continuing to service the assets throughout their life.

In other words, securitization enables the originators of the loans to enjoy most of the benefits of lending money without bearing the risks involved. Those risks are shifted to the institutional investors who acquire the ABSs and the funds they manage. By removing loans from the banking sector, the development of the ABS market has also reduced the contingent liabilities of the government, which, through the Federal Deposit Insurance Corporation (FDIC), insures the banks' depositors. However, at the same time, those risks are shifted back to individuals whose pension accounts would take a hit in the event of large-scale defaults in the assets underlying the ABSs that are held in their retirement account and mutual funds. The economic slowdown is likely to expose such weakness, particularly since sub-prime home-equity loans have become the fastest-growing sector of the ABS market in recent years. There are growing concerns that ABSs have given rise to moral hazard on the part of those who originate and sell the repackaged loans.

Figure 6.15 shows a breakdown of outstanding asset-backed securities by major types of credit.

Figure 6.15 Asset-backed securities outstanding by major types of credit, 2001 (US$ billion)

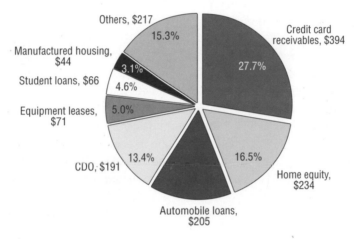

Source: The Bond Market Association, *Research Quarterly*, August 2002.

Commercial Banks. One rule of thumb should always be kept in mind regarding credit quality: it always appears high at the peak of the business cycle. So long as credit expansion continues, borrowers have no trouble repaying their loans, even if they have to take out new loans to pay back the old loans. Only when new credit begins to dry up does credit quality deterioration begin in earnest. It would seem that the U.S. credit market has just passed that watershed. Credit expansion is slowing and bankruptcies are beginning to blow out.

The total loans of commercial banks contracted in the first quarter of 2002 relative to the previous quarter, albeit by only US$2 billion. That was the first quarterly contraction in lending since the first quarter of 1997. Relative to the first quarter of 2001, lending increased by 1.6%. Banks lent generously to individuals, but curtailed their commercial and industrial loans. Loans to individuals increased by US$52 billion, or 8.7%, compared with one year earlier, while commercial and industrial loans contracted by US$78 billion, or 7.5%.

Thus far, consumers have shown greater resilience in the face of the economic downturn than have corporations. The continued rapid expansion of consumer credit is the principal reason why. As will be seen below, both sectors are in trouble. Banks will either continue to rein in credit or soon wish they had. Bank balance sheets are in for a retrenchment. They are unlikely to issue much new debt of their own as they call in loans to their clients. Foreign investors will have to look somewhere other than commercial banks if they are to reinvest their dollar surpluses.

The Rest of the Financial Sector. Little explanation is required for saving institutions other than to point out again that, as with commercial banks, the relative stagnation in their level of debt to GDP is largely explained by the development of the ABS market which has enabled these groups to shift assets and liabilities off their balance sheets and into special-purpose vehicles. The "Others" category depicted in the preceding figures is comprised of credit unions, life insurance companies, finance companies, mortgage companies, REITs, brokers and dealers, and funding corporations. This category is relatively small, equivalent to only 14% of GDP. Also, it has not grown relative to GDP over the last 20 years. For these reasons, no further comment will be made about these institutions.

The Financial Sector: Concluding Remarks. The debt of the financial sector has grown much more rapidly than that of all other sectors of the economy over the last two decades. Within the finance sector, federally related mortgage pools, GSEs, and ABS issuers have grown at an extraordinary pace and now dominate the sector. The health of these groups cannot be considered independently from the health of the overall economy. Consumption has held up remarkably well in 2001 and 2002 despite the economic downturn and sharp slide in share prices. Many observers believe that the consumer's resilience is explained by the continuing aggressive extension of credit by the financial sector in the form of mortgages and consumer credit. Rising joblessness, stagnating wages, the loss of stock-market wealth, and a historically low savings rate all suggest that the financial sector will find the quality of their assets deteriorating rapidly during the months and years ahead. That process is already well under way. As the deterioration of their asset quality accelerates, they themselves will be perceived as less creditworthy and will find it increasingly difficult to issue new debt of their own. In an environment of generally deteriorating credit quality, foreign investors will be reluctant to provide further credit to the financial sector in the United States.

The Household Sector

If the U.S. economy has been the engine of economic growth in the world in recent years, it has been because the American consumer has been in the driving seat ... and speeding.

The household sector's credit market debt amounted to US$7.9 trillion at the end of the second quarter of 2002, making it the second-heaviest borrower in the credit markets after the financial sector. As a percentage of GDP, this sector's debt has risen rapidly to 77%, from 50% in 1980, enabling the American consumer to fuel the global economy.

Record low interest rates and wildly aggressive lending practices by creditors have allowed households to continue increasing their debt and their consumption. However, the deflation of the New Paradigm economic bubble has caused unemployment to rise, while knocking down the rate of increase in personal income to the lowest level in more than a generation. Moreover, the U.S. stock-market crash has erased US$8 trillion in wealth since March 2000. The ratio of consumer debt service payments to disposable personal income is climbing quickly toward a new record high and personal bankruptcy filings have already set a new benchmark. Equally disturbing, the personal savings rate very nearly became a personal dis-savings rate in 2000 and 2001 at the peak of the boom.

As these issues were described in some detail in Chapter 5, no further analysis is required here to conclude that the finances of the American household sector are rotten. They can only be expected to worsen as the economy and share prices weaken further. Households will have no choice but to borrow less and to repay part of what they currently owe. Foreign investors would be wise to reduce any credit exposure they might have to this sector. It is very unlikely that they would consider the debt of this sector as an attractive investment opportunity during the next several years (see Figure 6.16).

The Non-financial Corporate Sector

The story in the corporate sector is quite similar to that of the household sector: reckless borrowing and mind-boggling capital misallocation. The debt crisis in the corporate sector was described in the previous chapter, so a brief summation of the facts will suffice here. In the second quarter of 2002, this sector's credit market debt amounted to US$7 trillion, or 68% of GDP, up from US$1.5 trillion, or 53% of GDP, in 1980.

The corporate sector's liabilities are comprised of corporate bonds, 54%; bank loans, 17%; and other loans and advances, 14% (see Figure 6.17). That is, of course, if their accounts are to be believed. With new scandals and

Figure 6.16   Household sector credit market liabilities: US$7,800 billion in 2002 (Q2)

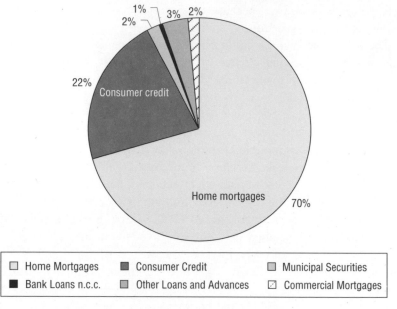

Source: Federal Reserve Board, *Flow of Funds*, Table L.100.

Figure 6.17   Non-financial commercial business credit market liabilities: US$4,866 billion in 2002 (Q2)

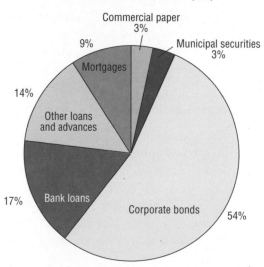

Source: Federal Reserve Board, *Flow of Funds*, Table L.102.

revelations of every type of corporate shenanigans dominating the front page of the newspapers week after week, there is every reason to suspect that this sector has drastically understated its liabilities, while there is absolutely no justification for extending yet more credit to the sector. The U.S. commercial banks reduced their commercial and industrial loans by US$78 billion, or 7.5%, in the first quarter of 2002 relative to one year earlier. A full-scale credit crunch crisis is now besetting the sector. Corporations must now reduce their liabilities. Many of them will have no option but to do so in the bankruptcy courts. Foreign investors purchased US$161 billion in U.S. corporate bonds in 1999, US$183 billion in 2000, and US$231 billion in 2001. In light of the losses that those investments must have generated, the surplus nations are very unlikely to consider U.S. corporate bonds as the investment vehicle of choice for recycling their dollar surpluses in the years immediately ahead.

It can be seen in Figure 6.18 that the increase in total credit market debt slowed (despite surging Treasury bond sales) during the last recession in the early 1990s as private investment fell and the growth in personal consumption expenditure slowed to a crawl. The same patterns will hold during this recession. Credit market debt will not expand sufficiently to allow the reinvestment of the surplus countries' dollar surpluses.

The U.S. Government

Out of all the major sectors issuing debt in the U.S. credit markets, the U.S. government is the least over-extended financially. Thanks to two tax increases in the 1990s and surging capital gains tax revenues during the New Paradigm bubble, the federal government achieved a budget surplus for four straight years beginning in 1998 (although many in government might hesitate before signing affidavits swearing to the accuracy of those accounts in light of the treatment of contributions to Social Security). Those fiscal surpluses put an end to a long string of budget deficits that added US$3.1 trillion to the government's publicly held debt between 1980 and 1998. Consequently, the ratio of government debt (held by the public) to GDP declined from 50% in 1993 to 33% in early 2002. In absolute amounts, the government's publicly held debt peaked in 1997 at US$3.8 trillion before falling back to US$3.4 trillion in 2001.

Now, however, the budget deficit is back, thanks to the recession and the stock-market crash. The Office of Budget and Management has forecast a deficit of US$165 billion in 2002 and US$109 billion in 2003. Events are likely to prove the estimate for 2003 to have been wildly optimistic. As the economy slows further and share prices continue their slide, tax revenues will be considerably weaker than currently anticipated, while expenditures,

Figure 6.18   Investment, consumption, and credit in the United States, 1981–2001 (percent change)

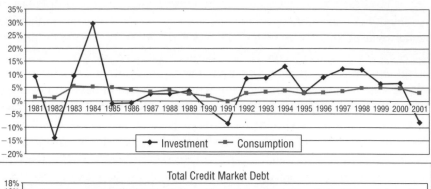

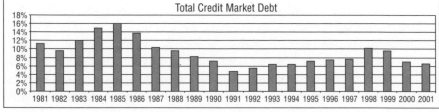

Source: IMF, *International Financial Statistics Yearbook 2001.*

augmented by additional spending to mitigate the impact of the slump, will be considerably higher. By 2004, it is quite probable that the budget deficit will exceed its old record of US$290 billion set in 1992 and continue to deteriorate from there.

A large new supply of Treasury bonds may be the salvation for the dollar in the near term. The United States' trading partners will leap at the opportunity to invest their dollar surpluses in bonds with the full faith and backing of the U.S. government.

The surplus nations need approximately US$500 billion worth of sound investment vehicles each year in which to invest their dollar surpluses. The prospects that such large amounts of sound credit instruments could be found within the financial sector, the household sector, or the non-financial corporate sector are not at all promising given the factors highlighted earlier in this chapter. Therefore, a large U.S. budget deficit could not occur at a more opportune time from the perspective of the surplus nations.

However, to what extent, and for how long, will the budget deficits satisfy the requirements of the rest of the world for secure dollar-denominated assets?

At present, the foreign holdings of privately held U.S. Treasuries come to 40% of the total outstanding. Such a large holding of Treasuries by other countries could be viewed as something of a security risk by the U.S.

government. For example, should other countries decide to sell Treasury bonds aggressively into the market either for economic or political reasons, a great deal of turmoil could arise in financial markets in the United States and around the world. For this reason, it seems realistic to assume that the foreign holdings of all new Treasury issues are unlikely to exceed 50% of the total.

Under those assumptions, budget deficits as high as US$500 billion would only provide half of the new supply of dollar-denominated assets the United States' trading partners need. The other US$250 billion would have to be found within the U.S. private sector. That would require the surplus nations to find US$1 trillion of sound investment vehicles in the U.S. private sector over the next four years. If they are not willing to risk a trillion dollars in private-sector investments over that time horizon, then the dollar must decline sharply as the dollar surpluses of the surplus nations are converted into other currencies.

Scenarios other than the one outlined above are conceivable. However, it is hard to imagine any realistic combination of events that would support the dollar at its current level for very much longer. For example, a budget deficit of less than US$500 billion is quite possible, but that would mean that the surplus nations would have to find a larger amount of secure investments in the private sector, which would be quite tough. On the other hand, a much larger budget deficit, say of US$800 billion or more, is not inconceivable, but a deterioration of the budget of that magnitude would imply a very serious economic collapse, which would mean even fewer sound private-sector investments. Finally, a systemic crisis in the banking sector or a collapse of one or more large GSEs would bring about an immediate upsurge in the supply of Treasury bonds, but would inflict extraordinary losses in other parts of the credit markets.

In the best case, then, it would appear that increasing U.S. budget deficits may provide part of the safe, dollar-denominated assets the rest of the world needs and thereby relieve part of the pressure on the dollar. However, the supply of government bonds is likely to be too small to discourage dollar selling or else so large as to imply crisis elsewhere in the credit markets. A temporary reprieve arising out of higher budget deficits is, realistically, the best scenario imaginable for the dollar – even under the best circumstances.

Equities

The rest of the world bought US$194 billion in U.S. corporate equities at the top of the market in 2000 and another US$129 billion in 2002. Between March 2000 and mid-July 2002, the S&P 500 Index fell 48%, inflicting great pain on U.S. and foreign investors alike (see Figure 6.19). Approximately US$8 trillion in wealth was destroyed in crashing U.S. equity markets during that period.

Two points may be sufficient to show why the U.S. equities market will not be considered a safe place for the surplus nations to invest their dollar surpluses in the years ahead.

First, the market capitalization of U.S. equity markets has fallen by US$8 trillion since they peaked in early 2000. They do not as easily absorb hundreds of billions of dollars of foreign investment as they once did.

Second, equities remain very overvalued by historical standards. Between 1900 and 1990, the average price-to-earnings (PE) multiple of the S&P Index was less than 15 times historic earnings. In mid-2002, after its 48% collapse, the index is still trading on 30 times historic earnings. Yes, investors should base their calculations on a company's prospects rather than its past, and therefore consider prospective earnings rather than historic earnings. However, given the ongoing revelations of accounting fraud among an extraordinary number of previously reputable companies and the slumping economy, a further sharp fall in earnings seems at least as probable as a sharp earnings recovery (see Figure 6.20).

Once the virtuous upward spiral of the bubble expansion within an economy gives way to the vicious downward spiral, earnings evaporate very quickly. That process, in large part, accounts for the 75% decline in the

Figure 6.19 Dow Jones Industrials, 1970–2002 (monthly averages)

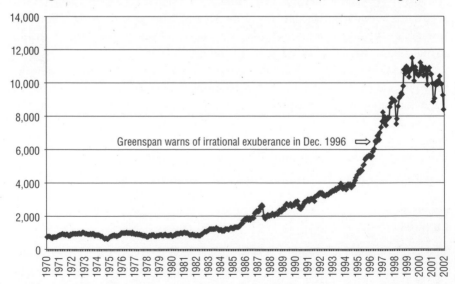

Source: Economagic.

Figure 6.20 Price-to-earnings multiples for the S&P 500, 1986–2001
(based on year-end prices and historic earnings)

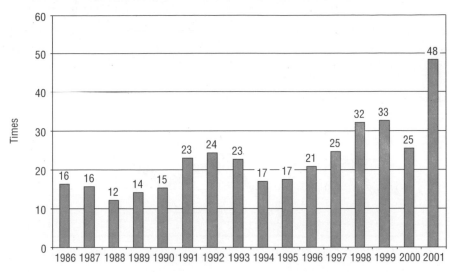

Source: Bloomberg.

Japanese stock market and the 88% collapse in Thailand's stock market following the implosion of their bubble economics. With the S&P down only 48% and the Dow Jones Industrial Index down only 30% from their highs, U.S. shares remain overvalued and are likely to fall considerably further and then remain depressed for years to come. The surplus nations would be well advised to invest their surpluses elsewhere.

By the way, when the US stock market crashed in 1929, it fell 88% before it bottomed. It did not recover to its 1929 high until 1954, 25 years later (see Figure 6.21). It does not always pay to buy on dips!

Foreign Direct Investment in the U.S.

The remaining major investment category available as a receptacle for the rest of the world's dollar surpluses is foreign direct investment into the United States. There has been substantial foreign direct investment into the U.S. in recent years. The amount rose as high as US$301 billion in 1999, before falling back to US$158 billion in 2001.

Foreign investors will continue to buy companies in the United States. However, the extinction of the dot.coms, the fiasco in the telecommunications industry, the scandalous behavior of some of the largest banks, and the risks arising from the conflicts of interest within the accounting profession have undermined confidence in the American business model. These factors are

Figure 6.21   Dow Jones Industrial Average, 1920–55 (monthly close)

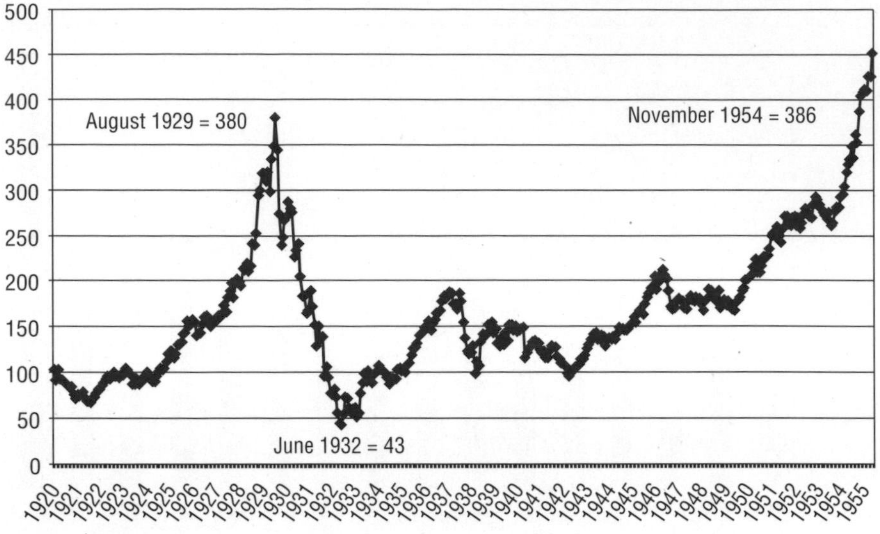

Source: Economagic.

likely to cause investors from other countries to think twice before making a direct investment in a U.S. company.

The slowing U.S. economy will also make the earnings prospects of most direct investment targets less attractive than before, which will further deter foreign investors. Finally, most investors prefer liquid assets that can be sold quickly and with little effort. The assets to be acquired through direct investment are therefore not acceptable to the majority of would-be foreign investors. Moreover, some of the countries with large current account surpluses with the United States may feel that directly investing in illiquid real assets in the U.S. is too risky from a political point of view. China, which now has the largest trade surplus of any country vis-à-vis the U.S., could fall into that category in light of its history of turbulent relations with the United States.

For all the reasons cited above, the United States' trading partners are likely to make fewer direct investments in the U.S. in the years immediately ahead instead of making more.

CONCLUSION

The dollar is destined to collapse because the U.S. economy will soon no longer be able to generate a supply of secure U.S. dollar-denominated investment vehicles sufficiently large to enable the rest of the world to recycle its annual half a trillion dollar current account surplus.

The countries running large current account surpluses against the United States need to continue buying U.S. dollar-denominated assets to avoid converting their dollar surpluses into their own currencies. Conversion would cause their currencies to appreciate and their exports to decline, throwing their economies into crisis. To avoid that scenario, the surplus nations have to buy either existing U.S. dollar-denominated assets or new dollar-denominated assets as they are issued.

Because the amounts involved are approaching the equivalent of 5% of U.S. GDP, if the surplus nations buy existing assets, they will drive up their prices from already inflated levels and thereby fuel new, unsustainable asset price bubbles in the U.S. On the other hand, in light of the current economic crisis and the weak financial condition of many of the largest businesses, very few U.S. corporations are likely to be able to bring substantial new debt or equity issues to the market in the near to intermediate term. Only the U.S. government will have the debt-servicing capacity to issue large amounts of new debt over the next five years.

The fate of the dollar in the near term may hinge on how quickly and by how much the U.S. budget deficit widens. Very large deficits exceeding US$500 billion annually would supply the secure dollar-denominated assets needed to recycle the rest of the world's dollar surpluses. Even that, however, would only give the dollar a temporary reprieve. Not even the U.S. government could sustain budget deficits of that size indefinitely.

The international monetary system is unstable. Because the post-Bretton Woods system has no inherent adjustment mechanism to ensure balanced trade, giant trade imbalances have arisen. As explained in Chapter 1, those trade imbalances are flooding the world with liquidity and generating excessive credit creation. Even if the dollar does not crash immediately, that does not mean that the global economy would stabilize, even temporarily. So long as the dollar remains at or near its current levels, the U.S. current account deficits will continue to generate unsustainable asset price bubbles and deflation around the world. Those very undesirable side effects are the subjects of Chapters 7 and 8.

▶ REFERENCES

1   *The Federal Reserve System*, 50th Anniversary Edition (Washington, D.C.: The Federal Reserve, 1963).
2   The Federal Reserve Board, *Flow of Funds*, Table Z-1.
3   The Bond Market Association.

Chapter 7

Asset Bubbles and Banking Crises

The excess credit which the Fed pumped into the economy spilled over into the stock market — triggering a fantastic speculative boom.

— Alan Greenspan, 1967[1]

Before the Bretton Woods international monetary system collapsed in 1973, all the money in the world was backed by gold. In other words, paper money was convertible into gold – at least at the government level, even if the rights of individuals to convert their paper money into gold had become increasingly curtailed as the 20th century progressed. Gold had long been the internationally accepted store of value for many reasons, one of the most important of which was that it could not be easily manipulated or debased by governments. Gold was always as good as gold; while government debt and paper money very frequently throughout history had proved to be far less good than gold – and sometimes completely worthless.

The collapse of Bretton Woods severed the last meaningful ties between paper money and gold. Very quickly, U.S. dollars replaced gold as the world's reserve currency in which most international trade transactions were conducted. International trade began to expand very rapidly because transactions could be settled in paper money, which could be printed without limit by governments; whereas before 1973, far less trade could be financed, since only gold (or currencies fully backed by gold) was accepted as payment and the amount of gold was limited.

International reserves had increased at a snail's pace prior to 1973, but exploded thereafter as rapidly increasing amounts of foreign exchange, primarily U.S. dollars, began flooding into every country in the world. This chapter will demonstrate how this inundation of dollars caused asset price bubbles around the world. Once that process is understood, it becomes apparent that this surge in international liquidity has also been to blame for the extraordinary outbreak of systemic banking crises that have grown in frequency and intensity all around the world during the last 30 years.

The cause-and-effect relationship between surging international reserve assets and systemic bank failures is very direct: the enormous trade imbalances that have occurred during the post-Bretton Woods international monetary regime have flooded the world with liquidity, the surge in liquidity has caused asset price bubbles in shares and property markets, and the implosion of those bubbles has caused systemic banking failures. The chapter will conclude with an examination of the severe damage that has been inflicted on government finances in those countries where asset price bubbles have popped and explain that the specter of fiscal collapse will make it impossible for many governments to bail out failed banking systems going forward. The growing possibility that asset price bubbles will end in fiscal crises is another reason why the current disequilibrium in the global economy cannot persist.

ASSET PRICE BUBBLES

When gold from South America began flooding into Europe in the 16th century, it set off severe inflationary shock waves across the continent. The inflationary impact of the conquistadors' gold is one of the most thoroughly analyzed events in economic history. It should not come as a surprise to economists, then, that the near exponential increase in dollar-denominated reserve assets has caused hyperinflation in asset prices in the modern world. It is easy to demonstrate that this has been the case.

This chapter begins by presenting six instances where asset price bubbles arose in a country (or group of countries) immediately after the influx of large amounts of capital from abroad. Each example will make reference to the increase in reserve assets that preceded or accompanied the episode of asset price inflation. By way of comparison, keep in mind that between 1949 and 1969, total reserve assets in the world rose by only 55%.

The South American Bubble of the 1970s

The first extraordinary manifestation of this process was in South America during the 1970s, when the American banks recycled OPEC's "petrodollar" deposits into loans to countries south of the U.S. border. Initially, as dollar loans poured into South America, economic growth rates accelerated. Brazil is the best example. Between 1971 and 1978, Brazil's reserve assets rose 600%, from US$1,696 million to US$11,826 million, and the economy grew at an average real rate of 8.5% a year. Brazil's "economic miracle" captured the attention of the world.

However, by the early 1980s, the boom had deflated into bust – not just in Brazil, but across most of Latin America. In August 1982, Mexico announced a moratorium on the repayment of its international loans. It soon became known that Mexico was not the only country unable to service its international debt. Concerns spread quickly that one or more of the largest

Table 7.1   U.S. banks' exposure as a percentage of capital, end 1982

	Argentina	Brazil	Mexico	Venezuela	Chile	Total
Citibank	18.2	73.5	54.6	18.2	10.0	174.5
Bank of America	10.2	47.9	52.1	41.7	6.3	158.2
Chase Manhattan	21.3	56.9	40.0	24.0	11.8	154.0
Morgan Guaranty	24.4	54.3	34.8	17.5	9.7	140.7
Manufacturers Hanover	47.5	77.7	66.7	42.4	28.4	262.7
Chemical	14.9	52.0	60.0	28.0	14.8	169.7

Source: William R. Cline, *International Debt: Systemic Risk and Policy Response* (Washington, D.C.: Institute for International Economics, 1984).

banks in the United States would fail – with systemic consequences (see Table 7.1). The first Third World debt crisis had begun.

Fortunately, the worst was averted. None of the large U.S. banks failed as a direct result of their international lending. However, the heavy external indebtedness of most South American countries contributed to depressed economic activity there throughout the 1980s, South America's decade of lost growth.

The Great Japanese Bubble of the 1980s

The rise of the Great Japanese bubble serves as the next example. Large current account surpluses produced large increases in the amount of dollars in Japan, as reflected in the 260% increase in Japan's international reserves between 1985 and 1988. Those dollars entered the Japanese banking system and set off a lending boom that caused an incredible bubble in the stock market and the property market. The link between the dollar inflows and the hyperinflation in asset prices is demonstrated in Figure 7.1. It is rather hard to believe the two events are merely a coincidence. Additional details can be found in Chapter 2.

Scandinavia's Property Bubble of the Early 1990s

Next consider Sweden and Finland in the early 1990s (see Figures 7.2 and 7.3). The reserve assets of each country doubled between 1984 and 1987. This influx of foreign capital quickly sparked off a boom in residential property prices. After the property bubble burst, non-performing loans as a percentage of total bank loans climbed to 9% in Finland and 11% in Sweden by the early 1990s. The fiscal cost of restructuring the financial sectors has been estimated at 11% of GDP in Finland and 4% in Sweden.[2]

Figure 7.1   Japan: Dollar reserves surge and so does the stock market, 1973–90

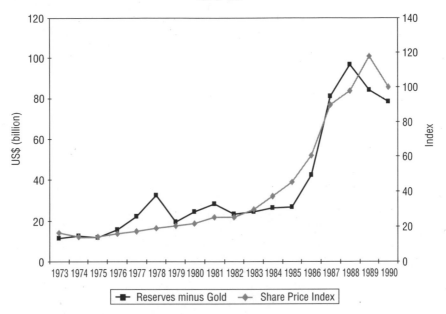

Source: IMF, *International Financial Statistics*.

Figure 7.2   Finland: Capital inflows cause property boom, 1984–88 (residential property)

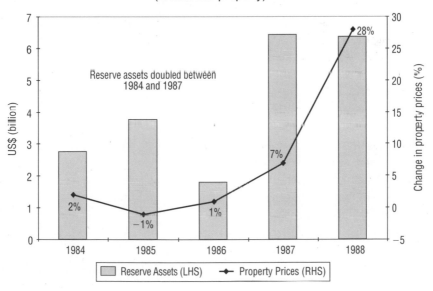

Sources: IMF, *International Financial Statistics* and *World Economic Outlook*.

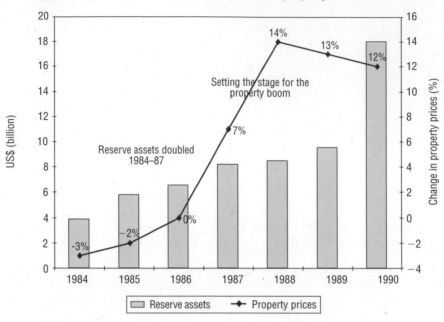

Figure 7.3 Sweden: Capital inflows cause property boom, 1984–90

Source: IMF, *International Financial Statistics* and *World Economic Outlook*

The Asian Miracle Bubble

Then there was the Asia Crisis. The pattern was quite similar for all the crisis-affected countries: Indonesia, Malaysia, South Korea, and Thailand. Amazing Thailand's amazing bubble was described in Chapter 2, so Malaysia will serve as a proxy for the Asia Crisis countries here (see Figures 7.4 and 7.5).

Between 1991 and 1993, as waves of foreign capital flooded into the Asian "dragon" economies, Malaysia's reserve assets rose 150% and the Kuala Lumpur Stock Exchange (KLSE) Index "miraculously" jumped 129%. Banks, which were flush with deposits as a result of all the capital that had entered the country, went on a lending spree. Between 1991 and 1997, bank loans skyrocketed by almost 190% and the country's GDP grew by more than 9% annually.

When the Asian Miracle bubble popped, the Malaysian government responded promptly and set up special-purpose vehicles to resolve the financial sector crisis. Non-performing loans (NPLs) as a percentage of all loans peaked at more than 30% when combining the loans acquired by Danaharta, the government's special-purpose vehicle, and the NPLs left

Figure 7.4 Malaysia: Surging reserves caused the stock market bubble, 1990–97

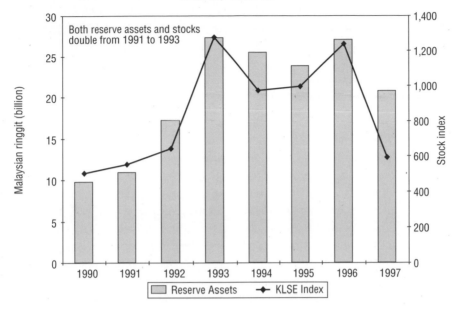

Sources: IMF, *International Financial Statistics Yearbook;* Bank Negara Malaysia.

Figure 7.5 Malaysia: Capital inflows facilitated the lending boom, 1990–97

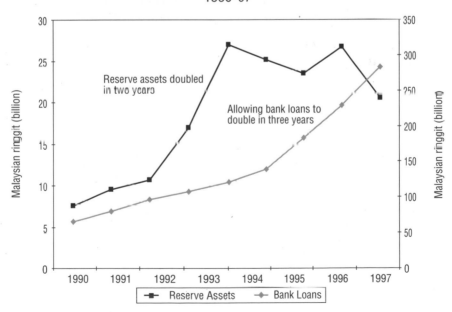

Sources: IMF, *International Financial Statistics Yearbook;* Bank Negara Malaysia.

within the banks. In a World Bank study, the fiscal cost of the crisis was estimated at 16.4% of GDP for the period between 1997 and mid-2000, but at the time that study was published, its authors considered the crisis to be "ongoing."[3] As of the third quarter of 2002, the KLSE Index remained 44% below its 1993 peak.

The Bubble that Matters Most

That brings us to "The Bubble that Matters Most." The pattern that led to the New Paradigm bubble in the United States is very similar to all the others examined above, with one exception. Because the United States is the country that issues the new international reserve currency, the U.S. dollar, the wave of capital inflow into the U.S. does not appear as an increase in the United States' reserve assets. It shows up as a surplus on the U.S. financial account. The United States' reserve assets are relatively small compared with those of many of its trading partners. For example, at the end of 2000, the United States' total reserves minus gold of US$56.6 billion amounted to only one-third those of China.

In that crazy game of marbles described by Jacques Rueff and outlined in Chapter 3, America's trading partners return to the U.S. the dollars they earn through their current account surpluses with the U.S. in order to avoid converting those dollars into their own currencies, which they do not wish to cause to appreciate. When the U.S. financial account surplus began to surge in the early 1980s as the result of the blow-out in the U.S. current account deficit, the U.S. stock market finally shot through the 1,000 level, and rose 54% between 1983 and 1987 (see Figure 7.6). It had first breached the 1,000 mark in 1972, but had failed to sustain itself above that benchmark for another 11 years.

The October crash of 1987 proved to be only a temporary, although shocking, correction, with share prices plunging 23% in one day. The real bonanza began in the second half of the 1990s when the U.S. financial account surplus (that is, the current account deficit) began to run amok. By 1996, when the financial account surplus/current account deficit surpassed its earlier peak set in 1987, irrational exuberance was already firmly entrenched. Thereafter, the party went into full swing as the surplus/deficit climbed to more than 4% of U.S. GDP in 2000.

Once again, the pattern was the same. Liquidity entered the economy from abroad – despite the twist that in this case the liquidity that entered the United States was dollars, but foreign-owned dollars. The liquidity surge caused a bubble. The bubble is now popping.

Figure 7.6 United States: Stocks surge with financial account surplus, 1983–2000

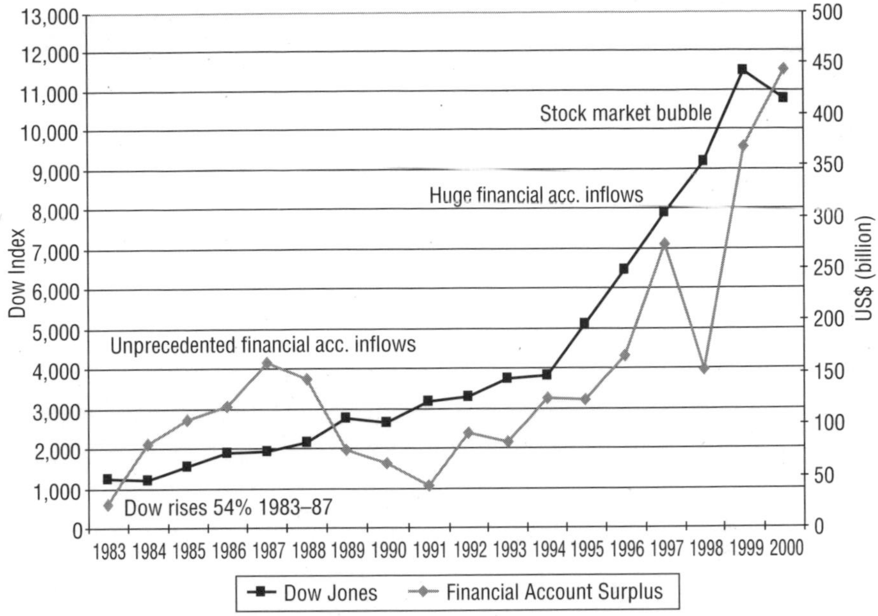

Sources: IMF, *International Financial Statistics*; Economagic.

The Jazz Age Bubble

The final example that will be used to demonstrate the connection between capital inflows and asset price bubbles is chronologically the first. There are several reasons why it is worthwhile describing again here the sequence of events that led to the Great Depression, even though that was the concern of Chapter 4. First, it is useful to re-emphasize that the breakdown of the gold standard at the outbreak of World War I led to huge trade imbalances, surging international liquidity, and hyperinflation in asset prices, just as the breakdown of the Bretton Woods system did 60 years later. Two cases demonstrating how the breakdown of a gold-based international monetary regime caused an economic crisis are better than one. Second, it is important to examine the systemic banking crisis in the United States that followed the collapse of the stock-market bubble in 1929, as well as the political response to that wave of bank failures.

Figure 7.7 shows that an enormous amount of gold flowed into the United States between 1914 and 1924. In fact, the amount of gold that entered the country during that 10-year period was considerably more than

Figure 7.7 United States: The gold component of high-powered money inside and outside the Treasury, 1910–29

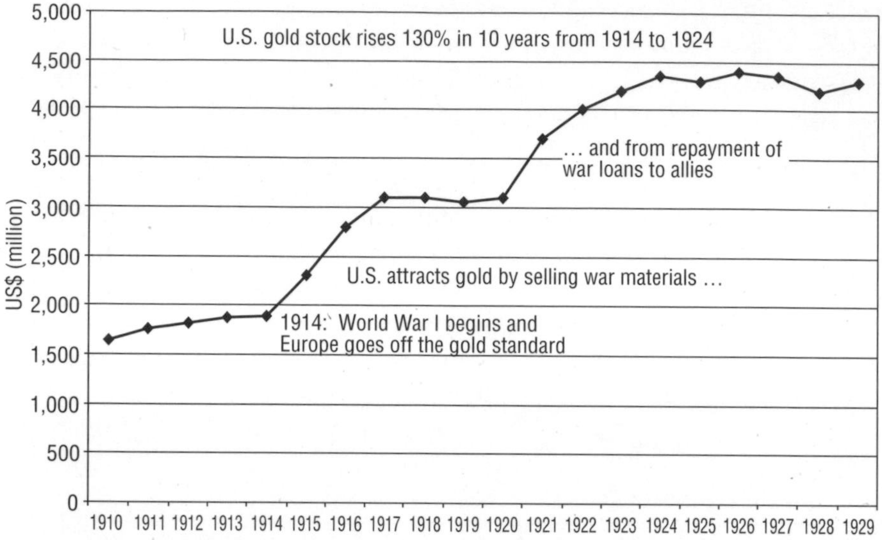

Source: Milton Friedman and Anna Jacobson Schwartz, *A Monetary History of the United States, 1867–1960* (Princeton: Princeton University Press, 1963).

all the gold that the United States had accumulated throughout its 138-year history leading up to 1914. That inflow of gold caused the Great Depression by first causing the Roaring Twenties.

When World War I erupted in 1914, all the major European powers went off the gold standard to enable them to finance the war by printing paper money and issuing debt. Had they continued to allow their currencies to be convertible into gold, their gold reserves would have quickly been depleted as the growing amounts of paper money in circulation were redeemed for the more reliable precious metal. After all, according to Gresham's Law, in free markets, good money always drives out bad money.

The European Great Powers had to conserve their gold in order to buy war materials from overseas. Their largest supplier was the United States. Until the United States entered the war in 1917, it demanded gold in exchange for its goods, as was common practice under the gold standard. Consequently, the U.S. gold reserves rose by 64% between 1914 and 1917. Once the U.S. entered the war, it allowed its allies to continue buying war materials on credit. For that reason, U.S. gold reserves ceased to expand over the following three years. However, once the war ended, war debts had to be repaid. England and France received war reparations from Germany and the other defeated nations and used those sums to repay the United

States for the debt they had accumulated in the final years of the war. In that way, gold reserves in the United States rose a further 40% between 1920 and 1924, resulting in a cumulative increase of 130% between 1914 and 1924.

Many fascinating arrangements in the international capital markets evolved during the 1920s. For instance, the United States lent Germany a great deal of money, which Germany used to pay war damages to England and France. That money then returned to the United States as England and France repaid their war debts to the Americans. Those inflows back into the U.S. allowed the Americans to lend still more to Germany, enabling the Germans to pay subsequent installments of reparations to the victors, pay interest on the earlier loans from the U.S., and, according to historians of the period, spend freely all across Germany on infrastructure and entertainment facilities such as concert halls and public swimming pools. Eventually, it all ended in hyperinflation and many of the largest German and Austrian banks went kaput. In *The Economic Consequences of the Peace*,[4] John Maynard Keynes warned that forcing Germany to pay crippling war reparations would end in disaster. It did. The economic collapse in Germany contributed to Hitler's rise to power.

Returning to the subject at hand, however, in the United States, once the war ended, the Roaring Twenties began. The country was rich. It had more than twice as much gold as before the war, at a time when gold mattered (see Figure 7.8). The European gold that had been used to pay for American goods was deposited into U.S. banks. Those gold deposits allowed credit creation to occur. Bank lending boomed from 1916 to 1920, averaging 16% growth per year. Lending contracted by approximately 6% a year in 1921 and 1922 after the Fed, established only in 1913, tightened credit. However, in 1923, lending accelerated again. Loans grew by 9.6% in 1923 and by an average of 5.5% a year from 1923 right up until the stock market crashed in 1929. Consequently, economic output and share prices roared on the back of easy credit. By the second half of the decade, investment had turned into speculation. Eventually, the bubble burst when the credit extended to finance the speculative ventures could not be repaid. Every bubble ends the same way.

▶ SYSTEMIC BANKING CRISES, OLD AND NEW

When bubbles explode, banks fail. One-third of all the banks in the United States went under between 1929 and 1933. Unlike today, there was no deposit insurance. When banks failed, the depositors lost their savings. Then, governments did not borrow money in order to refund the deposits that had been lost in the failed banks. As an aside, it is worth noting that much of the money that was deposited in those failed banks had been earned during the

Figure 7.8 United States: Gold reserves doubled; the stock market tripled, 1910–29

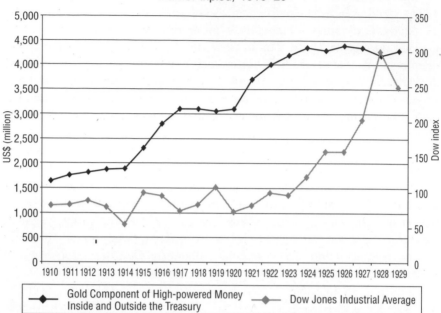

Sources: Milton Friedman and Anna Jacobson Schwartz, *A Monetary History of the United States, 1867–1960* (Princeton, N.J.: Princeton University Press, 1963); Economagic.

period of prosperity – prosperity that had resulted from easy credit. Had there been less credit extension, the economy would have grown much more slowly and there would have been fewer profits to deposit. In other words, much of the deposits that were destroyed in the banking crash were created due to the economic bubble that preceded the crash. This subject will be developed in the next chapter.

Be that as it may, when the banks failed and the deposits were destroyed, the money supply collapsed along with the deposit base, since M2 is comprised of currency in circulation plus deposits at banks. The destruction of so much wealth in the banking system – or, expressed differently, the sharp drop in the money supply – was the main reason the Great Depression was so severe and protracted.

During the decades that followed the Depression, a consensus built up among policymakers and economists as to what steps should be taken to ensure that the mistakes of the 1920s and early 1930s would be avoided in the future. For instance, in the United States, the *Glass-Steagall Act* was passed to prohibit commercial banks from engaging in stockbroking or the insurance business, because it was believed that the banks' involvement in those industries had, in many cases, contributed to bank failures. It may prove to be both ironic and tragic that the *Financial Services Modernizations Act* of 1999 effectively repealed *Glass-Steagall* less than a year before the second great speculative bubble of the 20th century began to implode.

A consensus also emerged that governments should regulate the banks more carefully. Finally, in the United States, laws were passed that provided deposit insurance to the public through the Federal Deposit Insurance Corporation. Lawmakers believed that deposit insurance would strengthen the public's faith in the banking system and, thereby, make bank runs and bank failures less likely. It was also believed that, in the event of any bank failures, deposit insurance would mitigate the negative impact on the money supply and the economy in general.

All in all, the government of the United States adopted the view that banks should be carefully regulated and monitored so that they would not fail. However, in case any bank did fail, the government's policy was to intervene by refunding the money the bank had lost to the bank's depositors in order to prevent one bank failure from spreading to other banks through depositor panic and in order to prevent the economy from being damaged by a contracting money supply.

For a number of decades after the 1930s, far fewer banks failed and banking crises ceased to pose systemic risks. World War II ended in American hegemony and the introduction of the Bretton Woods international monetary system. During the Bretton Woods era from 1946 to 1973, there were relatively few systemic banking failures around the world. However, once Bretton Woods broke down and the United States' balance of payments deficits began inundating the world with foreign exchange reserves, economic crises accompanied by systemic banking crises began to erupt all around the world with increasing frequency and intensity.

In June 2001, the Bank of England published a study entitled "Costs of Banking System Instability: Some Empirical Evidence." The first paragraph of that study concisely sums up the ongoing crisis in global banking:

> Over the past quarter of a century, unlike the preceding 25 years, there have been many banking crises around the world. Caprio and Klingebiel (1996, 1999), for example, document 69 crises in developed and emerging market countries since the late 1970s. In a recent historical study of 21 countries, Bordo, Eichengreen, Klingebiel and Martinez-Peria (2001) report only one banking crisis in the quarter of a century after 1945 but 19 since.[5]

From Tables 7.2 and 7.3, it is readily apparent that the rise in banking crises parallels the surge in international reserves described in earlier

Table 7.2 Selected banking crises: Non-performing loans and costs of restructuring financial sectors

Crisis countries	Years	Duration (years)	Non-performing loans (percentage of total loans)	Bank credit/GDP percent*	Fiscal and quasi-fiscal costs/GDP	GNP per head (US$ 000s PPP)	Currency crisis as well (pre-fix)
High-income countries							
Finland	1991–93	3	9.0	89.9 (89.9)	11.0	15.8	Yes
Japan	1992–98	7	13.0	119.5 (182.5)	8.0 (17)	21.5	No
Korea	1997–		30–40	70.3 (82.2)	34.0	14.7	Yes
Norway	1988–92	5	9.0	61.2 (79.6)	8.0	17.3	No
Spain	1977–85	9	n/a	68.1 (75.1)	16.8	4.7	Yes
Sweden	1991	1	11.0	50.8 (128.5)	4.0	17.2	Yes
United States	1984–91	8	4.0	42.7 (45.9)	3.2	15.2	No
Average		5.5	13.5	71.8 (97.7)	12.1	15.2	
Medium- and low-income countries							
Argentina	1980–82	3	9.0	29.8 (33.0)	55.3	6.4	Yes
Argentina	1995	1	n/a	19.7 (20.0)	1.6	10.5	No
Brazil	1994–96	3	15.0	31.7 (36.5)	5–10	6.1	No
Chile	1981–83	3	19.0	58.8 (60.2)	41.2	2.7	Yes
Colombia	1982–87	6	25.0	14.7 (14.7)	5.0	2.9	Yes
Ghana	1982–89	8	n/a	25.2 (25.2)	6.0	0.9	Yes
Indonesia	1994	1	n/a	51.9 (51.9)	1.8	2.5	No
Indonesia	1997–		65–75	60.8 (60.8)	50–55	3.0	Yes
Malaysia	1985–88	4	33.0	64.5 (91.8)	4.7	3.3	No
Mexico	1994–95	2	11.0	31.0 (36.3)	20.0	7.2	Yes
Philippines	1981–87	7	n/a	23.2 (31.0)	3.0	2.4	Yes
Sri Lanka	1989–93	5	35.0	21.3 (21.3)	5.0	1.9	No
Thailand	1983–87	5	15.0	44.5 (48.5)	1.5	1.7	No
Thailand	1997–		46.0	118.8 (134.9)	42.3	6.2	Yes
Turkey	1994	1	n/a	14.2 (15.3)	1.1	5.4	Yes
Uruguay	1981–84	4	n/a	33.4 (47.8)	31.2	4.6	Yes
Venezuela	1994–95	2	n/a	8.9 (12.3)	20.0	5.6	Yes
Average		3–7	27.8	38.4 (43.6)	17.6	4.3	
Average all countries		4.2	22.4	48.1 (59.4)	16.0	7.5	
of which: twin crises		4.1	2.6	46.5 (56.5)	22.9		
banking crisis alone		4.3	17.7	50.8 (64.2)	4.6		

Source: Bank of England, *Financial Stability Review*, June 2002, p. 162.

*Note: Credit to private sector from deposit money banks. The figures in brackets also include credit from other banks.

Table 7.3 The fiscal cost of banking crises

Country	Period	Fiscal cost (% of GDP)	Country	Period	Fiscal cost (% of GDP)
1 Argentina	1980–1982	55.1	21 Mexico	1994–ongoing	19.3
2 Argentina	1995	0.5	22 New Zealand	1987–1990	1.0
3 Australia	1989–1992	1.9	23 Norway	1987–1993	8.0
4 Brazil	1994–1996	13.2	24 Paraguay	1995–ongoing	5.1
5 Bulgaria	1996–1997	13.0	25 Philippines	1983–1987	13.2
6 Chile	1981–1983	41.2	26 Philippines	1988–ongoing	0.5
7 Colombia	1982–1987	5.0	27 Poland	1992–1995	3.5
8 Cote d'Ivore	1988–1991	25.0	28 Senegal	1988–1991	9.6
9 Czech Republic	1989–1991	12.0	29 Slovenia	1992–1994	14.6
10 Ecuador	1996–ongoing	13.0	30 South Korea	1997–ongoing	26.5
11 Egypt	1991–1995	0.5	31 Spain	1977–1985	5.6
12 Finland	1991–1994	11.0	32 Sri Lanka	1989–1993	5.0
13 France	1994–1995	0.7	33 Sweden	1991–1994	4.0
14 Ghana	1982–1989	3.0	34 Thailand	1983–1987	2.0
15 Hungary	1991–1995	10.0	35 Thailand	1997–ongoirg	32.8
16 Indonesia	1992–1994	3.8	36 Turkey	1982–1985	2.5
17 Indonesia	1997–ongoing	50.0	37 Turkey	1994	1.1
18 Japan	1992–ongoing	20.0	38 United States	1981–1991	3.2
19 Malaysia	1985–1988	4.7	39 Uruguay	1981–1984	31.2
20 Malaysia	1997–ongoing	16.4	40 Venezuela	1994–1997	22.0

Source: Patrick Honohan and Daniela Klingebiel (The World Bank), "Controlling Fiscal Costs of Banking Crises," April 17, 2000.

Figure 7.9 Total international reserve assets, 1949–2000

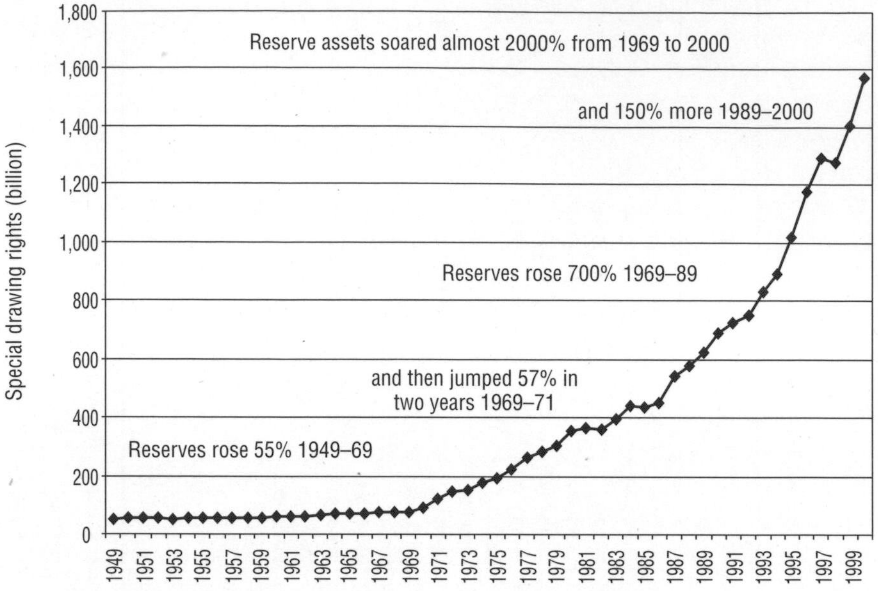

Source: IMF, *International. Financial Statistics* and annual reports.

chapters. It does not require a great stretch of the imagination to understand that the latter is responsible for the former. The linkages between capital inflows, accelerating credit expansion, the development of asset price bubbles, followed by systemic banking crises, is so obvious that the burden of proof should be on anyone who would argue otherwise. During the Bretton Woods era, when international reserve assets grew only slowly, systemic banking failures were not a concern. After Bretton Woods collapsed, they became pandemic. The near exponential expansion of the world's monetary base is indisputably the reason why (see Figure 7.9).

FROM BANKING CRISES TO FISCAL CRISES?

Tables 7.2 and 7.3 also demonstrate the great fiscal cost involved in resolving systemic banking crises. Under the influence of the International Monetary Fund, most countries that experienced systemic banking crises during the last 30 years raised government debt to give depositors money to replace their lost savings. This policy was generally pursued regardless of whether or not a formal deposit insurance scheme had been in place before the banking sector collapse. Typically, as the banking crisis unfolded, the government would announce a government guarantee of all deposits in the banking system if no such scheme had previously existed. By so doing, most countries were able to prevent runs on the banking system that would have resulted in still further damage to the banking sector, the money supply, and the economy. On the other hand, however, by guaranteeing all deposits, governments became obligated to pay for most of the losses incurred by any bank or banks that did fail.

Bailing out the depositors of failed banks has become very expensive. As shown in the preceding tables, the fiscal costs have been as much as 55% of GDP for some countries. According to Table 7.2, the fiscal costs amounted to the equivalent of 16% of GDP on average for the 24 banking crises in that study. Furthermore, several countries have experienced two or more banking crises since 1980: Argentina, Indonesia, Malaysia, Philippines, Thailand, and Turkey. Finally, it should be noted that many of the crises listed in the preceding tables are still ongoing. The current banking crisis in Argentina, for example, is so severe that the already heavily indebted government has been unable to raise enough debt to repay the public's savings. Depositors have reacted violently to their losses. Bloody rioting has toppled several governments over the last year, and political instability reigns.

Next, consider Japan. Japanese banks have been in crisis for more than 10 years. The Japanese depositors have not yet lost any of their savings, but that is only because the government has spent huge sums to keep the banks afloat. The crisis there is not yet resolved, but the Japanese government's debt has risen to 140% of GDP, causing rating agencies to downgrade Japan's sovereign debt rating to a level similar to Nigeria's.

As explained above, disequilibrium in international balance of payments is responsible for the wave of systemic banking crises sweeping the world. Unfortunately, there is every reason to fear that the number of banking crises will continue to increase and their severity continue to intensify. This is because the international balance of payments disequilibrium has been exasperated in recent years as the U.S. current account deficit ballooned to unprecedented levels. So long as the world continues to be flooded with dollar liquidity spun off from the American trade deficits, new rounds of asset price bubbles must be anticipated.

This cycle of surging dollar inflows, followed by rapid credit expansion, hyperinflation in asset prices, systemic banking crises, and big government bailouts, cannot continue indefinitely, however. Finite government resources will prove to be the limiting factor. Unless the plague of bank failures ceases, in the not too distant future, fiscal crises may become as common as banking sector crises are today.

When bubble economies deflate, there are generally two types of costs that a government must bear in order to prevent the subsequent recession from spiraling into crisis. The first is the direct cost of bailing out the depositors of the failed banking system. The second is the cost of annual fiscal deficits that come about as a combination of lower, post-bubble tax revenues and higher expenditure on stimulus programs and social safety nets.

Consider Japan, the world's second-largest economy. During the final years of the Great Japanese bubble, the government was able to reduce its debt relative to GDP from 71.6% in 1987 to 61.1% in 1991. As the 1990s progressed, the bubble in property and share prices deflated. By the end of that decade, the government's debt to GDP had nearly doubled to 115.8%, and it has continued to expand sharply since then. The OECD expects the Japanese government's debt to climb to the equivalent of 152% of GDP by the end of 2003.

By early 1999, the Japanese government had infused ¥10 trillion (US$83 billion) in capital into the banking industry. In addition to that, the government spent aggressively on fiscal stimulus programs to support economic growth. In 2002, Japan's fiscal deficit is expected to amount to more than 7% of Japan's GDP (see Figure 7.10).

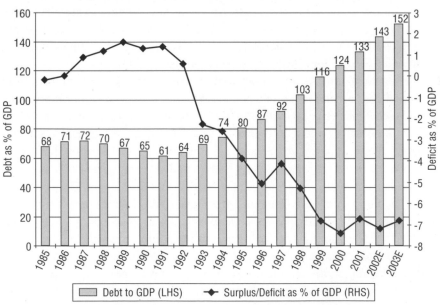

Figure 7.10   Japan: Deficits and debt, 1985–2003E

Source: OECD.

Because of the scale of the government intervention, Japan has avoided the kind of economic depression that engulfed the United States when the 1920s' bubble popped. The Japanese economy remains fragile nonetheless. Despite the massive intervention by the government, the economy has endured three recessions since the bubble began to deflate in the early 1990s.

Moreover, Japan's banking industry remains in serious trouble. According to Standard & Poor's, "Japan's banks are vastly undercapitalized. Whereas the FSA (Financial Services Agency) states that the (banking) system's impaired assets total ¥43 trillion (8.3.% of GDP) at the end March 2001, Standard & Poor's estimates the figure on a forward-looking basis to be three times as high." And, in a separate report, Standard & Poor's wrote, "entering 2002, the banking industry is thus in a worse condition than at any time in the past decade."[6]

Now, there are growing concerns about how much longer the Japanese government will be able to continue its aggressive fiscal stimulus campaign. No other industrialized country has accumulated such large government debt in the post-war era. These and other concerns prompted Standard & Poor's to lower Japan's credit rating twice in 2001 and a third time in 2002. Following the most recent downgrade, Japan's credit rating is now on par with that of some developing nations.

The economic situation in Japan is all the more precarious because the economy is still heavily reliant on selling its products to the United States. In 2000, Japan's trade surplus with the U.S. was US$81.6 billion,[7] the equivalent of almost 2% of Japan's GDP. Furthermore, that figure understates the importance of the U.S. market to Japan, since significant portions of the goods that Japanese corporations sell to U.S. consumers are made outside Japan in low-wage nations or within the United States itself in Japanese-owned factories. Should the U.S. recession worsen, the Japanese government would have to augment its deficit spending to keep the economy afloat. The world has begun to wonder how much more debt Japan will be able to service without resorting to the dangerous expedient of printing money.

Japan is not alone in its fiscal difficulties. Many countries around the world are in fiscal distress – distress often resulting from systemic banking crises. The list is quite long and expanding practically every month. So long as the global economic disequilibrium persists and continues to produce hyperinflation in asset prices, more governments will be added to that list as more banking systems collapse.

The fiscal health of the government of the United States is of the greatest concern for the global economy. And there, the outlook is not encouraging. As a percentage of GDP, U.S. government debt declined during the years of irrational exuberance in the second half of the 1990s, even though in absolute terms the dollar amount of the debt rose every year (see Figure 7.11). Now, however, one year into this post-bubble downturn, the budget deficit has returned with a vengeance.

If history is any guide, the United States is very likely to be hit by a systemic crisis in the financial sector. The development of securitization may have shifted the risks away from commercial banks. Nevertheless, the unwinding of the excesses of the 1990s is very likely to inflict extraordinary damage on some other parts of the financial sector. Regardless of whether the crisis manifests itself within the insurance industry, within one or more of the government-sponsored enterprises, or within the banking sector, the government will probably be compelled for political reasons to spend very large sums of money cleaning up the mess.

The cost of the financial sector bailout will come on top of record fiscal deficits over the next five years that will grow as tax revenues decline further and expenditures on stimulus programs increase. None of this is encouraging, particularly in light of the government's huge unfunded Social Security obligations.

Other countries will be confronted with similar fiscal strains during the global slump.

Figure 7.11   United States: Deficits and debt, 1985–2002E

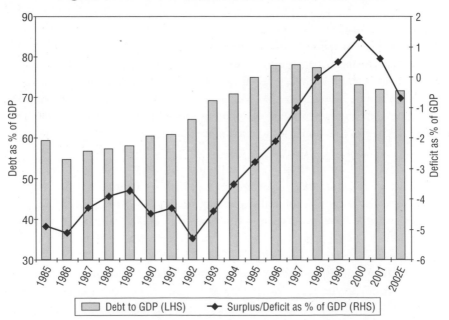

Source: OECD.

Tables 7.4 and 7.5 provide details for the debt and annual deficits of the industrialized countries within the OECD. The finances of the non-OECD developing world are generally more strained still.

CONCLUSION

The bank failures of the 1930s and the wave of systemic banking crises over the last 25 years both originated from a very similar chain of events. In both instances, when a gold-based international monetary system broke down, trade imbalances facilitated credit creations and resulted in hyperinflation in asset prices. When those asset price bubbles popped, banks failed.

The lesson policymakers learned from the banking crises of the Great Depression was that governments should bail out depositors when banks fail. The lesson that may be learned from the current set of crises is that governments themselves may go bankrupt in attempting to bail out the depositors. During the next five years, Japan may be the case that proves the point. It may soon be seen that fiscal crises are even more damaging than financial sector crises.

Global economic stability will only be restored when policymakers implement measures that eliminate the disequilibrium in the international balance of payments that has caused these crises.

REFERENCES

1   Alan Greenspan, "Gold and Economic Freedom," an essay published in Ayn Rand's *Capitalism: The Unknown Ideal* (New York: The Penguin Group, 1967).
2   Glenn Hoggarth and Victoria Saporta (Bank of England), "Costs of Banking System Instability: Some Empirical Evidence," *The Financial Stability Review*, June 2001, Appendix A.
3   Patrick Honohan and Daniela Klingebiel (World Bank), "Controlling Fiscal Costs of Banking Crises," April 17, 2000.
4   John Maynard Keynes, *The Economic Consequences of the Peace* (New York: Harcourt, Brace and Howe, 1920).
5   Hoggarth and Saporta, op. cit.
6   Standard & Poor's: reports published May 7, 2002 and January 31, 2002, respectively.
7   U.S. Census Bureau, Foreign Trade Division.

Table 7.4 General government structural balances, 1985–2003 (surplus (+) or deficit (−) as a percentage of potential GDP)

	1985	1986	1987	1988	1989	1990	1991	1992	1993	1994	1995	1996	1997	1998	1999	2000	2001	Projections 2002	2003
Australia	−5.2	−3.9	−2.1	−0.5	−0.3	−0.9	−2.5	−4.6	−4.6	−4.1	−3.4	−2.0	−0.3	0.5	1.4	−0.2	0.0	0.2	0.3
Austria	−1.9	−3.2	−3.7	−3.1	−3.4	−3.1	−3.8	−2.7	−4.1	−4.9	−5.0	−3.8	−1.8	−2.7	−2.6	−2.4	0.0	0.1	0.3
Belgium	−8.0	−8.0	−6.8	−8.0	−9.4	−9.1	−9.2	−9.2	−6.0	−3.9	−3.3	−2.1	−1.1	0.0	−0.1	−0.5	0.2	0.9	0.6
Canada	−8.4	−7.1	−6.2	−6.0	−6.1	−6.5	−6.9	−7.1	−6.8	−5.9	−4.6	−1.6	1.0	1.0	1.5	2.5	2.3	0.9	0.7
Denmark	–	–	–	0.5	0.3	−0.5	−1.6	−0.8	−0.2	−2.4	−2.5	−1.5	−0.8	−0.2	1.8	0.7	1.8	1.6	1.7
Finland	3.9	4.4	1.2	3.6	3.9	3.3	1.8	0.6	0.8	0.8	1.0	0.5	0.0	1.7	2.0	5.7	5.0	4.3	4.2
France	−1.3	−1.7	−0.7	−2.1	−2.2	−2.7	−2.7	−4.2	−5.0	−4.6	−4.6	−2.8	−1.8	−2.0	−1.3	−1.7	−1.7	−1.8	−1.8
Germany	0.0	−0.6	−1.1	−2.1	−0.1	−3.2	−3.6	−3.2	−2.1	−1.7	−2.7	−2.4	−1.7	−1.3	−0.8	−1.3	−2.0	−1.5	−1.1
Greece	−10.7	−8.8	−7.5	−10.7	−14.7	−15.9	−11.8	−12.4	−11.9	−8.4	−8.7	−6.1	−3.3	−1.3	−0.9	−0.5	−0.4	0.2	0.6
Iceland	−1.3	−4.9	−3.4	−3.5	−5.2	−3.7	−2.6	−0.5	−1.9	−3.4	−1.2	−1.0	0.4	0.1	2.0	1.4	−1.3	−0.4	−0.1
Ireland	−9.4	−7.7	−6.2	−3.1	−1.5	−4.0	−2.8	−2.1	−0.9	0.0	−1.3	0.5	1.0	2.3	1.6	2.8	−0.4	−0.4	−0.5
Italy	−11.7	−11.5	−11.4	−11.8	−12.6	−12.6	−12.1	−10.4	−8.8	−8.4	−7.6	−6.9	−2.5	−2.7	−1.1	−1.4	−0.8	−0.4	−0.5
Japan	−0.2	0.0	0.9	1.2	1.6	1.3	1.4	0.6	−2.3	−2.6	−3.9	−5.1	−4.1	−5.3	−6.8	−7.4	−6.7	−7.2	−6.8
Netherlands	−3.6	−5.4	−5.8	−4.3	−6.0	−7.6	−4.8	−5.4	−3.5	−4.7	−4.3	−2.1	−1.6	−1.7	−0.7	0.3	0.3	0.9	0.5
New Zealand	–	−7.9	−3.0	−4.4	−3.0	−3.1	−0.5	0.0	0.8	2.6	2.1	2.1	1.2	0.7	1.0	1.4	0.5	0.0	−0.2
Norway	−0.9	1.1	0.3	0.8	0.2	−1.5	−4.4	−6.4	−6.7	−5.6	−2.2	−2.1	−1.4	−2.7	−1.2	0.1	0.0	−0.9	−1.5
Portugal	−4.7	−4.1	−4.3	−3.5	−3.4	−6.4	−7.8	−4.1	−5.2	−4.4	−3.3	−3.1	−2.1	−2.4	−2.5	−2.4	−2.5	−2.0	−1.4
Spain	−4.6	−4.9	−3.3	−3.8	−4.7	−5.6	−5.5	−4.3	−5.4	−4.6	−4.9	−2.9	−1.5	−1.5	−0.7	−0.4	0.1	0.2	0.3
Sweden	−3.8	−2.1	2.2	0.7	2.2	1.6	−2.1	−5.2	−7.2	−7.9	−6.0	−0.9	0.6	3.5	1.6	3.4	5.4	2.8	2.5
United Kingdom	–	–	−2.7	−1.8	−1.3	−2.9	−2.2	−4.2	−5.6	−5.6	−5.0	−3.7	−2.0	0.4	1.4	1.5	0.9	−0.6	−1.4
United States	−4.9	−5.1	−4.3	−3.9	−3.7	−4.5	−4.3	−5.3	−4.4	−3.5	−2.8	−2.1	−1.0	0.0	0.5	1.3	0.6	−0.7	−0.5
Euro area	−3.7	−4.0	−3.9	−4.6	−4.5	−5.8	−5.8	−5.3	−4.5	−4.1	−4.3	−3.2	−1.7	−1.6	−0.9	−1.0	−1.1	−0.7	−0.7
Total of above European Union countries	−4.1	−4.3	−3.8	−4.1	−3.9	−5.2	−5.1	−5.2	−5.0	−4.6	−4.6	−3.4	−1.8	−1.2	−0.5	−0.5	−0.6	−0.6	−0.7
Total of above OECD countries	−3.9	−4.0	−3.3	−3.2	−3.0	−3.9	−3.7	−4.4	−4.4	−3.9	−3.7	−3.0	−1.7	−1.3	−1.0	−0.7	−0.9	−1.6	−1.5

Source: OECD.

Table 7.5 General government gross financial liabilities, 1985–2003
(as a percentage of nominal GDP)

	1985	1986	1987	1988	1989	1990	1991	1992	1993	1994	1995	1996	1997	1998	1999	2000	2001	Projections 2002	Projections 2003
Australia	–	–	–	25.9	23.8	22.6	23.2	28.2	31.6	41.4	43.2	40.3	38.5	33.2	27.5	23.4	24.4	24.3	23.4
Austria	49.1	53.6	57.5	58.9	58.1	57.2	57.5	57.2	61.8	64.7	69.2	69.1	64.7	63.9	64.9	63.6	61.7	60.4	57.4
Belgium	118.1	123.3	127.6	127.6	123.7	128.2	130.1	131.4	138.1	136.8	133.9	130.1	124.7	119.3	115.0	109.3	108.2	104.4	99.5
Canada	84.2	88.9	89.2	88.8	90.0	93.1	102.1	110.4	116.0	117.4	120.4	120.3	118.4	115.2	113.2	103.0	101.6	99.7	96.2
Denmark	74.9	71.8	68.6	66.7	65.0	65.8	66.7	70.6	83.8	77.7	73.9	68.1	64.4	59.7	54.9	50.1	46.4	43.4	40.2
Finland	–	–	–	–	–	14.3	22.6	40.6	56.0	58.0	57.2	57.1	54.1	48.8	46.8	44.0	43.6	41.7	40.9
France	38.0	38.8	40.1	40.0	39.9	39.5	40.3	44.7	51.6	55.3	59.3	62.3	64.7	65.0	64.6	64.1	64.8	65.6	65.7
Germany	40.6	40.6	41.6	42.1	40.8	41.4	38.8	41.8	47.4	47.9	57.1	60.3	61.8	63.2	60.9	64.1	64.8	61.3	60.9
Greece	47.1	47.7	53.0	62.7	65.8	89.1	91.1	97.6	110.3	108.0	108.7	111.3	108.2	104.9	103.8	102.7	99.7	98.6	97.5
Iceland	32.7	30.2	27.6	31.2	36.8	36.5	38.6	46.3	53.4	55.8	59.3	56.7	54.1	49.2	44.4	41.8	47.0	42.0	37.3
Ireland	99.5	110.6	111.8	108.2	98.9	101.4	102.8	100.1	96.2	90.4	82.6	74.2	65.1	55.1	49.6	38.8	36.5	33.8	30.9
Italy	81.9	86.2	90.4	92.5	95.3	103.7	107.4	116.1	117.9	124.0	123.1	121.8	119.6	117.5	115.9	111.4	108.7	106.3	103.1
Japan	67.7	71.2	71.6	69.6	66.7	64.6	61.1	63.5	69.0	73.9	80.4	86.5	92.0	103.0	115.8	123.5	132.8	143.3	152.0
Korea	16.3	14.4	12.6	9.8	9.1	8.2	7.2	4.8	5.8	6.1	6.3	6.2	6.0	6.3	6.0	5.6	5.5	13.8	12.4
Luxembourg	–	–	–	–	–	4.4	3.9	4.8	5.8	5.4	5.6	6.2	6.0	6.3	6.0	5.6	5.5	4.8	5.0
Netherlands	68.7	70.6	73.	76.0	76.0	76.7	76.9	77.6	78.8	75.7	77.2	75.2	69.9	66.8	63.1	56.0	53.2	50.8	49.0
New Zealand	–	–	–	–	–	–	–	–	70.6	63.9	57.2	51.8	49.8	50.4	48.3	45.5	44.6	43.7	42.7
Norway	32.5	40.9	33.5	33.0	33.0	29.5	27.8	32.4	40.8	37.2	34.7	31.0	27.9	26.6	27.6	30.9	26.8	25.9	25.9
Portugal	55.8	54.0	60.8	61.0	59.0	55.6	57.1	54.8	61.1	62.1	64.3	62.7	58.9	54.8	54.2	53.5	55.6	55.6	54.2
Slovak Republic	–	–	–	–	–	–	–	–	–	25.0	22.8	27.4	29.7	29.7	29.8	33.5	37.3	39.9	41.4
Spain	49.0	49.8	49.0	45.3	46.9	48.8	49.9	52.4	63.5	65.7	73.6	81.3	80.7	81.3	75.4	72.1	69.1	67.5	65.4
Sweden	64.7	64.1	57.0	51.2	46.5	42.7	51.5	69.0	73.7	77.9	76.9	74.5	73.6	72.6	68.2	60.6	52.9	48.9	46.6
Switzerland	–	–	–	–	–	–	–	–	–	–	–	–	–	–	–	–	–	–	–
United Kingdom	59.2	53.4	56.	49.7	43.0	44.4	44.3	49.2	58.1	55.8	60.6	60.1	60.5	61.4	56.4	54.0	52.5	51.8	51.6
United States	59.0	62.6	64.	64.7	65.0	66.6	71.4	74.1	75.8	75.0	74.5	73.9	71.4	68.3	65.3	59.4	59.5	58.9	57.6
Euro area	52.9	54.6	56.	57.3	58.0	60.4	60.7	64.5	69.0	70.8	74.8	77.8	77.9	77.2	75.1	72.9	71.9	71.5	70.0
Total of above European Union countries	56.8	53.0	59.	58.3	57.2	58.8	59.0	63.6	69.9	71.3	75.4	76.5	76.1	75.6	72.9	70.5	69.1	68.4	67.1
Total of above OECD countries	59.2	61.7	62.	61.6	60.8	61.7	63.4	66.9	71.0	72.1	74.5	75.6	75.2	75.5	75.2	72.8	73.5	74.5	74.7

Source: OECD.

Chapter 8

Deflation

Deflation and the bad-loan problem are feeding each other in a vicious cycle.

— Heizo Takenaka, Japanese Economic and Fiscal Policy Minister,
November 5, 2002

Over the last 20 years, increasing trade between industrialized countries and low-wage, developing nations, in combination with an international monetary system incapable of guaranteeing balanced trade, have created a structural imbalance in the global economy that is highly deflationary in nature. There are two reasons why the current trade arrangements are deflationary. The first is very straightforward: an increasing proportion of the manufactured goods in the world are made with very low-cost labor; consequently, the price of those goods is falling because they cost less to make. The second reason is more complicated. Trade imbalances generate reserve assets that fuel credit creation and over-investment. Over-investment causes excess capacity, and excess capacity causes deflation. This chapter will describe how both these processes exert downward pressure on prices. Part Three of this book will examine the role that deflation will play in the coming global recession.

WORLDWIDE DISINFLATION

For more than 10 years, inflation rates have been falling sharply around the world, in the advanced economies and the developing world alike (see Figure 8.1 and 8.2). This bout of disinflation is particularly unusual in light of the very strong economic growth in the world's largest economy, the United States, during the second half of the 1990s.

FREE TRADE IS DEFLATIONARY

Things cost less when they are made by workers who are paid less than US$5 a day. In one sentence, that sums up one of the two main reasons why inflation rates have recently fallen to their lowest level in 30 years despite the very strong economic growth in the United States. The first half of this

Figure 8.1 World dis(inflation), 1970–2001

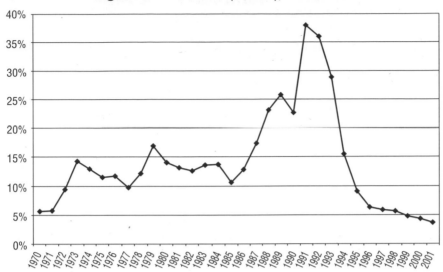

Source: IMF, The World Economic Outlook Database, April 2002.

Figure 8.2 Disinflation in advanced economies and developing economies, 1970–2002

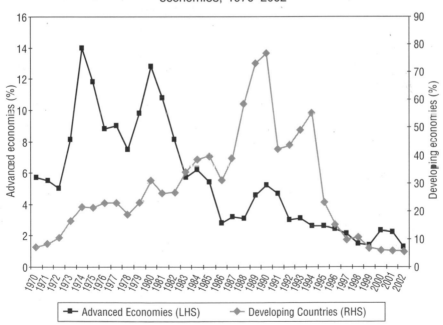

Source: IMF, The World Economic Outlook Database, April 2002.

chapter highlights the deflationary consequences of trade liberalization. Excess capacity, the other important source of deflationary pressure, is examined in the second half of the chapter.

Almost any labor-intensive product that can be made in the United States, Western Europe, or Japan can be made at considerably less cost in China or a dozen other low-wage nations. Impediments once thrown up by transportation problems or capital shortages have long since been overcome by technological developments and the removal of capital controls. Today, the most capital-intensive manufacturing processes can be financed and built in any number of developing countries, so that the most advanced facilities can be combined with the lowest-cost labor. The resulting output is the most price-competitive in the world. Transportation costs are no barrier. Large items such as cars can be shipped on super cargo ships; small items such as semiconductors can be sent overnight on cargo jets. If all trade barriers were removed in 2003, practically nothing would be manufactured in the "industrialized," advanced countries by 2010.

Europe and Japan manage to maintain overall trade surpluses through a combination of their trade surpluses with the United States and numerous official and cultural barriers to imports from low-wage nations. However, the United States, which constitutes approximately one-third of the global economy, has embarked on an unprecedented experiment involving huge trade deficits over the last 20 years.

Initially, in the early 1980s, these deficits expanded because of the economic overheating in the United States brought about by the Reagan administration's ill-fated experimentation with supply-side economics which produced a string of budget deficits that amounted to nearly US$3 trillion between 1982 and 1997 (see Figure 8.3).

The U.S. trade deficit hit its peak for the decade at US$159 billion in 1987 and then declined over the next four years as the dollar weakened and the U.S. economy cooled. From a trough of US$76 billion in 1991, the U.S. trade deficit began to expand again the following year. It hit a new high of US$164 billion in 1994, the year the North American Free Trade Agreement (NAFTA) came into force. The World Trade Organization (WTO) was established in 1995. Between 1994 and 1999, the U.S. trade deficit more than doubled to US$343 billion, and the following year it increased a further 30% to US$450 billion, or 4.5% of U.S. GDP.

The blowout in the trade deficit in the second half of the 1990s was due, in part, to the strong U.S. economy. The large currency devaluations by many of the United States' trading partners played an equally important role, however. Between 1990 and June 2002, the dollar rose 75% against the Chinese yuan, 211% against the Mexican peso, 72% against the Korean won, 41% against the Malaysian ringgit, and 60% against the Thai baht.

Figure 8.3   The infamous twin deficits: The U.S. budget deficit and U.S. trade deficit, 1971–2002F

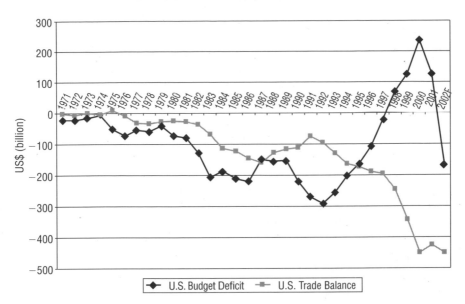

Sources: Budget: Office of Management and Budget, The Executive Office of the President; trade: IMF, *International Financial Statistics Yearbook 2001,* 2002 estimated.

Over that 12-year period, the dollar actually fell 23% against the Japanese yen. However, the yen peaked in June 1995 at a rate of ¥84.6 per dollar. Between then and June 2002, the dollar rose by 39% against the yen.[1]

By the mid-1990s, U.S. policymakers appear to have come to the conclusion that U.S. trade deficits could be used to support the economic growth of its trading partners at little to no cost to the United States. One must wonder when the realization set in within Washington that U.S. trade and current account deficits actually benefited the United States – at least in the short term – since surplus nations were compelled to reinvest their dollar surpluses in U.S. dollar-denominated assets if they were to avoid the appreciation of their own currencies and the disappearance of their trade surpluses, which a conversion of their dollar surpluses into their own currencies would have caused. Thereafter, it could be said that the United States adopted a trade deficit policy.

Every recent U.S. administration has trumpeted the benefits to be derived from trade liberalization while simultaneously protecting selected industries. Farmers are heavily subsidized, and the textile industry is sheltered behind trade barriers. The American automobile industry has survived only because Japan agreed to accept "voluntary" import quotas in the 1980s. The semiconductor industry enjoyed similar protection. Most recently, in 2002, quotas were required to rescue the U.S. steel industry. Despite the rhetoric that free trade benefits consumers by lowering prices, apparently some industries are too politically important to be subjected to the full discipline of international competition.

Nevertheless, the influx of cheap imports was sufficient to bring about disinflation at the same time that the U.S. economy enjoyed its longest-ever period of uninterrupted expansion.

In earlier business cycles, wage pressures would have mounted as full employment was reached; and wage-push inflation would have forced the Fed to increase interest rates in order to keep inflation in check. Higher interest rates would have caused the economy to cool down and would have taken the upward pressure off wage rates. That was the typical post-World War II business cycle pattern.

The pattern in the 1990s' expansion was very different. The possibility of relocating manufacturing facilities to countries with low-cost labor kept wage rates under pressure despite the strong economic growth. With low levels of inflation at the consumer price level, the Fed saw no reason to increase interest rates, even though the economy was expanding at a rate considerably above what had been considered to be a sustainable, non-inflationary trend rate.

There can be no question that the United States gained in the short term from the disinflationary impact of rapidly rising imports from low-wage countries. Consumers benefited from lower prices. Perhaps even more importantly, low inflation rates permitted low interest rates, and low interest rates spurred economic growth by lowering the cost of borrowing. The housing market gained, in particular. Share prices also rose, since investments in shares appeared relatively more attractive than the low interest rates available on bank deposits.

In retrospect, however, it is now clear that very low interest rates also created serious longer-term problems – namely, economic overheating and the stock market bubble. The Fed had no mandate to prevent asset price inflation, only consumer price inflation. Consequently, the FOMC (the Fed's Federal Open Market Committee) left interest rates unchanged or even reduced them as the stock market inflated to ridiculous heights. Moreover, even after the bubble in share prices began to deflate in mid-2000, an aggressive series of interest rate reductions by the Fed over the following 18 months brought about a bubble in the property market.

The problems arising out of the government's trade deficit policy are now reaching a new, and potentially much more dangerous, stage. As the overheated U.S. economy falls deeper into recession, there is a very high chance that disinflation will mature into deflation. There is no built-in mechanism within the current trade regime that stops low-wage imports from exerting additional downward pressure on product prices just because the inflation rate has fallen to zero. So long as the United States continues to support the economic growth of the rest of the world through its trade deficits, the downward pressure on product prices will persist. Furthermore, disinflation could be transformed into deflation very quickly should the over-indebted U.S. consumer be forced to rein in his spending, resulting in a sudden lurch down in aggregate demand.

There is no reason to believe that the U.S. trade deficit will return to balance if left to market forces. In fact, the trade deficit is very likely to continue widening. American consumers will carry on buying the cheaper imported goods made with low-wage labor. The developing countries are too poor to afford to buy sufficient amounts of the technologically advanced products in which the U.S. has a competitive advantage. So long as the existing trade regime is in place, more and more U.S. manufacturing will be shifted to low-wage countries such as Mexico or China. The differential in wage rates between the United States and the developing world is simply too immense to allow any other outcome.

Data on wage rates for every country are not available. However, much can be learned by comparing the per capita GDP of various countries. Consider Table 8.1.

There are 36 countries with a lower per capita GDP than that of Vietnam. However, because most of those countries do not currently have suitable infrastructure to host large-scale manufacturing operations for multinational corporations, they have not been included on this list.

Table 8.1 A comparison of GDP per capita, 2001

	2001 per capita GDP in U.S. dollars	As % of U.S. per capita GDP
Vietnam	392	1.1
India	466	1.3
Indonesia	682	1.9
China, P.R.: Mainland	911	2.5
Philippines	916	2.5
Thailand	1,811	4.9
Malaysia	3,679	10.0
Mexico	6,031	16.4
Korea	8,855	24.1
United Kingdom	23,765	64.7
Japan	32,637	88.9
United States	36,716	100.0

Source: IMF, The World Economic Outlook Database, April 2002.

There are two significant ways in which per capita GDP differs from the average amount earned by each person in the country. First, in most countries, the wealthiest 5% of the population earns a significantly larger portion of the country's total income than the poorest 20%. Consequently, the GDP per capita is significantly higher than the average income of the population. As the distribution of income differs from country to country, there is no easy way to adjust the per capita numbers for this factor. The second difference is that in much of the developing world, up to half of the population is too young to be in the workforce. Therefore, assuming that only half of the population is employed, the per capita GDP numbers should be doubled to more closely reflect the income earned by the part of the population that actually works. The first consideration causes the per capita numbers to be overstated relative to the actual wages earned, while the second factor causes them to be understated.

Despite the shortcomings of this methodology, Table 8.1 still clearly illustrates that the income gap (and therefore the difference in wage rates) between the developing world and the United States is enormous. Even if we doubled China's per capita income of US$911 to US$1,822 to take a stab at the amount earned by the working population, we would find that there are still hundreds of millions of Chinese people who earn less than 5% of the per capita income of the United States. Presumably, those workers would be quick to accept a job with almost any multinational company willing to pay them some premium above what they are currently earning.

Although the minimum wage for most countries is not available, the minimum wage in Thailand is known. It is 165 baht (US$3.80) per day in Bangkok, and less in the provinces. Since Thailand's per capita GDP is more than twice as high as that of the first five countries shown in Table 8.1, it is reasonable to assume that the minimum wage in those countries is lower than that paid in Thailand. The combined populations of those five countries amount to approximately 45% of the world's total population. So, quite clearly, there is no shortage of workers in the world willing to work for US$4 per day. Moreover, considering that a very large percentage of the population of those countries is currently less than 20 years old, demographic trends are more likely to put downward pressure on wages as more young people enter the workforce. So long as wage rates are determined by the law of supply and demand, wages are more likely to fall than to increase, since the number of manufacturing jobs will not increase as rapidly as the global workforce.

The series of currency devaluations over the last 10 years has also had the effect of reducing the purchasing power of many countries as measured in U.S. dollars. For example, the per capita dollar income in Thailand was lower in 2001 than in 1992 (see Figure 8.4).

Figure 8.4 Thailand: Per capita GDP, 1990–2001

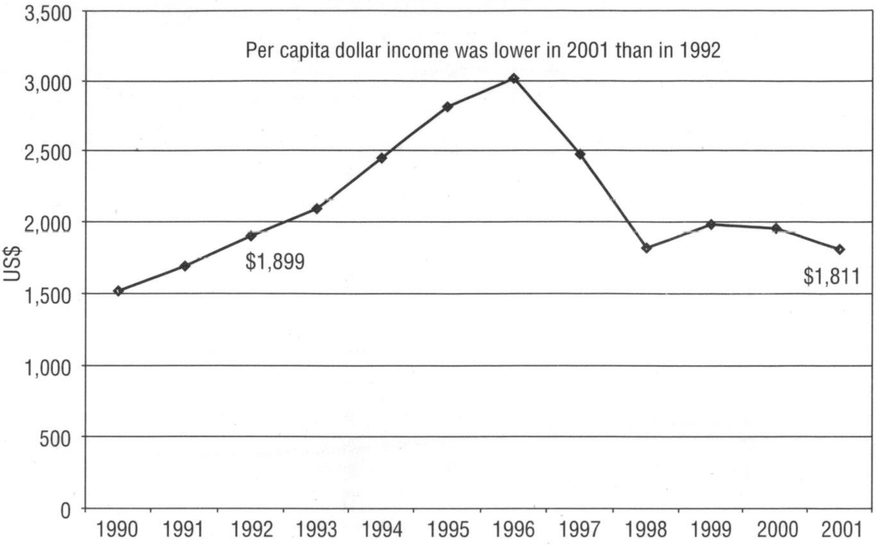

Per capita dollar income was lower in 2001 than in 1992

$1,899

$1,811

US$

1990 1991 1992 1993 1994 1995 1996 1997 1998 1999 2000 2001

Source: IMF, The World Economic Outlook Database, April 2002.

The Bush administration is currently seeking to establish a free trade zone with all of South America. As can be seen in Figure 8.5, GDP per capita in South America ranges between US$1,000 and US$4,400, with the exception of Uruguay where per capita income is US$5,800. In eight out of the 10 countries shown in the figure, per capita GDP has fallen since 1995 – from 3% in Uruguay to 45% in Argentina. It is difficult to understand how further trade liberalization with the poor countries of South America could fail to exacerbate the U.S. current account deficit.

For all these reasons, the current account deficit of the United States can only continue to widen in the years ahead, unless and until the dollar falls very significantly against the currencies of all the United States' major trading partners. As the imports from low-wage nations flood into the U.S., they are very likely to cause the current disinflationary trend to continue and to mature into deflation.

It has become sacrilege to cast doubt on the sanctity of free trade in recent decades. To question the benefits to be derived from free trade is to invite ridicule in much the same way as it was considered contemptible to question the invulnerability of the New Paradigm economy as recently as 2000. Sadly, the fact of the matter is that existing trade arrangements are destabilizing the global economy and cannot continue without ending in economic disaster.

Figure 8.5 South American countries: GDP per capita flat to falling in most countries, 1995–2002

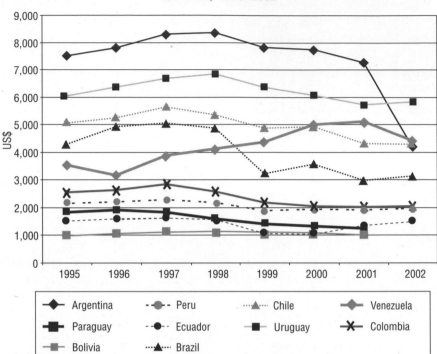

Source: IMF, The World Economic Outlook Database, April 2002.

Let's return to first principles. David Ricardo (1772–1823) was among the first and most influential advocates of free trade. His Theory of Comparative Advantage was particularly important in swaying public opinion in favor of trade liberalization. However, Ricardo demonstrated the benefits to be derived from trade between England and Portugal – not between England and Guangdong Province.

Most crucially, it is important to understand that Ricardo's theories were constructed at a time when gold was the currency in which trade was transacted. In Ricardo's world, trade imbalances resulted in a change of relative prices as gold left the deficit nations and entered the surplus nations. Any country with a large and persistent trade deficit would have suffered a loss of gold and, consequently, a contraction of credit, recession, falling prices, and falling wages, until its products became competitive enough to restore its trade balance. Later in the 19th century, when England experienced extended trade deficits with China due to its appetite for Chinese tea, it resorted to war and forced China to buy its (Indian) opium to prevent the loss of England's precious metals.

Were the gold standard that Ricardo understood still in place, the United States would have seen its entire gold holdings completely depleted long ago as a result of its trade deficits in the 1980s. Thereafter, further deficits would have been impossible because the country would have had no means left with which to pay for them. For example, according to IMF statistics, the United States currently has 262 million ounces of gold among its international reserve assets, an amount worth US$83.8 billion, assuming a value of US$320 per ounce of gold. In 2001, the United States' trade deficit with China alone was US$83 billion, enough to wipe out all the U.S. gold reserves in just one year.

If Ricardo were restored to life, he would be bewildered, at least temporarily, by the international trade and monetary framework in place at the turn of the 21st century. However, it would not take him long to understand that once the dollar replaced gold as the primary international reserve asset, the world economy became flooded by dollar liquidity due to a long series of monumental trade imbalances. Also, he would quickly understand that it was this inundation of dollars that was responsible for the economic overheating and hyperinflation in asset prices that has destabilized the global economy during the 1980s and 1990s.

At this point in history, it should not be forgotten that David Ricardo was the economist who developed the Theory of the Iron Law of Wages, as well as the Theory of Comparative Advantage. With his Theory of the Iron Law of Wages, Ricardo asserted that: (1) "the natural price of labor is that price which is necessary to enable the laborers, one with another, to subsist and to perpetuate their race, without either increase or diminution"; and (2) "However much the market price of labor may deviate from its natural price, it has, like commodities, a tendency to conform to it."[2] In other words, Ricardo believed that wage rates generally tend not to rise above the minimum level sufficient to keep the working class alive, working, and procreating.

As wage rates in the global manufacturing sector fall toward US$4 per day, at least Ricardo's Theory of the Iron Law of Wages looks set to be validated by developments in the 21st century. In a world where trade imbalance results in destabilizing credit creation, rather than a change in relative prices, it is far less certain that the same can be said for his Theory of Comparative Advantage.

EXCESS CAPACITY

The relocation of a rapidly increasing proportion of the world's manufacturing facilities to low-wage developing countries is exerting strong downward pressure on the prices of manufactured goods. However, there is also a second way in which the existing trade arrangements generate deflationary pressure. The United States' current account deficit, which has grown to the equivalent of 1.5% of global GDP per annum, generates very large amounts of reserve assets which fuel credit creation. Too much credit extension allows over-investment and ends in excess capacity. Excess capacity causes deflation.

Excess capacity is the industrial equivalent of an asset price bubble. Both are caused by too much credit extension, and both can cause bank failures.

It is easy to increase aggregate supply in any economy. Simply increase the flow of credit to the manufacturing sector. It is much more difficult to increase aggregate demand, which is ultimately linked to the purchasing power of the public. Rising asset prices can temporarily cause purchasing power to increase through a wealth effect. But even asset prices are capped by the underlying ability of the public to acquire and finance those assets. Ultimately, aggregate demand is determined by wages. When aggregate supply – that is, industrial production – increases faster than wage growth, excess capacity results. Excess capacity causes falling product prices, deteriorating profitability, corporate-sector distress, and, finally, financial-sector distress. The extraordinary surge in international reserve assets over the last 30 years has allowed excessive credit extension that has resulted in a surge in industrial production around the world. However, the purchasing power of the world's population has not expanded at the same pace. Consequently, today there is a glut of industrial capacity on a global scale.

Worldwide disinflation supports this view, but beyond pointing to price trends, it is not easy to document global excess capacity. For instance, there are no data series on global capacity utilization. Nor are there data series showing the "global" price for most types of manufactured goods, such as a global car price index, or a global textile price index. The task of demonstrating the existence of global excess capacity is made yet more complicated by the differing characteristics of various national economies. For example, some economies are export-oriented, such as the Japanese and Chinese economies, while others – that of the United States, in particular – could be described as import-oriented. In a global economy, excess capacity cannot always be determined by comparing domestic supply with domestic demand. For example, the ratio of private investment to personal consumption tends to be higher in export-oriented countries, since businesses there invest to supply the world market, not only a domestic market.

Despite the difficulties involved in substantiating the presence of global excess capacity, it is well known that there is too much capacity in many industries on a global scale. The steel, semiconductor, automobile, and telecommunications equipment industries are some of the best-known examples. The rest of this chapter will demonstrate how excessive credit expansion resulted in the over-investment that is now culminating in deflation.

Japan: Deflation Nation

Consider first Japan (see Figure 8.6). Between 1985 and 1988, Japan's reserve assets practically quadrupled. In three years, the country's reserves rose from US$27 billion to US$97 billion. Immediately thereafter, Japan's already high rate of credit growth accelerated. The expansion of credit fueled an investment boom – not only in property and shares, but also in industrial production (see Figure 8.7).

The late 1980s were glorious years for Japan and its corporations and banks. The economy seemed unstoppable. The country was then in the midst of the virtuous spiral stage of its credit bubble. As businesses expanded their investments, employment and salaries increased. Moreover, the more banks lent, the higher asset prices rose. Rising wages and the booming property and stock markets allowed personal consumption to rise as well. All of those factors supported higher corporate profitability. All segments of the economy were expanding and contributing to the growth of all the other segments through their expansion.

Figure 8.6   Japan: 1. Reserves rose sharply; 2. Credit growth expanded; 3. Investment accelerated, 1981–90

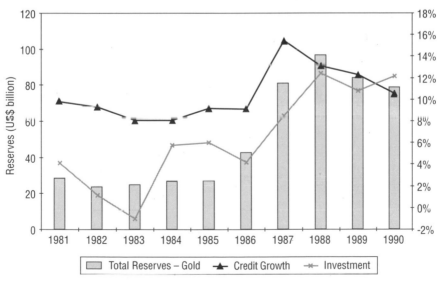

Source: IMF, *International Financial Statistics Yearbook 2001*.

Figure 8.7   Japan: Industrial production index, 1980–2000

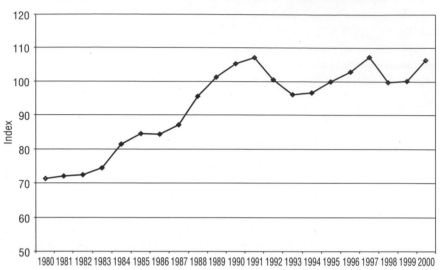

Source: IMF, *International Financial Statistics Yearbook 2001.*

Then, in the early 1990s, the expansion stopped. It stopped because the growth in consumption did not keep pace with the growth in investment. Wages and personal income had risen during the boom years – just not as much as aggregate supply. This can be seen in the sharp rise in the ratio between private investment (gross fixed capital formation) and personal consumption (see Figure 8.8). That ratio rose from 51% in 1986 to 61% in 1990.

As mentioned above, it is very easy to expand industrial capacity if enough credit is available. The hard part is selling all the merchandise that the expanded capacity can produce. The purchasing power of the public is the limiting factor. During credit booms, the increase in industrial capacity outstrips the growth in purchasing power. When supply exceeds demand (that is, demand supported by sufficient purchasing power), prices must fall.

And thus it was in Japan. The vicious downward spiral stage of the credit bubble took hold in the early 1990s. As product prices fell, corporate profitability fell. Consequently, wages and bonuses were cut back and unemployment began to rise. Consumers, with less money in their pockets and less certainty about the future, began to rein in their consumption. Less consumption dealt still another blow to profitability. Share prices fell along with consumption and profits. Very quickly, businesses were forced to curtail new investment. Demand for loans declined because existing capacity was already excessive, and because excess capacity made further investment

Figure 8.8   Japan: The ratio of private investment to personal consumption, 1983–2000

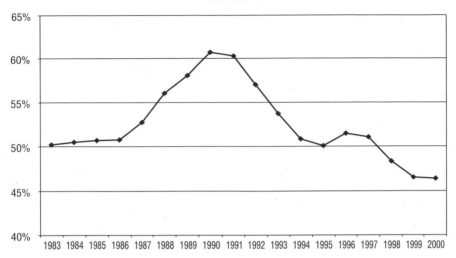

Source: IMF, *International Financial Statistics Yearbook 2001.*

unprofitable. As each weak part of the economy inflicted damage on all the other parts, aggregate demand in the economy fell, but the industrial capacity remained in place. Interest rates fell, but that did not help. Businesses will only borrow and invest if the rate of return they expect to make on their investment exceeds the rate of interest they must pay to borrow funds. In Japan's post-bubble economy, the excess capacity was so great that almost any new investment would have resulted in a loss – not a profit. Even when interest rates fell to just above 0%, businesses were not interested in borrowing, due to the dearth of profitable investment opportunities.

During the course of the 1990s, the non-performing loans of the banks and the debt of the government both accelerated steadily, but prices fell (see Figure 8.9). Deflation was first recorded in 1995. Prices inched up again in 1997 and 1998, but deflation set in again in 1999 and prices have fallen every year since.

Falling prices are very hard on corporate profitability. Deflation also makes it more difficult for businesses to service their debt, since each year they must achieve higher turnover just to compensate for the falling sales prices. The Japanese government has spent fiendishly attempting to kick-start the economy. While those efforts have failed to renew economic growth, they have at least managed to prevent Japan's long recession from becoming a depression. Still yet, the outlook for Japan's economy is not encouraging. Property and share prices continue to fall, the global export market is weakening as the U.S. recession worsens, the government's fiscal

Figure 8.9   Japan: From inflation to deflation, 1970–2002

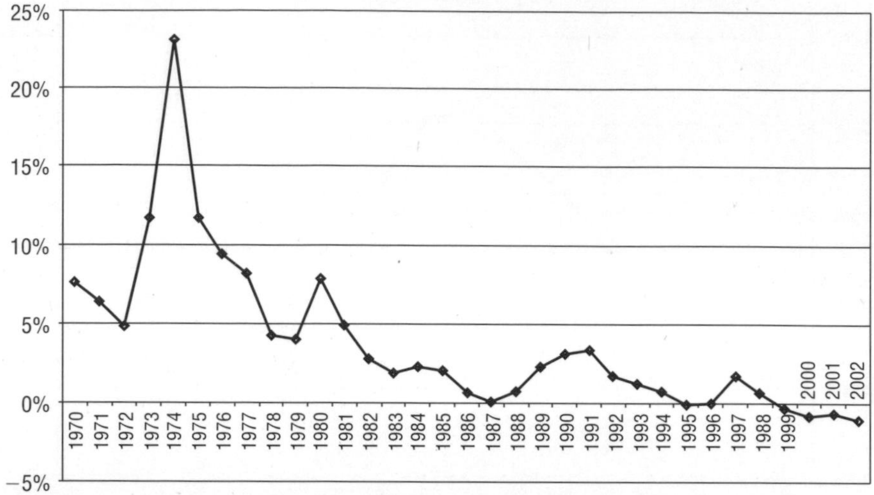

Source: IMF, The World Economic Outlook Database, April 2002.

position is deteriorating, and, according to Standard & Poor's, the non-performing loan problem at Japan's banks is worse now than ever before. Finally, China's recent entry into the WTO is certain to exacerbate the deflationary pressures in Japan, since China's per capita GDP is only 3% of that of Japan. Anything that can be manufactured in Japan can be manufactured much more cheaply in nearby China. Only Japanese trade barriers could prevent China's cheap manufactured goods from exerting more downward pressure on Japanese prices; and the rules of the WTO are designed to remove all such impediments to trade.

Disinflation in the Asia Crisis Countries

A few figures will be sufficient to demonstrate that the same chain of events took place in the Asia Crisis countries in the 1990s. First, the reserve assets of Indonesia, Korea, Malaysia, and Thailand ballooned beginning in the late 1980s (see Figure 8.10).

Next, credit expanded at an extraordinary pace right up until 1997 (see Figure 8.11). As a rule of thumb, any country that experiences loan growth of more than 10% per annum for a period of five or more consecutive years is very likely to suffer a systemic banking crisis. The Asia Crisis countries racked up much higher loan growth than that for 10 straight years before their banks failed.

Figure 8.10 Bubble fuel: Total reserves minus gold, 1970–96
(percent change)

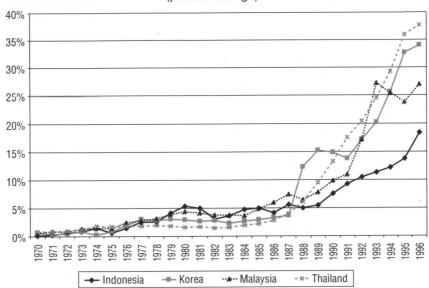

Source: IMF, *International Financial Statistics Yearbook 2001*.

Figure 8.11 Asia Crisis countries: Credit growth, 1983–97

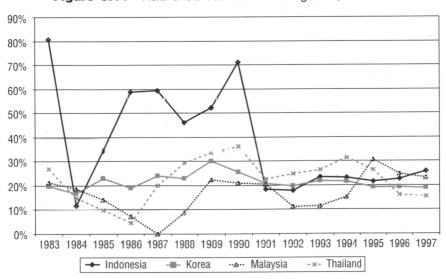

Source: IMF, *International Financial Statistics Yearbook 2001*.

Excessive loan growth allowed over-investment, as can be seen in Figure 8.12 showing the ratio of private investment to personal consumption. As in Japan, and, as we will see, elsewhere around the world, investment expanded faster than consumption in each of these countries during their boom years. The resulting excess capacity ended in economic collapse.

In order to help weakening corporations avoid defaulting on their loans, the banks in the Asian Miracle countries had been rolling over a good portion of their loan portfolios for a number of years before the financial house of cards eventually collapsed in 1997. When it did, domestic demand, which had been pumped up by easy credit, wage increases, and hyperinflation in asset prices, plunged ... but the industrial capacity remained in place.

After a jump in inflation in 1998 due to the imported inflation that accompanied the sharp devaluation of the Asia Crisis currencies, disinflation quickly set in across the region (see Figure 8.13). Indonesia was the exception. The economic collapse there was so overwhelming, the government was forced to print money to save what they could of the banking system. Hyperinflation was the result. Prices rose 58% in 1998 and another 21% in 1999.

Figure 8.12 Asia Crisis countries: Ratio of private investment to personal consumption, 1980–99

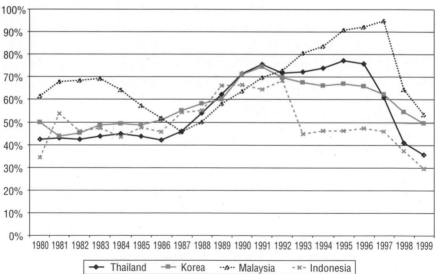

Source: IMF, *International Financial Statistics Yearbook 2001.*

Figure 8.13 Asia Crisis countries: Average inflation rate (excluding Indonesia), 1990–2002

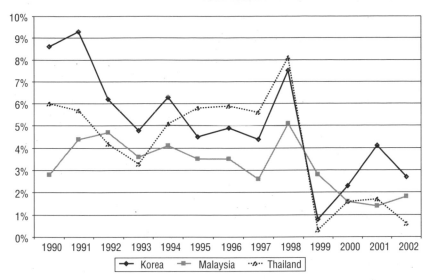

Source: IMF, The World Economic Outlook Database, April 2002.

China: Deflation in Boom-time

China is the next case of interest. China's economic bubble has not yet popped. In all other respects, the pattern is the same as that experienced in Japan and the Asia Crisis countries. Between 1986 and 2000, China's reserve assets rose from US$11.5 billion to US$168 billion, and domestic credit skyrocketed from 794 billion yuan to 11.9 trillion yuan.[3] The flood of credit allowed an over-investment binge that caused the ratio of private investment to personal consumption to peak at 83% in 1993 and to remain above 70% thereafter (see Figure 8.14).

During the second half of the 1980s and the first half of the 1990s, inflation was a serious concern for China. However, by 1995 disinflation had taken hold, as the supply of almost every manufactured product exceeded the demand that the purchasing power of the Chinese population could afford. In 1998, China experienced deflation despite an economic growth rate of almost 8%. In 1999, the Chinese economy continued to boom, but prices fell again. In 2000, prices inched up only 0.4%.

It would be difficult to discover any (peacetime) nation during the industrial age that had strayed further away from any kind of sustainable economic equilibrium than China has over the last 15 years. Between 1980 and 2000, domestic credit in China expanded at an average rate of 22% per

Figure 8.14   China: Ratio of private investment to personal consumption, 1980–99

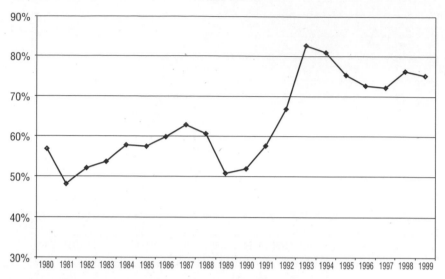

Source: IMF, *International Financial Statistics Yearbook 2001.*

annum to an amount equivalent to 133% of the country's GDP. That credit growth has been one of the two driving forces behind the country's extraordinary economic growth – exports being the other. The trouble is that up to half of those loans have become non-performing and may never be repaid.[4] The economy has grown dependent on double-digit loan growth to keep loss-making state-owned enterprises in business and China's huge workforce employed. However, now that the country faces excess capacity and deflation at home, most new investments (undertaken to expand industrial capacity still further) can only be loss making if targeted at the domestic market. In such an environment, the majority of new loans that are extended within China are destined to become non-performing. If the banks continue to extend credit aggressively, the cost that the government will have to bear to bail out China's depositors may quickly exceed fiscal resources – if it has not done so already. On the other hand, if the banks cease to aggressively extend credit, then domestic demand would slump, China's economy would slow rapidly, deflationary pressures would worsen, unemployment would rise, and social stability would be threatened. It is a terrible dilemma that confronts Chinese policymakers.

Meanwhile, on the international markets, China's exports are the most price-competitive in the world. Not only do Chinese manufacturers enjoy a workforce that is highly skilled and very low-cost, but they also have access to credit that, in many cases, they may never be forced to repay. China is an

Figure 8.15 China: Deflation, 1970–2001

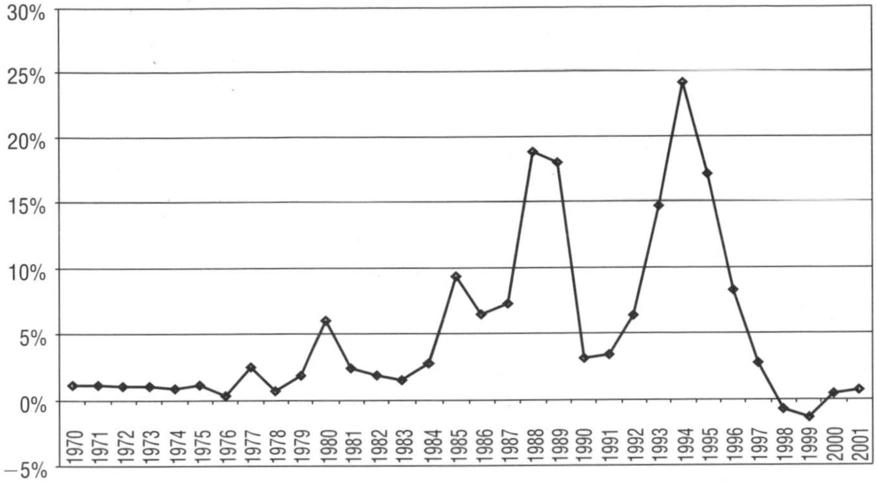

Source: IMF, The World Economic Outlook Database, April 2002.

exporting powerhouse. Its primary export to the rest of the world is deflation (see Figure 8.15).

Boom-time Disinflation in the United States

Finally, consider the economy of the United States, which comprises approximately one-third of global economic output. During the second half of the 1990s, as that country's current account deficit exploded to mind-boggling levels, its trading partners acquired U.S. dollar-denominated assets with the dollars they earned through their surpluses. Consequently, by the end of the decade, the U.S. financial account surplus exceeded US$1 billion a day. Those dollar inflows, which played an important role in creating the stock-market bubble in the United States, also contributed to over investment in the real economy there. Consider the increase in the ratio of private investment to personal consumption (see Figure 8.16). That ratio rose sharply throughout the 1990s and, between 1998 and 2000, it remained at an unusually high level last exceeded in 1985.

Evidence of the investment binge can also be seen in the rate of growth in the United States' industrial capacity in the late 1990s. Between October 1996 and April 1999, industrial capacity grew at an annualized pace of between 5% and 7%. During the 1970s, the highest rate of growth in industrial capacity was 4.4% at the beginning of the decade. The highest rate during the 1980s was 3.2% in 1985. After mid-1999, as much of that investment proved to be uneconomical, the rate of capacity expansion slowed very sharply, falling to only 1% in June 2002 (see Figure 8.17).

Figure 8.16 United States: Ratio of private investment to personal consumption, 1986–2001

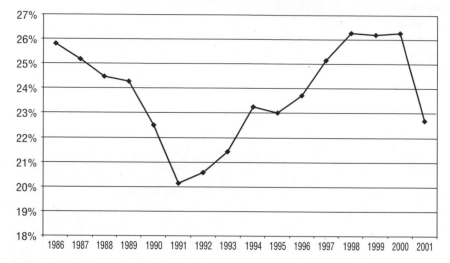

Source: U.S. Dept. of Commerce, Bureau of Economic Analysis, National Accounts Data.

Figure 8.17 United States: Industrial capacity: Total industry, 1968–2002

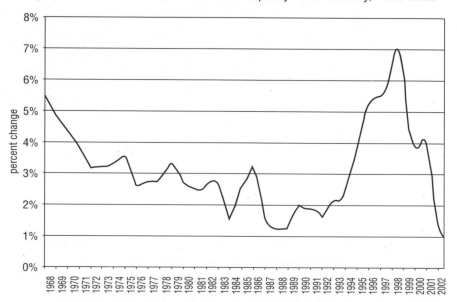

Source: Federal Reserve Statistics, *Industrial Production*.

Once industrial capacity is put in place, it does not go away just because it is not needed – even if it is loss-making. When the downturn comes, production falls off, causing a drop in the capacity utilization rate. In December 2001, the capacity utilization rate in the United States fell to 74%. Lower capacity utilization rates have only been recorded twice since 1967, once in 1975 and again in 1982, when it fell as low as 71% (see Figure 8.18).

Inflation in consumer prices was 1.1% at an annualized rate in June 2002 (see Figure 8.19). It had not been lower since 1963. The low rate of inflation is due to both the importation of goods made with very low-cost labor and to falling product prices across numerous industries where over-investment during the second half of the 1990s resulted in excess capacity.

Deflationary pressures are greater still at the producer price level. As Figure 8.20 shows, prices of manufactured goods at the producer level fell for 10 consecutive months from October 2001 to July 2002, the most recent month with available data.

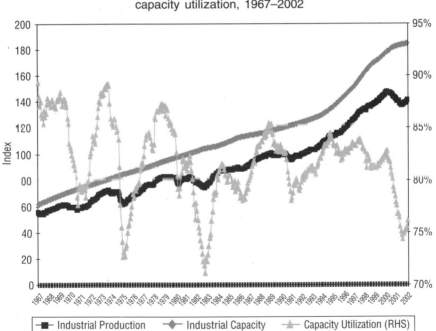

Figure 8.18   United States: Industrial production, capacity, and capacity utilization, 1967–2002

Source: Federal Reserve Statistics, *Industrial Production*.

Figure 8.19   United States: Consumer Price Index: Disinflation, 1970–2002

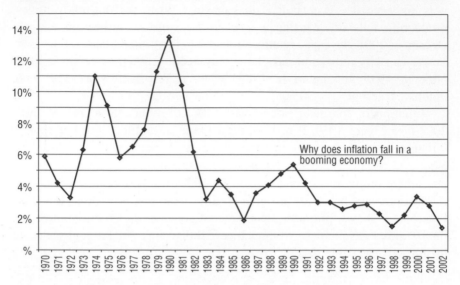

Source: IMF, The World Economic Outlook Database, April 2002.

Figure 8.20   United States: Producer Price Index: Manufactured goods, 1980–2002 (% change year-on-year)

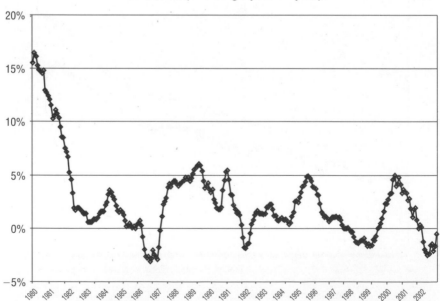

Source: U.S Bureau of Labor Statistics, *Producer Price Indexes.*

▶ THERE IS WORSE TO COME

The current weakness in prices is particularly worrying because the U.S. economy has only just begun to enter the vicious downward spiral stage of this credit bubble cycle. The consumers, who, after all, are the end buyers in the economy, are extraordinarily over-indebted. It is only a matter of time before they are forced to rein in their consumption, pay down their debts, and rebuild their savings. That reduction in consumer spending will drive the United States – and the world – much deeper into recession. Aggregate demand will contract, but industrial capacity will remain in place. Capacity utilization will fall further, providing a graphic illustration of the excess capacity in the economy. Product prices will fall due to the excess capacity, and corporate profitability will suffer as a result. One bad thing will lead to another in a negative, mirror-image of the virtuous upward spiral the economy enjoyed during the bubble years. Poor corporate profitability will result in higher unemployment, which in turn will cause a further reduction in consumption, still worse profitability, rising corporate bankruptcies, financial-sector distress, and credit contraction. Housing prices will deflate again once the aggressive credit expansion that fueled their rise is cut off.

The experience in the United States will be remarkably similar to that which unfolded in Japan and the Asia Crisis countries when their credit bubbles deflated. The economic crisis in the U.S. may be less severe than in those countries, since the property market bubble is not as extreme in America as it was elsewhere; on the other hand, there will be no "engine of economic growth," no export market of last resort, to help the United States export its way out of crisis in the way that the seemingly insatiable U.S. market helped the other post-bubble economies during the 1990s.

The global economy will soon enter a deflation-induced slump similar to the one that has gripped Japan for the last decade. Moreover, the two policy responses developed to treat economic downturns in the 20th century – Keynesianism and monetarism – are unlikely to be able to restore global growth this time around. Governments, which spent lavishly during recessions and economic expansions both over the last 50 years, now may not have sufficient fiscal firepower left to jump-start the economy at this time when fiscal stimulus is so badly needed. Fiscal stimulus has failed completely to restore economic growth in Japan. Worse still, an aggressive monetary response would do more harm than good. Excessive monetary expansion, in the form of international dollar liquidity, created the global economic bubble in the first place. Additional aggressive expansion of the global money supply would succeed, at best, only in creating a new round of asset price bubbles that would ultimately implode in an even more terrible economic collapse.

Monetary policy works through credit expansion. When the government wishes to expand the money supply, it buys assets (such as government bonds) from the banks, increasing their liquidity. In theory, the banks, in turn, lend more to businesses, which are expected to increase their investment and hire more workers, thereby eventually stimulating consumption and the economy overall. In a post-bubble economic environment, characterized by excess capacity, bankrupt corporations, and overly indebted consumers, monetary policy does not work. Although the liquidity position of the banks is improved by the government's actions, there are neither a sufficient number of creditworthy borrowers to lend to (given the very large number of debtors unable to repay their existing debts), nor a sufficient number of clients who want to borrow, due to the lack of money-making investment opportunities left in the glutted marketplace. Consequently, the increased money supply never reaches the consumers and personal consumption does not revive.

DO BANK BAILOUTS CAUSE LIQUIDITY TRAPS?

There is one other aspect of modern economic management that seems likely to depress price levels in the years ahead. Today, when banks fail – and, as explained in the last chapter, an extraordinary number of banks have failed in recent years – governments make every effort to bail out the depositors of those banks. This policy reassures the public that their deposits are safe and, in that way, reduces the risk of bank runs. It also serves to maintain consumer purchasing power and to prevent any contraction in the money supply, since deposits are the largest component of M2. Of course, it comes at a cost to the government. The Savings and Loan crisis in the United States during the 1980s is estimated to have cost the equivalent of 3% of U.S. GDP, while the systemic banking failure in Indonesia cost 50% of GDP between 1997 and 2000.[6] However, in a post-bubble economic environment, bailing out banks appears to have another consequence that is not yet fully appreciated: it contributes to the formation of liquidity traps that perpetuate deflationary pressure in the economy.

Bank failures are not new. In fact, they pre-date the Industrial Revolution. In earlier times, when banks failed, their depositors lost their savings and the available credit in the banking system contracted. When there were runs on other banks, credit contraction was felt throughout the economy. Less credit was available to finance new investments, unemployment rose, and the price level fell. Business conditions were poor and few people had the funds to take advantage of any new opportunities that did arise. However, anyone who did still have financial resources was well placed to take advantage of the next upswing whenever it did come about.

Today, when banks fail, depositors generally do not lose their savings. The government intervenes and, if necessary, uses government funds to replace the savings that were lost by the failed banks. This policy serves to maintain consumer purchasing power. It also prevents the money supply from contracting and, thereby, helps avoid a credit crunch. Unfortunately, based on the experience of Japan and the Asia Crisis countries, in the current economic crisis this policy appears actually to perpetuate the existing deflationary pressures in a different way.

The current global economic crisis is a crisis of excess capacity that has resulted from excessive credit expansion. Initially, as the global money supply expanded on the back of surging dollar liquidity, a great deal of profits were generated and deposited into the banks around the world. Those deposits enabled banks to extend new loans that further stimulated the economic expansion. This expansionary cycle continued until asset price bubbles formed and excessive industrial capacity came into existence. At that point, a large portion of the loans that had fueled the boom could not be repaid, and a large portion of the deposits were lost.

In a post-bubble environment characterized by excess capacity, if governments refund to the public the savings that the banks lost, then there will continue to be too much credit available relative to profitable investment opportunities. In other words, the conditions that brought about the bank failures in the first place will continue to exist. There will be too much credit chasing too few profitable opportunities. Every potentially profitable opportunity that does arise will be instantly overwhelmed with financing offers; and well-funded competitors will replicate the venture until excess capacity makes that business unprofitable as well. Under such conditions, returns on investment are unable to rise. Keep in mind that a significant portion of the deposits that governments are forced to refund in such situations only came into existence in the first place as profits earned as a result of the unsustainable, credit-induced economic boom. The continued existence of that same pool of financing perpetuates the excess capacity and prevents the re-establishment of a normal rate of return.

With too much credit chasing too few viable investments, interest rates fall and a liquidity trap emerges. When interest rates fall close to zero and there are still no profitable investment opportunities, due to the excess capacity in the economy, the situation is called a liquidity trap. It is called a trap because there is no apparent way out. Interest rates can't be forced below 0%.

That is what has occurred in Japan and across most of the Asia Crisis countries. Interest rates in those countries have fallen to very low levels, and yet the return on investment is so low there that it is still not profitable for businesses to borrow and invest. It is likely that the same pattern will be repeated in the United States as the recession there worsens if the U.S. government bails out the losers (as it very probably will) when banks or other financial institutions begin to go under.

If it is true that bailing out banks under these conditions only results in bringing about liquidity traps by preserving too much credit in the economy, then, in a post-bubble environment, there is no way to prevent deflation by using existing policy tools. If banks fail and the government does not bail out the depositors, then the money supply will collapse, credit will contract, and prices will fall. On the other hand, if banks fail and the government does bail out the depositors, then the excessive supply of credit in the economy will persist and result in a liquidity trap that ensures that rates of return remain negative even though interest rates have fallen to zero. In that case, supply will continue to exceed demand and product prices will continue to fall.

CONCLUSION

Existing policy tools are likely to prove to be incapable of resolving the current global economic crisis. Keynesianism and monetarism have both been too abused during the preceding decades to be effective now. Similarly, bailing out the depositors of failed banks may solve one set of problems by preventing a collapse of the money supply, only to produce another set of problems by perpetuating the excessive pool of credit that was responsible for causing the crisis in the first place.

If some variation of a protracted, 1930s-type deflationary depression is to be avoided (without resorting to war or hyperinflation), then a new policy fix suitable to the current post-bubble economic environment will have to be devised (see Figure 8.21). Part Four of this book offers some recommendations that could boost global demand in our new global economy without relying on either fiscal or monetary stimulus. First, however, Part Three examines why the global economy cannot avoid being dragged down into a severe economic slump by the recession in the United States and the inevitable collapse in the value of the dollar.

Figure 8.21   United States: Consumer prices, 1914–40
(% change year-on-year)

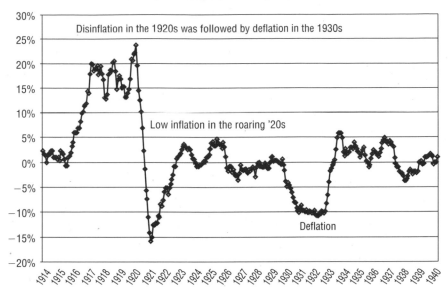

Source: U.S. Bureau of Labor Statistics, Consumer Price Index – All Urban Consumers.

▶ REFERENCES

1   Federal Reserve Economic Data: St. Louis Fed.
2   From *The Principles of Political Economy and Taxation* (London: J. M. Dent and Sons, 1873), pp. 52–63.
3   IMF, *International Financial Statistics Yearbook 2001*, lines 11.d and 32.
4   See Nicholas Lardy's *China's Unfinished Economic Revolution* (Washington D.C.: The Brookings Institution, 1998) for a detailed analysis of China's troubled banking sector.
5   Board of Governors of the Federal Reserve System, International Finance Discussion Papers, No. 729, June 2002, "Preventing Deflation: Lessons from Japan's Experience in the 1990s."
6   Patrick Honohan and Daniela Klingebiel (The World Bank), "Controlling Fiscal Costs of Banking Crises," Preliminary draft, April 17, 2000.

PART THREE

GLOBAL RECESSION AND THE DEATH OF MONETARISM

Part Two explained why the severe disequilibrium in the global economy cannot persist. Part Three assesses how badly the global economy will be impacted when that disequilibrium unwinds. It also explains why traditional monetary policy will continue to prove ineffective in fighting deflation or in restoring economic growth in a post-bubble environment.

The global economy suffered a severe shock in 2001. Economic growth rates decelerated abruptly, stock markets spiraled downward, commodity prices fell, and government finances came under strain all around the world. That shock was brought on by the first phase of the New Paradigm recession (NPR) in the United States during which private investment fell sharply and U.S. imports contracted by US$79 billion, or 6%, relative to the year before.

The second phase of that recession (NPR Phase II) is about to begin. It will result from a sharp decline in personal consumption expenditure. When the consumer credit bubble in the United States pops, falling consumption will cause a further drop in investment. Total aggregate demand will contract – possibly over a multi-year period. Consequently, U.S. imports will fall much more than during 2001. Worse still, the inevitable correction of the U.S. current account deficit will greatly compound the problems caused by the NPR Phase II. Chapter 9 considers when the next down leg of the global recession is likely to begin and gauges how hard the global economy is likely to be hit.

Chapter 10 begins by considering how far the U.S. dollar will have to fall against the currencies of all its major trading partners before the U.S. current account returns to equilibrium. During the second half of the 1980s, the dollar fell 50% against the yen and the mark before the U.S. current account deficit came back under control. This time, a 50% drop might not be enough. Moreover, this currency readjustment will involve a large number of currencies, not only the yen and the euro. The second half of the chapter examines how well prepared the rest of the world is to face the double onslaught of a U.S. recession and the correction of the U.S. current account deficit. The economic health of China, Japan, the other Asian exporting nations, Europe, and Mexico are each analyzed in turn. It will become clear that when the era of export-led growth comes to an end, a difficult new age will begin.

Part Three ends with an explanation of why monetary policy is incapable of overcoming deflation in a post-bubble environment. The United States' current account deficits have flooded the world with financial liquidity. That liquidity has fueled a global credit bubble that permitted over-investment, brought about excess capacity and asset price bubbles, and now is culminating in deflation. While it may be possible to fight fire with fire, you can't fight liquidity with liquidity. The Bank of Japan has tried and conceded that it doesn't work. Chapter 11 explains why monetarism is drowning … in the new global money supply that is gushing out of the disequilibrium in America's balance of payments.

Part Four will outline measures that could help mitigate the damage of the coming worldwide economic downturn and put in place the foundations for more balanced and sustainable growth in the decades ahead.

Chapter 9

Global Recession:
Why, When, and How Hard?

Never did a ship founder with a captain and crew more ignorant of the reasons for its misfortune or more impotent to do anything about it.

— E. J. Hobsbawm, 1968[1]

INTRODUCTION

The outlook for the global economy is profoundly disturbing. During the 1990s, the booming U.S. economy served as the world's engine of economic growth. Surging credit expansion in the United States allowed businesses to increase their investments and consumers to boost their consumption, producing the longest uninterrupted economic advance on record. The rest of the world profited handsomely from the powerful economic boom in the U.S. Between the end of 1991, when the expansion began, and the end of 2000, as it was coming to an end, U.S. imports jumped 150% to US$1.2 trillion. Moreover, not only did America's imports grow at an extraordinary pace, but the gap between what the United States bought from the rest of the world and what the rest of the world bought from the United States – the U.S. current account deficit – also widened enormously. The United States' trading partners expanded their industrial capacity to meet U.S. demand; and rising investment allowed increasing consumption as well. U.S. demand for imported goods meant more jobs, more corporate profits, and more economic growth throughout the rest of the world.

All that is coming to an end. The over-indebted American economy has entered a recession that is likely to be as extreme and prolonged as the economic boom that preceded it. The downturn began in 2001 with a sharp fall in U.S. private investment. The repercussions of that reduction in investment – primarily technology-related investment – were felt around the world. Despite the fall off in investment and rising unemployment, consumption in the United States remained robust in 2001 and 2002, providing a crutch for the wounded economy. A rapid reduction in interest rates to 40-year lows enabled American consumers to continue increasing their indebtedness and their consumption. Future developments, however,

175

will show that this aggressive monetary easing was nothing more than a palliative that merely prolonged and exacerbated the disequilibrium in the economy. The second, and more profound, phase of this recession will result in a steep decline in personal consumption. The American consumer is over-indebted and will soon be forced to curtail the profligate behavior he embraced during the 1980s and 1990s. The downturn in consumption will cause a further reduction in investment. Both combined will sharply reduce U.S. imports. Falling U.S. imports will throw the world into recession – just as booming U.S. demand fueled the global expansion in the second half of the 1990s.

This global recession will be exacerbated by the inevitable correction of the U.S. current account deficit. That deficit, which exceeded 4% of U.S. GDP in both 2000 and 2001, has provided tremendous economic stimulus to the global economy in recent years. However, it is patently unsustainable, for a number of reasons. If it corrects at the same time that falling consumption sharply curtails America's imports, the global economy will suffer a depression unlike anything experienced since the 1930s. If it corrects after the U.S. recession plays itself out, the recession that the rest of the world will have to endure will be a very extended one. In either case, the excesses of the 1990s will be regretted long into the future. This chapter will demonstrate why.

THE IMPORTANCE OF IMPORTS

The United States has become known as the world's engine of economic growth because of the extraordinary amount of goods it imports from the rest of the world, and because of the speed at which its imports have grown. In 1980, U.S. imports amounted to US$250 billion, the equivalent of 2.4% of global GDP or 12% of world exports. By 2000, U.S. imports had increased almost 400% to US$1,224 billion, the equivalent of 3.9% of global GDP or 19% of world exports. The growth in U.S. imports was particularly extraordinary in the late 1990s. During 1999 and 2000, the final two years of the New Paradigm bubble, U.S. imports jumped by US$307 billion, an increase of 33% over the level of 1998 (see Figure 9.1).

Although the growth in global trade has been very impressive over the last 30 years, it has been far from balanced. The United States' trading partners derived immense benefits from the surge in their exports to America. Nevertheless, in most cases, their demand for U.S. goods increased at a pace considerably slower than that at which their U.S. exports expanded. Consequently, a trade gap of unprecedented magnitude developed (see Figure 9.2).

Figure 9.1   United States: Merchandise imports, 1960–2001

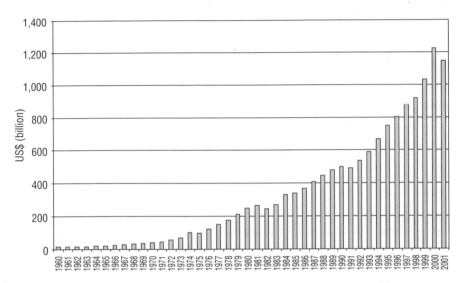

Source: Federal Reserve Economic Data: St. Louis Fed.

Figure 9.2   United States: Trade gap, 1960–2001

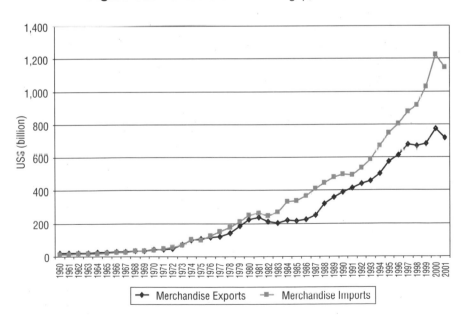

Source: Federal Reserve Economic Data: St. Louis Fed.

The persistence of the U.S. trade deficit first became noticeable in the second half of the 1970s. It was not until the following decade, however, when the Reagan tax cuts caused economic overheating in the United States, that the deficits became a serious cause for concern (see Figure 9.3).

Throughout this period, the United States' current account deficit (which incorporates the balance on services and income, as well as trade) was nearly as large as its trade deficit. In 1987, when the current account deficit approached 3.5% of U.S. GDP, it began to destabilize global capital markets and was considered to be among the causes of the 1987 stock market crash (see Figure 9.4).

A sharp decline in the value of the dollar and a U.S. recession helped bring the United States' balance of payments back closer to equilibrium in 1990 and 1991. Afterwards, however, both the trade and the current account deficits blew out to new all-time highs.

By 2001, the U.S. current account deficit was so large that it was exceeded only by the GDP of 13 countries. South Korea's GDP was US$422 billion in 2001. The Netherlands' GDP was US$380 billion. The United States' current account deficit, at US$393 billion, could be slotted neatly between the two. In fact, the size of this deficit was the equivalent of 1.3% of world GDP. A more accurate picture of the importance of this deficit to the United States' trading partners can by reached by deducting U.S. GDP from total world GDP in order to show the size of the economy of the rest

Figure 9.3   United States: Merchandise trade gap — out of control, 1960–2001

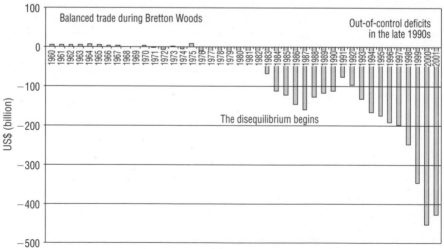

Source: Federal Reserve Economic Data: St. Louis Fed.

of the world without the United States. In that case, the U.S. current account deficit was equivalent to 1.9% of the non-U.S. portion of global economic output in both 2000 and 2001 (see Table 9.1).

Figure 9.4   United States: Current account balance: Subsidizing the rest of the world, 1960–2001

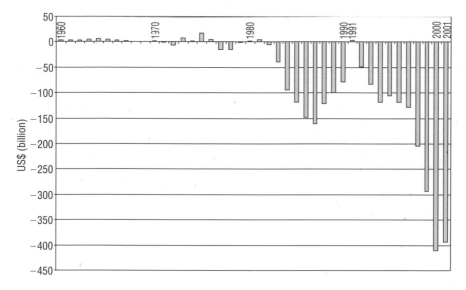

Source: Federal Reserve Economic Data: St. Louis Fed.

Table 9.1   The U.S. current account deficit directly contributes 1–2% of world GDP, 2001

	U.S. current account (US$ billion)	The U.S. current account deficit as % of:	
		World GDP	World GDP excluding U.S. GDP
1990	−79.0	0.35	0.47
1991	3.7	−0.02	−0.02
1992	−48.5	0.20	0.28
1993	−82.5	0.34	0.46
1994	−118.2	0.45	0.62
1995	−105.8	0.36	0.49
1996	−117.8	0.39	0.54
1997	−128.4	0.43	0.60
1998	−203.8	0.69	0.98
1999	−292.9	0.96	1.38
2000	−410.3	1.31	1.91
2001	−393.4	1.27	1.89

Sources: Current account, Federal Reserve Economic Data: St. Louis Fed; GDP: IMF, The World Economic Outlook (WEO) Database, April 2002.

It would be inaccurate to conclude from the preceding statement that the rest of the world's economic output would have been 1.9% less in each of those years had there been no U.S. current account deficit. Actually, the negative impact would have been considerably greater than 1.9%. The economic output of the United States' trading partners was further enhanced by a multiplier effect that resulted as their surpluses against the United States entered their economies. Had there been no U.S. current account deficit, the non-U.S. portion of the world economy would have grown considerably less during the last 20 years than it actually did.

The impact of the U.S. current account deficit on the growth in world trade has been equally extraordinary. For example, during 2001, the current account deficit was equivalent to 6.4% of total world exports (see Table 9.2).

Table 9.3 lists the 16 largest economies plus seven other export-oriented Asian nations in order to show which countries are net exporters and which are net importers. The United States' economy contributes approximately one-third of global economic output. The output of the 15 next-largest countries combined accounts for another 50% of world GDP. The remaining 160 national economies each contribute less than 1% of world GDP as measured in U.S. dollars.

Table 9.3 lists each country's net export position relative to the rest of the world. Table 9.4 provides details on each country's trade balance vis-à-vis the United States alone.

Table 9.2 The U.S. current account deficit accounts for 6.4% of world exports, 2001

	U.S. current account (US$ bn)	World merchandise exports (US$ bn)	The U.S. current account deficit as % of world exports
1990	−79.0	3,439	2.3
1991	3.7	3,530	−0.1
1992	−48.5	3,758	1.3
1993	−82.5	3,766	2.2
1994	−118.2	4,281	2.8
1995	−105.8	5,140	2.1
1996	−117.8	5,340	2.2
1997	−128.4	5,527	2.3
1998	−203.8	5,441	3.7
1999	−292.9	5,624	5.2
2000	−410.3	6,310	6.5
2001	−393.4	6,162	6.4

Sources: Current account: Federal Reserve Economic Data: St. Louis Fed; exports: IMF, *International Financial Statistics Yearbook 2001*.

Table 9.3 Exporters and importers, 2001

Rank	Country	Share of 2001 world output		Net exports as % of GPD		
		(US$ bn)	(%)	1998	1999	2000
1	United States	10,208	32.9	−1.7	−2.7	−3.9
2	Japan	4,149	13.4	1.8	1.5	1.4
3	Germany	1,847	6.0	1.7	1.1	0.4
4	United Kingdom	1,424	4.6	−0.9	−1.7	−1.9
5	France	1,307	4.2	2.6	2.5	1.4
6	China	1,159	3.7	3.8	2.9	n.a.
7	Italy	1,089	3.5	3.4	2.1	1.2
8	Canada	700	2.3	1.4	3.3	5.1
9	Mexico	618	2.0	−2.2	−1.6	−1.8
10	Spain	582	1.9	0.4	−1.2	−2.3
11	Brazil	504	1.6	−2.0	−1	n.a.
12	India	481	1.6	−1.4	n.a.	n.a.
13	Korea	422	1.4	13.5	6.9	2.8
14	Netherlands	380	1.2	6.7	4.9	5.2
15	Australia	357	1.2	−1.8	−2.7	−1.1
16	Russia	310	1.0	7.5	16.8	20.8
	The Asian Exporters:					
17	Taiwan	309	1.0	n.a.	n.a.	n.a.
26	Hong Kong	163	0.5	1.0	5.5	4.7
29	Indonesia	152	0.5	9.7	8.0	7.8
33	Thailand	122	0.4	15.9	12.6	8.2
40	Singapore	93	0.3	19.6	19.2	n.a.
41	Malaysia	90	0.3	21.8	24.8	19.9
43	Philippines	75	0.2	6.6	0.2	6.1

Sources: IMF, *International Financial Statistics Yearbook 2001*; The World Economic Outlook (WEO) Database, April 2002.

The importance of the trade surplus these countries enjoy vis-à-vis the United States cannot be over-emphasized. It should be borne in mind that these are not one-off gains. They are repeated annually. For many countries, the cumulative total of their trade surpluses with the United States over several years amounts to a very large number. Those sums have a profound effect on corporate profitability, employment, money supply growth, asset prices, and fiscal revenues of the surplus countries. They also boost the amount of trade that is conducted between the surplus countries themselves. For example, because both Malaysia and Indonesia have a trade surplus with the U.S., both countries are able to afford to buy more products from one another than they would if neither of them had a trade surplus with the U.S. Inter-Asian trade is expanding, but in large part that expansion is due to the balance of payments surplus that each of those countries enjoys with the United States. In other words, the U.S. deficits play a vital role in promoting the growth in world trade by providing a substantial portion of the funds that finance that trade.

Table 9.4 The importance of trade with the United States

	Trade balance with U.S. (+ = Surplus, − = Deficit) US$ bn		GDP US$ bn	US$ bn	Trade balance as % of GDP	
	2000	2001	2000	2001	2000	2001
Japan	81.6	69.0	4,768	4,149	1.7	1.7
Germany	29.1	29.1	1,871	1,847	1.6	1.6
United Kingdom	1.8	0.7	1,433	1,424	0.1	0.0
France	9.4	10.5	1,301	1,307	0.7	0.8
China	83.8	83.1	1,080	1,159	7.8	7.2
Italy	14.0	13.9	1,076	1,089	1.3	1.3
Canada	51.9	52.8	711	700	7.3	7.5
Mexico	24.6	30.0	581	618	4.2	4.9
Spain	−0.6	0.6	562	582	−0.1	0.1
Brazil	−1.5	−1.4	594	504	−0.3	−0.3
India	7.0	6.0	460	481	1.5	1.2
Korea	12.5	13.0	462	422	2.7	3.1
Netherlands	−12.2	−10.0	371	380	−3.3	−2.6
Australia	−6.0	−4.5	381	357	−1.6	−1.3
Russia	5.6	3.5	260	310	2.2	1.1
The Asian Exporters:						
Taiwan	16.1	15.3	309	282	5.2	5.4
Hong Kong	−3.1	−4.4	163	162	−1.9	−2.7
Indonesia	8.0	7.6	152	146	5.3	5.2
Thailand	9.8	8.7	122	115	8.0	7.6
Singapore	1.4	−2.7	93	88	1.5	−3.1
Malaysia	14.6	13.0	90	88	16.2	14.8
Philippines	5.1	3.7	75	71	6.8	5.2
World	436.1	411.9	31,332	30,993	1.4	1.3

Sources: Trade balance: U.S. Census Bureau, *U.S. Trade by Country*; GDP: IMF, The World Economic Outlook (WEO) Database, April 2002.

The expansion of the U.S. current account deficit has been accelerating over the last decade. The cumulative deficit in the three years between 1999 and 2001 alone came to US$1.1 trillion. There is no question that the global economy would have been considerably weaker without that windfall. Not only would the surplus countries have achieved far less economic growth, corporate profitability, and money supply growth, but the United States would have had to do without US$1.1 trillion in capital inflow on its financial account. In that sense, this system could be described as "karma capitalism," because what goes around (the U.S. current account deficits) really does come back around (as the U.S. financial account surpluses).

If the United States' imports and its current account deficit could continue expanding at an accelerating rate forever, there would be far less to worry about. Unfortunately, they can't. As explained in earlier chapters, the business cycle is alive and well. The 2001 recession was only the first phase of a multi-year economic contraction in the United States. It was caused by a decline in investment. The second phase will result from a fall in consumer spending. Unfortunately, when consumption declines, investment will fall further as well. In 2001, U.S. imports fell by US$79 billion, or 6%. That slump will appear mild relative to the decline (most probably) in 2003 and 2004 that accompanies a simultaneous reduction in both investment and consumption expenditure.

A worsening of the U.S. recession during the years immediately ahead appears almost unavoidable. The extent of the damage that the U.S. recession will inflict on the rest of the world will depend in large part on whether the correction in the U.S. current account deficit occurs at the same time as the recession or subsequently. As explained in Chapters 6–8, there are at least three reasons why the disequilibrium in the U.S. current account cannot persist. First, for the deficit to persist, it would require the United States to continue going deeper into debt to the rest of the world by approximately the same amount as the current account deficit each year. Given that the net investment position of the United States was already in deficit by the equivalent of 23% of GDP as of the end of 2001, and that the current account deficit exceeded 4% of GDP in both 2000 and 2001, it would not be long at this rate before the United States could not service its growing debt burden.

Second, in the surplus countries, the capital inflows cause asset price bubbles that result in systemic banking crises when they pop. Twenty years of large U.S. current account deficits have generated pandemic banking crises around the world. The fiscal cost of bailing out depositors has been enormous. Pandemic fiscal crises will be next if the fountain of credit creation resulting from the U.S. deficits does not soon cease gushing. Argentina's government has succumbed. Brazil has a very high fever. And most troubling of all, Japan has been downgraded to critical condition by the ratings agencies.

The final reason these deficits can't continue is that they are deflationary and undermine corporate profitability around the world by facilitating over-investment and excess capacity. Even in the United States and Europe, the financial sector could not long survive an extended period of corporate losses.

If the U.S. current account deficit does persist at 4% or more of U.S. GDP for a number of more years, it will continue to destabilize the global economy by causing excessive debt creation in the United States, and asset price bubbles, deflation, and systemic banking crises around the world. The longer the disequilibrium carries on, the more painful the inevitable adjustment process will be when it corrects. Sooner or later, the United States' trading partners will be deprived of this US$400 billion to US$500 billion in annual economic subsidy from the United States. It will come as a very hard blow.

> ### HOW HARD?

Economic models are difficult to design and are generally inaccurate. Therefore, it is very difficult to forecast with any certainty how much the rest of the world will suffer as a result of the imminent second phase of the U.S. recession and the eventual correction in the U.S. current account deficit. History should serve as good a guide as any other.

In 2001, the imports into the United States fell by US$79 billion, or 6.3%, to US$1,180 billion. The U.S. current account deficit fell by only US$17 billion, or 4.1%, to US$393 billion. That reduction in U.S. demand for foreign products had a profound impact on the rest of the world. World merchandise exports shrank by 4% in value in 2001, the largest annual decrease since 1982.[2]

The economic growth rates of all the United States' major trading partners decelerated abruptly. Stock markets spiraled downward, commodity prices fell, and government finances came under strain.

Table 9.5 shows that economic growth rates in 2001 slowed greatly in every region of the world except Africa. The slowdown in growth ranged from 24% in the transition countries to 91% in the newly industrialized Asian economies.

Exports contracted in 11 out of the 16 largest economies and in all of the export-oriented Asian economies. Taiwan was hardest hit, suffering a 17% drop in exports. Japan, the Philippines, Korea, and Singapore all recorded a two-digit drop in exports, with Malaysia close behind.

Table 9.5 World economic growth slowed sharply in 2001

| | Gross domestic product, constant prices (annual % change) | | | | Decline in growth rate (%) |
	1998	1999	2000	2001	2001 vs. 2000
Advanced economies	2.7	3.3	3.9	1.2	−69
Major advanced economies	2.8	2.9	3.5	1.1	−69
Other advanced economies	2.2	5.0	5.3	1.6	−70
European Union	3.0	2.7	3.4	1.7	−50
Euro area	2.9	2.6	3.4	1.5	−56
Newly industrialized Asian economies	−2.4	8.0	8.5	0.8	−91
Developing countries	3.5	3.9	5.7	4.0	−30
Africa	3.4	2.6	3.0	3.7	23
Developing Asia	4.0	6.1	6.7	5.6	−16
Middle East and Turkey	3.9	1.0	5.8	2.1	−64
Western hemisphere	2.3	0.2	4.0	0.7	−83
Countries in transition	−0.8	3.6	6.6	5.0	−24

Source: IMF, The World Economic Outlook Database, April 2002.

Table 9.6. From boom to bust: What a difference one year (and a small correction in the U.S. current account deficit) can make

Country ranked by GDP:	Exports (value) (% change) 2000	Exports (value) (% change) 2001	GDP (% change) 2000	GDP (% change) 2001	Change in growth rate 2001 vs 2000
Largest 16:					
1 United States	11.4	−6.5	4.1	1.2	−71
2 Japan	14.3	−15.6	2.2	−0.4	n.a.
3 Germany	1.5	3.2	3.0	0.6	−80
4 United Kingdom	4.7	−4.0	3.0	2.2	−27
5 France	C.2	−1.7	3.6	2.0	−44
6 China	27.7	6.8	8.0	7.3	−9
7 Italy	C.9	1.5	2.9	1.8	−38
8 Canada	1E.0	−5.2	4.4	1.5	−66
9 Mexico	22.0	−4.7	6.6	−0.3	n.a.
10 Spain	1C.4	−3.8	4.1	2.8	−32
11 Brazil	14.7	5.7	4.4	1.5	−66
12 India	1E.8	3.5	5.4	4.3	−20
13 Korea	1E.9	−12.5	9.3	3.0	−68
14 Netherlands	E.7	−1.4	3.5	1.1	−69
15 Australia	1E.9	−0.8	3.2	2.4	−25
16 Russia	3E.4	−2.2	9.0	5.0	−44
Others:					
17 Taiwan Prov. of China	22.1	−17.1	5.9	−1.9	n.a.
26 China, P.R.: Hong Kong	1E.2	−5.9	10.5	0.1	−99
29 Indonesia	27.7	−8.7	4.8	3.3	−31
33 Thailand	1E.2	−7.0	4.6	1.8	−61
40 Singapore	2C.2	−11.7	10.3	−2.1	n.a.
41 Malaysia	1E.2	−9.8	8.3	0.4	−95
43 Philippines	8.8	−15.6	4.0	3.4	−15

Sources: Merchandise exports: World Trade Organization; real GDP, local currency: IMF, The World Economic Outlook Database, April 2002.

All 23 countries in this survey experienced substantially lower economic growth rates in 2001 (see Table 9.6). Japan, Mexico, Taiwan, and Singapore saw their economic output contract relative to 2000. Growth rates slowed by more than 50% in nine other countries. China fared best with only a 9% reduction in growth.

Global commodity prices were also hit by the slowdown in U.S. demand. Prices fell for almost two-thirds of the commodities shown in Table 9.7, with more than one-third suffering double-digit declines. The prices of fats and oils, timber, fertilizers, and metals and minerals were all under considerable pressure. Only the price of grains and other food increased.

Table 9.7 Commodity price data, 2000 and 2001

| | | Annual averages | | |
	Units	2000	2001	% change
Energy				
Coal, Australia	$/mt	26.25	32.31	23.1
Crude oil, Brent	$/bbl	28.27	24.42	−13.6
Non-energy commodities				
Agriculture				
Beverages				
Cocoa	cents/kg	90.6	106.9	18.0
Coffee, arabica	cents/kg	192	137.3	−28.5
Tea, average 3 auctions	cents/kg	187.6	159.8	−14.8
Food				
Fats and oils				
Coconut oil	$/mt	450.3	318.1	−29.4
Copra	$/mt	304.8	202.1	−33.7
Groundnut oil	$/mt	713.7	680.3	−4.7
Palm oil	$/mt	310.3	285.7	−7.9
Soybean meal	$/mt	189.2	181	−4.3
Soybeans	$/mt	211.8	195.8	−7.6
Grains				
Maize	$/mt	88.5	89.6	1.2
Rice, Thai, 5	$/mt	202.4	172.8	−14.6
Sorghum	$/mt	88	95.2	8.2
Wheat, Canada	$/mt	147.1	151.5	3.0
Other food				
Bananas, EU	$/mt	712.4	777.2	9.1
Beef	cents/kg	193.2	212.9	10.2
Fishmeal	$/mt	413	486.7	17.8
Lamb	cents/kg	261.9	291.2	11.2

Table 9.7 (*cont'd*)

		Annual averages		
	Units	2000	2001	% change
Oranges	$/mt	363.2	595.5	64.0
Shrimp	cents/kg	1513	1517	0.3
Sugar, world	cents/kg	18.04	19.04	5.5
Raw materials				
Timber				
Logs, Malaysia	$/cum	190	159.1	−16.3
Plywood	cents/sheet	448.2	409.8	−8.6
Woodpulp	$/mt	664.3	517.3	−22.1
Other raw materials				
Cotton, "A Index"	cents/kg	130.2	105.8	−18.7
Jute	$/mt	277.4	329.4	18.7
Rubber, Malaysia	cents/kg	69.1	60	−13.2
Sisal	$/mt	631.8	699.2	10.7
Wool	cents/kg	437	418.7	−4.2
Fertilizers				
DAP	$/mt	152.2	147.7	−3.0
Phosphate rock	$/mt	43.8	41.8	−4.6
Urea, Black Sea	$/mt	112.1	105.3	−6.1
Metals and minerals				
Aluminum	$/mt	1549	1444	−6.8
Copper	$/mt	1813	1578	−13.0
Gold	$/toz	279	271	−2.9
Iron ore	cents/dmtu	28.79	30.03	4.3
Lead	cents/kg	45.4	47.6	4.8
Nickel	$/mt	8638	5945	−31.2
Silver	$/toz	499.9	438.6	−12.3
Steel products index	1990 = 100	76.4	66.8	−12.6
Tin	cents/kg	543.6	448.4	−17.5
Zinc	cents/kg	112.8	88.6	−21.5

Source: World Bank.

The stock markets were a disaster zone. The selling began in half of the largest stock markets in 2000. In 2001, share prices fell sharply in 10 out of the 14 markets shown in Table 9.8. And the selling continued on into 2002. As at the beginning of August 2002, 12 out of the 14 markets were experiencing losses for the year. Over the 32-month period from January 2000 to August 2002, Japan's stock market fell by half, those of Germany, France, Brazil, India, and the Netherlands fell by more than 40%, and those of the U.S., the U.K., and Spain dropped by one-third. Trillions of dollars of wealth evaporated.

Falling share prices, lower corporate profitability, and rising unemployment took their toll on government revenues. Fiscal heath deteriorated in most countries in 2001, with much worse projected for 2002 (see Table 9.9).

A couple of excerpts from the mid-year 2002 budget review of the United States' Office of Management and Budget shed a great deal of light on the new post-bubble fiscal realities confronting policymakers around the world.

> After surging for more than seven years, revenue growth slowed dramatically in 2001, even before accounting for the 2001 tax relief act, and then fell in 2002. The reversal was driven predominantly by

Table 9.8 Stock markets' slide, 2000–02

		% change			% change
		2000	2001	2002 to Aug.	Jan. 00 to Aug. 02
United States	S&P 500	−2	−17	−18	−33
Japan	N225	−29	−28	−2	−50
Germany	XETRA	−1	−25	−28	−46
UK	FTSE 100 Index	1	−18	−16	−31
France	CAC 40	6	−26	−24	−40
China	SSE Composite	35	−28	10	7
Italy	n.a.				
Canada	n.a.				
Mexico	IPC	−1	7	−11	−6
Spain	Madrid Gen Index	−1	−17	−18	−33
Brazil	Bovespa	8	−28	−25	−42
India	BSESN	−17	−23	−7	−41
Korea	KOSPI	−35	21	−4	−24
Netherlands	AEX Index	5	−22	−26	−40
Australia	All Ordinaries	6	3	−9	0
Russia	Moscow Times Index	8	87	26	153

Source: Reuters.

Table 9.9 Increasing fiscal strains: General government balance, 1998–2002F (% of GDP)

	1998	1999	2000	2001	2002F
Advanced economies	−1.4	−1.0	0.0	−1.2	−2.0
United States	−0.1	0.6	1.5	0.1	−1.4
Euro area	−2.2	−1.3	0.2	−1.4	−1.6
Newly industrialized Asian economies	−0.6	−0.7	0.2	0.5	−0.2

Source: IMF, The World Economic Outlook Database, April 2002.

the recession and the stock market's decline. Moreover, the drop in receipts has been notably larger than the decline in economic growth. The difference between receipts growth and GDP growth in 2002, even after adjustments for the 2001 tax relief and the 2002 stimulus act, is projected to reach eight percentage points. This is a much larger divergence than during the 1990–91 recession, even when adjusted for tax legislation at that time. The current receipts situation is similar to those experienced during the far more severe recessions of the 1970s and early 1980s. ... Receipts in 2002 are now estimated to decline outright by [US]$124 billion, or six percent, from 2001 levels. The last time revenues fell to that extent was in 1955.[3]

Politicians who had foolishly extrapolated the bubble revenues of the late 1990s into the distant future are now waking up to the unpleasant impact that the down leg of the business cycle has on government budgets. Tax receipts fall and expenditures on social safety nets and stimulus programs rise during recessions. These difficulties are very frequently compounded by the additional cost of bailing out the depositors of failed banks. Japan is now familiar with all these problems. The ratio of that country's government debt to GDP has risen to 140% and is projected to rise to 200% by 2010, according to Standard & Poor's.[4]

WHEN?

When the U.S. property bubble pops. In 2002, the global economy is being supported by an American shopping spree that is being financed by a bubble in the U.S. property market. Mortgage rates have fallen to record lows, creating two windfalls for the American consumer. The first is a straightforward wealth effect. Record low mortgage rates – combined with the ample financing being extended by Freddie Mac and Fannie Mae – are driving up property prices. In addition to that, falling interest rates and the rapid increase in home prices has sparked off a refinancing extravaganza that is putting more money in the hands of consumers even as every other aspect of the U.S. economy worsens. The housing bubble is the main explanation for the resilience of the American consumer. Sadly, bubbles pop.

In August 2002, the 30-year fixed-rate mortgage fell to a record low of 6.13%[5] (see Figure 9.5). Rarely has global prosperity relied so heavily on one number.

The three largest government-sponsored enterprises have made sure there was plenty of fuel to fire the property boom. The total assets of Fannie Mae, Freddie Mac, and the Federal Home Loan Bank (FHLB) system

Figure 9.5   United States: Thirty-year conventional mortgage rates, 1971–2002

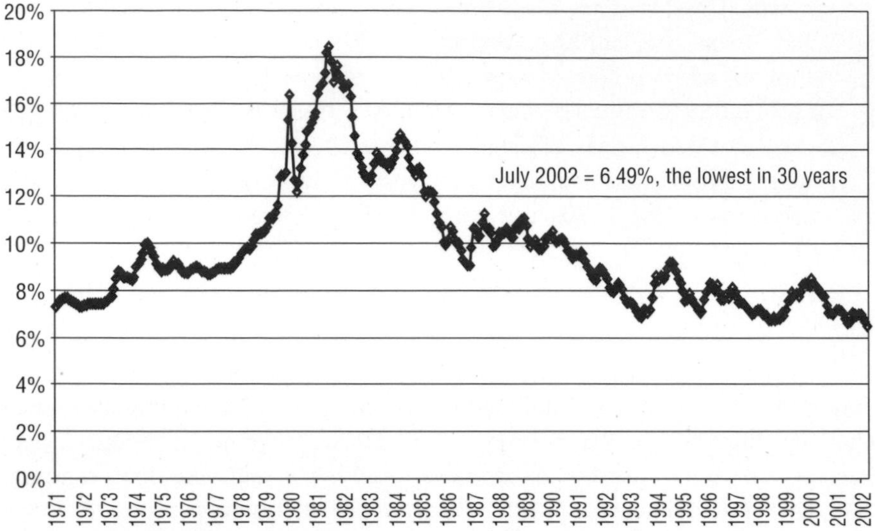

July 2002 = 6.49%, the lowest in 30 years

Source: Federal Home Loan Mortgage Corporation.

ballooned US$248 billion, or 13%, during the four quarters ended June 2002; increased by US$550 billion, or 33%, between June 2000 and June 2002; and increased by US$1.16 trillion, or 133%, between June 1998 and June 2002.[6] The average single-family home price rose by 10.4% in June 2002 compared with one year earlier and rose an astounding 24% compared with the price level in 1999 (see Table 9.10). There should be little doubt as to why U.S. property prices have skyrocketed.

Mortgage origination boomed against this background of plentiful credit availability, rising to more than US$2 trillion in 2001, up from US$639 billion in 1995. By August 2002, refinancing activity represented 71% of total mortgage loan applications.[7] Essentially, what this means is that Americans are sucking out the increased equity value from their homes – and spending it – just as quickly as the value of their homes increases. Moreover, many lenders are now providing mortgages based on a loan-to-value ratio of as high as 120% of the home's worth. Sub-prime lenders have been particularly aggressive and instrumental in fanning the property mania.

How much longer this bubble in the U.S. property market can continue to expand depends on two things: how much longer mortgage rates continue to fall; and how much longer Americans can continue to finance home prices that are rising at a considerably faster rate than the increase in their wages and personal income.

Table 9.10 The property bubble: Sales price of existing single-family homes in the United States, 1999–2002 (US$)

Year	United States	Northeast	Midwest	South	West
			Average (Mean)		
1999	168,300	177,300	140,000	150,000	224,800
2000	176,200	182,200	145,500	161,000	231,300
2001	185,300	190,500	152,200	171,100	243,500
			Not Seasonally Adjusted		
2001 June	191,100	197,100	153,300	182,200	246,700
Jul	190,600	201,200	161,000	175,700	242,500
Aug	193,500	202,100	158,000	179,900	251,400
Sept	185,200	182,600	151,900	171,100	248,300
Oct	181,800	186,200	145,600	167,700	244,200
Nov	182,900	187,700	144,700	173,400	240,400
Dec	192,200	197,900	158,900	182,600	243,700
2002 Jan	190,600	206,000	148,900	179,100	249,000
Feb	189,600	199,500	155,100	173,600	249,800
Mar	194,600	199,400	156,100	179,500	260,800
Apr	196,500	203,100	160,600	178,500	263,300
May (revised)	199,600	207,600	153,700	186,300	270,100
June (preliminary)	211,000	215,100	174,400	196,000	275,400
June 2002 vs. June 2001	10.4%	9.1%	13.8%	7.6%	11.6%
June 2002 vs. 1999	25.4%	21.3%	24.6%	30.7%	22.5%

Source: National Association of Realtors.

Mortgage rates could continue to decline from their current record lows, considering that the supply of credit is considerably greater than the demand for credit in a post-bubble economy characterized by excess capacity and few profitable investment opportunities. The blow-out in the fiscal government deficit (a US$147 billion deficit during the first 10 months of fiscal 2002, compared with a surplus of US$172 billion during the same period in the prior year) could check the decline in interest rates through the old-fashioned "crowding-out effect," as very large amounts of Treasury bonds are offered on the capital markets. However, if the experience in Japan and other post-bubble countries is anything to go by, the growing borrowing needs of the government will not be sufficient to offset the declining borrowing requirements of the private sector.

Instead of rising interest rates, affordability may be the pin that finally pricks the U.S. property bubble. The National Association of Realtors' Housing Affordability Index (HAI) is useful in illustrating the limits of affordability (see Table 9.11).

The HAI is shown in the last column. The higher the number is, the more affordable houses are. An explanation of the methodology may be helpful.

Table 9.11 National Association of Realtors' Housing Affordability Index

Year	Median priced existing single family home (US$)	Mortgage rate (%)	Monthly P & I payment (US$)	Payment as % of income	Median family income (US$)	Qualifying income (US$)	Affordability index composite
1999	133,300	7.33	733	18	48,950	35,184	139.1
2000	139,000	8.03	818	19.3	50,890	39,264	129.6
2001	147,800	7.03	789	18.2	51,995	37,872	137.3
2001 June	152,200	7.18	825	19.2	51,442	39,600	129.9
July	151,700	7.19	823	19.2	51,534	39,504	130.5
Aug	153,700	7.06	823	19.1	51,627	39,504	130.7
Sept	147,400	6.93	779	18.1	51,719	37,392	138.3
Oct	145,400	6.73	753	17.4	51,811	36,144	143.3
Nov	147,100	6.62	753	17.4	51,903	36,144	143.6
Dec	153,100	6.77	796	18.4	51,995	38,208	136.1
Jan	150,300	6.89	791	18.2	52,082	37,968	137.2
2002 Feb	149,400	6.85	783	18.0	52,168	37,584	138.8
Mar	153,200	6.84	802	18.4	52,255	38,496	135.7
Apr	154,500	6.95	818	18.8	52,342	39,264	133.3
May (revised)	155,000	6.82	810	18.5	52,429	38,880	134.8
Jun (preliminary)	163,500	6.70	844	19.3	52,516	40,512	129.6 This Month
Northeast	167,900	6.44	844	17.9	56,467	40,512	139.4
Midwest	137,100	6.36	683	14.5	56,472	32,784	172.3
South	155,100	5.90	736	18.3	48,230	35,328	136.5
West	224,500	5.97	1,073	24.6	52,343	51,504	101.6

Source: National Association of Realtors.

To interpret the indices, a value of 100 means that a family with the median income has exactly enough income to qualify for a mortgage on a median-priced home. An index above 100 signifies that a family earning the median income has more than enough income to qualify for a mortgage loan on a median-priced home, assuming a 20% down payment. For example, a composite HAI of 120.0 means a family earning the median family income has 120% of the income necessary to qualify for a conventional loan covering 80% of a median-priced existing single-family home.[8]

From Table 9.11 it can be seen that as of June 2002, the HAI has been falling and is as low as at any point during the last three-and-a-half years, although, at 129.6, the index indicates that housing is still affordable under the terms described in the index methodology. At the same time, it can also be seen that the median family income has risen by only 7.3% since 1999, whereas the median-priced existing single-family home has jumped by 22.6% over the same period. Of course, it has been the decline in mortgage rates to 6.7% in June 2002 that has prevented the affordability index from falling further.

There is one factor that should not be overlooked here that undermines the reliability of this index as a true reflection of affordability. The affordability index takes for granted the 20% down-payment that is a critical part of its calculations. A 20% down-payment on a US$133,300 (1999) home is US$26,660, whereas a 20% down-payment on a US$163,500 home (June 2002) is US$32,700, 23% more. Not every American family with a median family income of US$52,516 has an extra US$32,700 lying around to use as a down-payment on a new home, particularly following the greatest stock market crash since 1929.

Consider the property market in "the West." There, the median home price is US$224,500. Twenty percent of that amount is US$44,900, 86% of the median family income. In a world of way-out-of-the-money stock options, property out west appears rather out of line with purchasing power – regardless of its 101.6 reading on the HAI.

With home prices rising three times faster than family income at the national level, affordability is diminishing much more than the HAI would suggest. Aggressive mortgage lending may continue to drive property prices higher for some time yet. However, it becomes increasingly difficult to sustain an asset price bubble over time. Property prices cannot continue rising faster than income for much longer. And, needless to say, if interest rates begin to rise for whatever reason, the game is up. Property prices will fall, the refinancing will stop, and consumption will fall.

Capital gains on home sales and home equity extraction through refinancing have provided tremendous support to consumption. In January 2002, Fed Chairman Greenspan made the following remarks on the subject:

> Moreover, attractive mortgage rates have bolstered both the sales of existing homes and the realized capital gains that those sales engender. They have also spurred refinancing of existing homes and the associated liquification of increases in house values. These gains have been important to the ongoing extraction of home equity for consumption and home modernization. ... Cash-outs (from refinancing) rose from an estimated annual rate of about [US]$20 billion in early 2000 to a rate of roughly [US]$75 billion in the third quarter of last year (2001).[9]

Refinancing slowed in late 2001 when interest rates temporarily rose, but reaccelerated in mid-2002. According to the Mortgage Bankers Association, its Refinance Index in mid-August 2002 was "just short of the record of ... the week ended November 9, 2001." They also reported that "Refinancing activity represented 70.8% of total (mortgage loan) applications" in mid-August 2002.

The booming U.S. property market and the opportunity it creates for "home equity extraction" is the most important prop supporting U.S. consumption. It is not certain when the property boom will cease, but it is certain that it *will* cease. The longer it goes on, the more the economy will suffer when it does end. In all probability, home prices will fall, and delinquency rates and defaults on mortgages will rise. When the wealth effect from the property bubble turns negative rather than positive, the Great American Shopping Spree will be over and the second phase of the New paradigm recession will begin.

Personal consumption expenditure amounted to nearly US$7 trillion in 2001. As of June 2002, this, the largest component of U.S. GDP, was still growing at an annualized rate of more than 3%, representing a growth in personal consumption of approximately US$210 billion when annualized (see Figure 9.6). It will be a severe shock to the global economy when, rather than continuing to expand, this figure begins to contract as it did in 1974, 1980, and 1991 – not to mention earlier and much more painful episodes in U.S. economic history.

CONCLUSION

As the tables in this chapter have illustrated, the US$78 billion fall in U.S. imports in 2001 gave a painful jolt to the global economy. That shock

Figure 9.6　United States: Consumption expenditure, 1991–2002
(% change year-on-year)

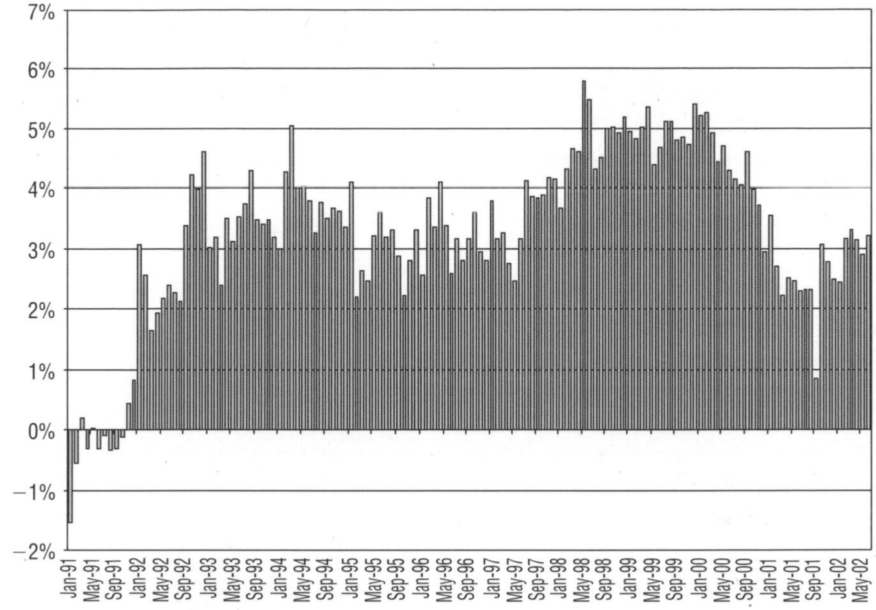

Source: Federal Reserve Economic Data: St. Louis Fed.

occurred despite the fact that the U.S. economy still grew at a rate of 0.3% during the year and despite the subsidy of nearly US$400 billion that the U.S. current account deficit provided to the rest of the world. Furthermore, the United States' imports in 2001 were still very high compared with earlier years. U.S. imports in 2001 were 11% higher than in 1999 and 53% higher than the level recorded in 1995. Meanwhile, the U.S. current account deficit was 270% higher in 2001 than in 1995.

The next few years seem certain to produce a much harsher economic environment than that experienced during 2001. When the consumer credit bubble in the United States pops, the U.S. economy is going to record a meaningful contraction in real economic output – very possibly over a multi-year period. Falling consumption expenditure will drag down investment expenditure with it. The overall shrinkage in aggregate demand will cause a much greater reduction in imports into the United States than during 2001 when the American economy was still expanding.

Also, compare the US$78 billion reduction in U.S. imports in 2001 with the United States' unsustainable US$400 billion to US$500 billion annual current account deficit. Harbor no illusions: that deficit is going to collapse. Equilibrium on the balance of payments will be restored. Most probably, that will occur as the result of a collapse in the value of the dollar. It is certain that equilibrium will not be restored by a sudden rush by the rest of the world to buy American goods – not at current exchange rates, in any case. They can't afford them.

If the U.S. current account deficit begins to correct during the impending second phase of the recession, U.S. imports could fall by US$300 billion to US$400 billion in 2003 relative to 2002 … and fall again in 2004 and 2005. In light of the economic problems that were caused by the US$78 billion decline in U.S. imports in 2001, imagine how much worse the global economy would fare under those conditions.

REFERENCES

1   E. J. Hobsbawm, *Industry and Empire* (London: Weidenfeld & Nicolson, 1968).
2   WTO, *Annual Report 2002*, Chapter II, World Trade Developments.
3   Office of Management and Budget, Executive Office of the President, Mid-Session Review, Budget of the United States Government Fiscal Year 2003, released July 2002.
4   Takahira Ogawa, "One Step Forward, Two Steps Back: Koizumi's Reform Setbacks," Standard & Poor's, August 18, 2002.
5   Mortgage Bankers Association of America, Weekly Application Survey, August 21, 2002.
6   Doug Noland, *Credit Bubble Bulletin*, August 23, 2000, PrudentBear.com.
7   Mortgage Bankers Association of America, August 21, 2002.
8   National Association of Realtors, Methodology for the Housing Affordability Index, 2002.
9   Remarks by Chairman Alan Greenspan at the Bay Area Council Conference, San Francisco, California, January 11, 2002.

Chapter 10

The End of the Era
of Export-led Growth

*I think the strong dollar policy has served us exceedingly well
over the past several years and still does.*

— Robert Rubin, 1998[1]

A QUESTION OF TIMING

Every economist and every securities analyst knows better than to say
"when" and "by how much" in the same sentence. Many a clever forecast
has been confounded by the problem of timing. It is one thing to see the
future. It is an entirely different matter to know when that future will occur.
Economic events often take much longer to unfold than economists
anticipate. For example, Thailand's economy was recognizable as a bubble
by 1993. That bubble didn't pop for another four years.

In order to forecast the outlook for the global economy now, it is
necessary to estimate the timing of two events. The first is the timing of the
collapse in consumer spending in the United States that will ring in the
second phase of the New Paradigm recession (NPR Phase II). That, in turn,
depends on when the U.S. property bubble bursts. As discussed in Chapter 9,
those events will probably occur in 2003 – or in 2004, at the latest. The
second event that must be timed is the correction of the U.S. current account
deficit. That painful adjustment could take place at the same time as the
NPR Phase II or subsequent to that event. The timing of that correction will
hinge on how long the U.S. dollar remains at its present, extraordinarily
overvalued level. The first section of this chapter speculates about the
lamentable fate of the dollar. The rest of the chapter will consider how
prepared the rest of the world is to face the double onslaught of a U.S.
recession and the correction of the U.S. current account deficit.

HOW MUCH MUST THE DOLLAR FALL?

The first time the U.S. current account deficit ran amok was in the mid-
1980s. Then, the deficit peaked at 3.4% of GDP in 1987, considerably less

than its level in 2000 and 2001, but very alarming nevertheless to those charged with maintaining economic stability at the time (see Figure 10.1).

The concerns over the ballooning U.S. current account deficits were such that in September 1985, the G-7 countries agreed upon the Plaza Accord which called for coordinated government intervention in the currency markets to pull down the overvalued dollar in order to help restore balanced trade. The Japanese yen and the German mark, the currencies of the United States' most important trading partners, reacted promptly and rose. Between its peak in February 1985 and the end of 1988, the dollar fell by 50% against both the mark and the yen (see Figure 10.2).

It took longer for the U.S. current account deficit to respond, however. That deficit continued to expand for another two years until 1987, when it topped out at 3.4% of U.S. GDP. Such a large imbalance in the current account of the world's largest economy spooked capital markets and was instrumental in the October 1987 crash on Wall Street that saw the Dow Jones Industrial Average fall 23% in one day.

Now, more than 15 years later, the United States, with a current account deficit that, on average, has exceeded 4% of GDP for three years in a row,

Figure 10.1 The U.S. current account deficit, 1980–2001 (as a % of U.S. GDP)

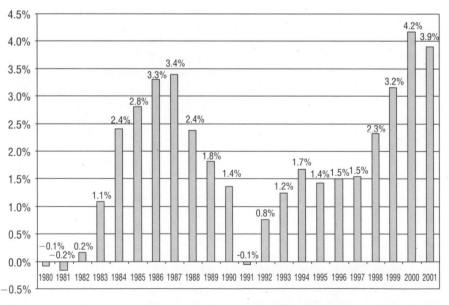

Sources: Current account: Federal Reserve Economic Data; St. Louis Fed; GDP: Bureau of Economic Analysis.

Figure 10.2   The last time the dollar fell by half: The U.S. dollar versus
the yen and the mark, 1971–2001

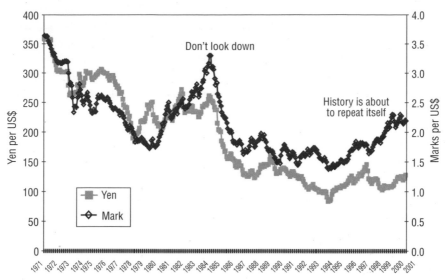

Source: Federal Reserve Economic Data, St Louis Fed.

has only tentatively begun to inch away from its famous "Strong Dollar
Policy." That policy could just as easily be called the United States' "Trade
Deficit Policy," since it has generated the largest trade imbalances in that
country's history and destabilized the global economy in the process.

There really can be no doubt that a new "accord" will soon be reached
that will drastically drive down the value of the dollar. What is not certain
is whether that accord will be reached by politicians and central bankers, or
imposed through a market panic and a run on the dollar. Current account
deficits, like economic bubbles, are inherently unsustainable. The collapse in
the value of the dollar is a matter of *when*, rather than *if*.

The dollar must fall – and not only against the yen and the euro, this
time. The pattern of global trade has changed. Now China has the largest
trade surplus with the United States, a surplus equivalent to 7% of China's
GDP. Then there are the Asian exporting nations and Mexico, all of which
are heavily dependent on their large trade surpluses with the United States.
Their currencies must rise very sharply as well in order for a restoration of
the international balance of payments to be achieved.

The key question, however, is: "How much must the dollar fall against
the currencies of all its major trading partners?" It is far from certain that a
50% plunge in the value of the dollar against the Chinese yuan would put

an end to China's giant trade surpluses against the United States, considering that such an adjustment would only push up the wages of Chinese industrial workers from around US$5 per day to around US$10 per day. With a workforce numbering in the hundreds of millions earning US$10 per day, China would still be wildly competitive against the United States as a manufacturer of almost any kind of industrial product.

The same is true for Indonesia, Vietnam, the Philippines, Thailand, Malaysia, and the United States' neighbor, Mexico. The dollar could fall by half against the currencies of all those countries and their trade surpluses with the United States might well continue expanding, given their ultra-low cost wage base. Japan, despite its high-cost wage base, still achieved a US$69 billion trade surplus with the United States in 2001 even though the dollar has fallen by two-thirds against the yen over the last 30 years. Clearly, given the magnitude of the Japanese surplus, that adjustment process has not yet gone far enough.

A collapse in the value of the dollar against the currencies of all its major trading partners is unavoidable. However, given the huge differential between wage rates in the United States and in the newly industrializing countries, a realignment of exchange rates alone may not be sufficient to end the United State's trade deficits. Additional quotas, accepted voluntarily or otherwise, and the imposition of other kinds of trade barriers will probably be put in place even after the dollar's fall.

The rise of the yen in the second half of the 1980s eventually put an end to the rise of Japan. Unfortunately, the collapse of the United States' trade deficit policy soon will have the same effect on a number of other countries. The Era of Export-led Growth is coming to a close. The transition to economic growth founded on rising domestic demand is bound to be a difficult one.

▶ AT THE DAWN OF A DIFFICULT NEW AGE

The global economic slowdown in 2001 was a foretaste of the much worse slump to come. The severity and duration of the global economic downturn will depend on when the correction in the U.S. current account deficit takes place. If the second phase of the U.S. recession and the correction in the U.S. current account deficit occur at the same time, the shock to the global economy will be very acute. If the current account deficit corrects after the U.S. recession plays itself out, then it will cause the global slump to be a very protracted one.

In either case, the global recession will resemble the 2001 slowdown. The difference will be in the magnitude of the impact. The coming global recession will hit world trade, commodity prices, stock markets, and government finances just as the 2001 slowdown did. However, it will hit them much harder.

Just as growth rates slowed almost everywhere in 2001, no country will escape the fallout of the impending global slump. Nevertheless, it is still useful to consider how countries or regions will be affected individually (see Table 10.1).

Table 10.1 The losers (ranked by their trade surplus with the United States, 2001)

	Trade surplus with the U.S. (US$ bn)	Exports to the U.S. (US$ bn)	2001 GDP (US$ bn)	As % of GDP	
				Trade balance with the U.S.	Exports to the U.S.
China	83	102	1,159	7.2	8.8
Japan	69	127	4,149	1.7	3.0
Asian exporters	54	152	1,374	4.4	13.0
Euro zone	45	169	6,631	0.7	2.6
Mexico	30	131	618	4.9	21.3

Sources: Trade: U.S. Census Bureau, *U.S. Trade by Country;* GDP: IMF, The World Economic Outlook Database, April 2002.

China

China has the largest trade surplus with the United States. In 2001, China's exports to the U.S. continued to increase despite the overall fall in U.S. imports. That year, China's exports to the U.S. rose by US$2.3 billion to US$102.3 billion. Compare those figures with the US$71.2 billion that China exported to the U.S. in 1998.

China's manufacturers have a tremendous advantage over those in the United States because of China's extraordinarily low wage rates and because many Chinese manufacturers have access to credit that they never repay. So long as there is no adjustment in the exchange rate between the dollar and the yuan, China's exports will continue to account for a growing percentage of the goods sold in the United States (see Figure 10.3).

Nevertheless, there is reason to believe that China's exports to the United States will nevertheless fall sharply in absolute terms during the second phase of the U.S. recession. The recession in 2001 was driven by a collapse in investment, especially in areas related to technology. Although China is making rapid progress in producing higher-value goods, its specialty is still in manufacturing cheap consumer goods. Consequently, China's exports did not suffer during the 2001 slump in high-tech imports

Figure 10.3   China: Exports to the United States, 1990–2002

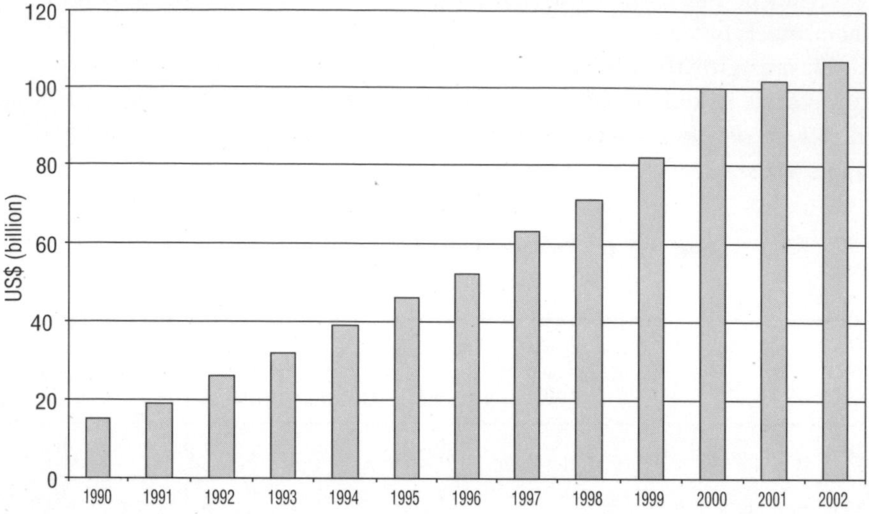

Source: U.S. Census Bureau.

into the United States. It is likely to fare much worse in the second phase of the recession when household consumption falls in the United States. Then U.S. demand for China's consumer goods will fall and China's exports to the United States will decline.

China's economic growth is driven by exports and bank loans. It may be that China compensates for the fall in its exports in the years ahead by having its banks accelerate their lending. Such a strategy could temporarily soften the blow of falling exports, but it must be seen as a warped kind of fiscal stimulus that China cannot afford. Loan growth in China has increased at a double-digit rate every year since the early 1980s. Not surprisingly, that explosion of credit resulted in over-investment and excess capacity across almost every industry on a grand scale. Deflation has arisen directly out of China's credit policy. Now, according to many estimates, the non-performing loans in China's banks have risen to as much as 50% of all loans. That amounts to more than US$500 billion in bad debt, a figure approaching 50% of China's GDP. China's tax collection system is far less effective than that of more developed nations. It brings in a far smaller percentage of GDP in taxes than most tax collectors in OECD countries. China will have a very hard time bailing out the depositors of its already technically insolvent banks when the time comes. The more it relies on credit growth to stimulate economic growth, the greater will be the price that it will one day have to pay for its dangerous experiment in bank-led Keynesian stimulus.

It is quite certain that if a country could manufacture economic prosperity for its people simply by forcing its banks to increase lending by 20% per annum, it would have been discovered centuries ago and we would all be living in an age of endless luxury today. Sadly, credit bubbles always have and always will end in disaster. In China's case, the repercussions of the eventual meltdown in its banking system could extend well beyond the economic realm.

Japan

Japan has been singing the post-bubble blues for more than a decade. Standard & Poor's estimates that the non-performing loans in Japan's banks amount to a figure equivalent to 10% of Japan's GDP. Moreover, in early 2002, that rating agency wrote that Japanese banks had never been in a worse condition.[2] The government's finances are in terrible shape (see Figure 10.4). The ratio of government debt to GDP is reported to be 140% currently, and it is forecast to rise to 200% by 2010.[3] These are levels well beyond anything experienced in any industrial nation since World War II.

The 2001 U.S. recession threw Japan into its third recession in 10 years – despite fiscal deficits exceeding 7% of GDP. That year, Japan's exports to the United States fell by 14% to US$126 billion from US$146

Figure 10.4   Japan: General government gross financial liabilities, 1985–2002 (est.)

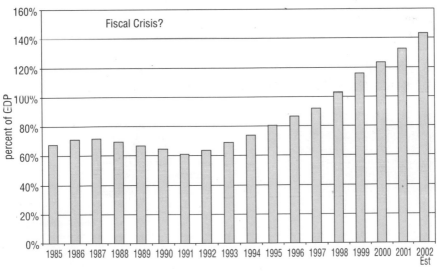

Source: OECD.

billion the year before. There can be little doubt that the second part of America's double-dip recession will be tough on Japan. The country's asset prices are still deflating from the bubble of the 1980s. At 5.3%, unemployment is near all-time highs.[4] The banks are in trouble. The government's finances are in trouble. Japan has a lot of great companies, such as Sony, but if global aggregate demand is falling, corporate profits will suffer regardless of whether Japan Inc. manufactures in Osaka, Kentucky, or Shanghai. Another drop in U.S. imports will exacerbate all of Japan's problems, and there are no remedies in sight.

During the 1990s, the Bank of Japan cut interest rates aggressively in an attempt to revive the economy, but without success (see Figure 10.5). The central bank cut its discount rate to virtually 0% in March of 2001 and still the economy continued to deteriorate and prices continued to fall.

Given Japan's overstretched and rapidly deteriorating fiscal position and the recognition by the Japanese central bank that monetary policy cannot help in this situation (see Chapter 11), the policy options available to help Japan mitigate the damage from the second phase of the U.S. recession appear rather constrained, to say the least. Government spending minimized the effect that the country's economic weakness had on the public during the 1990s. Government spending and guarantees also prevented a systemic banking crisis from destroying the public's savings. If concerns set in

Figure 10.5   Japan: Central bank discount rate, 1970–2002

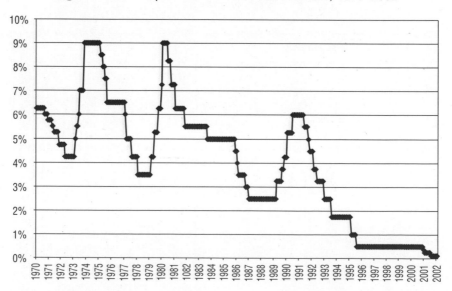

Source: Bank of Japan.

regarding the government's ability to repay its growing mountain of debt, the Japanese public may not be as lucky during this decade.

The Asian Exporters

The countries grouped together in this section, under the title of the "Asian exporters," are different in very many ways. Some are rich and well managed, some are impoverished and poorly managed, while still others are somewhere in between. Despite their differences, they all have two things in common: they are all very economically dependent on exporting to the United States; and they are all going to suffer when U.S. imports fall during the second phase of the New Paradigm recession and when the U.S. current account deficit corrects. Many of these countries are already in quite serious difficulty as a result of having been blown into bubble economies by balance of payments surpluses that were linked to the United States' deficits.

Table 10.2 ranks the eight Asian exporters by the size of their trade balance with the United States relative to their economic output. In 2001, on average (unweighted), their exports to the U.S. amounted to 13% of their GDP, while their trade surplus amounted to 4.4% of GDP. Malaysia appears most reliant on the U.S. market given that its exports to the United States are the equivalent of 25% of its GDP. In reality, those figures probably overstate the true gains Malaysia receives through its trade with the United States, because a large portion of its U.S. exports are shipped directly from U.S.-owned manufacturing facilities there – particularly computer chip plants. Those U.S. factories provide jobs for Malaysians, but not the full gains that would be derived had all Malaysia's exports originated from

Table 10.2 The Asian exporters: The importance of trade with the United States in 2001

(+ = Surplus, − = Deficit) (US$ bn)				As % of GDP	
	Export	Trade balance	GDP	Exports	Trade balance
Malaysia	22.3	13.0	88	25.3	14.8
Thailand	14.7	8.7	115	12.8	7.6
Taiwan	33.4	15.3	282	11.8	5.4
Philippines	11.3	3.7	71	15.9	5.2
Indonesia	10.1	7.6	146	6.9	5.2
Korea	35.2	13.0	422	8.3	3.1
Hong Kong	9.6	−4.4	162	5.9	−2.7
Singapore	15.0	−2.7	88	17.0	−3.1

Sources: Trade balance: U.S. Census Bureau, *U.S. Trade by Country*; GDP: IMF, The World Economic Outlook Database, April 2002.

plants fully owned by Malaysians. The same is true, but to a lesser extent, for most of the other Asian exporters and even more so for Mexico.

That many of the products being exported to the United States from Asia are made in American-owned factories should not obscure the staggering overall importance of U.S. demand for Asian prosperity. Every country in this group has aggressively pursued a strategy of export-led growth for several decades. It was a strategy that paid handsome dividends until most of these economies were blown into bubbles during the 1990s as a result of excess credit creation arising out of their balance of payments surpluses. The Asian Miracle was transformed into the Asia Crisis practically overnight following the collapse of the unofficial baht/dollar peg on July 2, 1997 (see Table 10.3).

Table 10.3 Economic growth among the Asian exporters:
Two bad years out of four, 1998–2001

Real GDP growth (local currency)				
	1998	1999	2000	2001
Hong Kong	−5.3%	3.0%	10.5%	0.1%
Indonesia	−13.1%	0.8%	4.8%	3.3%
Korea	−6.7%	10.9%	9.3%	3.0%
Malaysia	−7.4%	6.1%	8.3%	0.4%
Philippines	−0.6%	3.4%	4.0%	3.4%
Singapore	−0.1%	6.9%	10.3%	−2.1%
Taiwan	4.6%	5.4%	5.9%	−1.9%
Thailand	−10.5%	4.4%	4.6%	1.8%

Source: IMF, The World Economic Outlook Database, April 2002.

Three humbled tigers – Indonesia, Korea, and Thailand – had to resort to borrowing enormous sums from the International Monetary Fund to avoid defaulting on their international obligations. Malaysia narrowly avoided becoming the fourth. For the most part, the Philippines escaped the bust by having missed the entire boom in the first place. Taiwan, which had been damaged by an asset price bubble all its own at the end of the 1980s, came through the Asia Crisis least affected. Singapore and Hong Kong held up reasonably well, thanks in large part to the strong regulatory framework that governs their banks.

Every one of the Asian exporters except Hong Kong responded to the crisis by allowing (or, in several cases, submitting to) a large depreciation of their currency. Hong Kong defended its peg, but paid a price as domestic prices adjusted down, instead of the Hong Kong dollar.

With highly competitive currencies and against the backdrop of the wildly overheating U.S. economy, the economic growth rates of most of the Asian exporting countries bounced back strongly in 1999 and 2000. Despite strong economic growth rates, many of these countries were far from fully restored to robust health, however. Indonesia, Korea, Thailand, and Malaysia all experienced a systemic banking crisis in 1997 that is still not fully resolved. The fiscal cost of bailing out the savings of the public was high. The latter three countries were rewarded for their fiscal prudence and low government debt levels in the years before the crisis by being able to keep their banking system functioning, albeit with considerable difficulty. Indonesia was not so lucky. The Philippines could be said to have a slow-burning banking crisis that preceded the crisis and still lingers on today. And, for that matter, the banks in Taiwan are not without their problems. Only the banks in Hong Kong and Singapore entered the new millennium on a fully sound footing.

Interest rates declined sharply, but bank lending to the private sector fell almost everywhere across the region, as would be expected following a crisis caused by excessive lending and over-investment. Only governments needed to borrow from banks in order to fund the rescue programs for their failed banks. Later, the commercial banks flung credit at consumers in an attempt to grow loans and remain profitable. Greater access to credit inspired Asian consumers to spend and gave a boost to regional economies. However, individual bankruptcy rates are now soaring around the region as a result. It remains to be seen how long the credit-induced consumption boom will last or what percentage of those consumer loans will be repaid.

The first phase of the New Paradigm recession caught the Asian exporters by surprise in 2001. Economic growth rates dropped off sharply, and Singapore and Taiwan, the two strongest performers during the Asia Crisis, both went into recession. Almost everywhere, tax revenues fell and unemployment rose.

Regrettably, the outlook for the Asian Eight is pretty terrible for the foreseeable future. The economies of all these countries have been shaped by a strategy of export-led growth. Now they must face a crisis involving not only a serious double-dip recession and a decline in demand in their major export market, but also, on top of that, a correction in the U.S. current account deficit that has served as an extraordinarily important economic subsidy to them for the last 20 years. These countries enjoyed a combined trade surplus against the United States of US$54 billion in 2001. The unwinding of the United States' balance of payments disequilibrium will put an end to the Era of Export-led Growth in Asia. There is a real risk that many of the economic and social gains that were made during those years will be lost in the years ahead, when only balanced trading with the United States will be possible. Furthermore, these countries will have to meet these challenges with weakened government finances, damaged financial systems, and a generally depressed post-bubble economic environment. It may be that the Asian Miracle is succeeded by an extended Asian Malaise.

Europe

Europe is best positioned to ride out the approaching global recession – as far as it is possible to generalize across the continent. Germany appears to have the most to lose from a decline in U.S. imports and a correction in the U.S. current account deficit. By and large, however, Europe is much less reliant on exporting to the United States than either Japan or China. For example, China's trade surplus vis-à-vis the United States in 2001 was US$83 billion. Japan's was US$69 billion. By contrast, the combined surplus that the seven European countries listed in Table 10.4 recorded against the United States was only US$48 billion, with Germany accounting for US$29 billion of that amount.

Table 10.4 Europe's trade exposure to the United States, 2001

| | Exports to U.S. | | Trade balance with U.S. | |
	(US$ bn)	(% of GDP)	(US$ bn)	(% of GDP)
Germany	59.1	3.2	29.1	1.6
United Kingdom	41.1	2.9	0.7	0.0
France	30.4	2.3	10.5	0.8
Italy	23.8	2.2	13.9	1.3
Netherlands	9.5	2.5	−10.0	0.1
Russia	6.3	2.0	3.5	−2.6
Spain	5.2	0.9	0.6	1.1
Total	175.4		48.3	

Sources: Trade: U.S. Census Bureau, *U.S. Trade by Country*; GDP: IMF, The World Economic Outlook Database, April 2002.

Similarly, Europe's fiscal position is relatively stronger than that of Japan or China. The Japanese government's debt-to-GDP ratio has risen throughout the 1990s and is now estimated to be approximately 140%. China's government debt has also been rising sharply in absolute terms; moreover, the publicly available data are drastically understated in that they do not reflect the government's liabilities related to China's banking-sector fiasco. Europe's record on fiscal sobriety could have been better, but the constraints imposed by the Maastricht Treaty in preparation for the adoption of a single currency generally kept Europe's fiscal spending in check (see Table 10.5).

Figure 10.6 illustrates that, overall, the Euro-area countries did succeed in reducing the ratio of government debt to GDP during the second half of the 1990s. Only moderate praise is warranted, though, considering that the late 1990s represented the peak of the business cycle when government

Table 10.5 Europe's fiscal position, 2001

	General government gross financial liabilities (% of GDP)	General government structural budget (% of GDP)
France	64.1	−1.7
Germany	60.3	−2.0
Italy	108.9	−0.8
Netherlands	53.2	0.3
Spain	69.1	0.1
United Kingdom	52.5	0.9
Euro-area	71.9	−1.1

Source: OECD.

Figure 10.6 Euro area: General government gross financial liabilities, 1985–2001 (as a % of GDP)

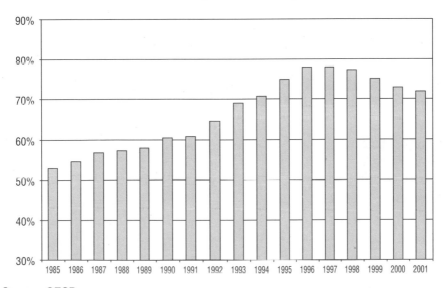

Source: OECD.

revenues were strong and, in many cases, boosted by extraordinary windfalls such as the sale of 3G licenses for absurd amounts of money. Moreover, an improvement of a few percentage points between 1997 and 2001 did little to repair the damage of the 25 percentage-point deterioration between 1985 and 1997.

Despite its relative strengths, Europe remains vulnerable to the next phase of the U.S. recession in a number of areas. Europe will be harmed by falling exports – directly as exports to the United States fall, as well as indirectly as demand for European exports from third countries declines due to the fall in their exports to the U.S.

Moreover, Euroland will suffer from the loss of tourist revenues. As the U.S. recession bites and the dollar falls against the euro, the number of American tourists vacationing in Europe will fall. There will also be fewer tourists arriving from other countries for similar reasons. Europe will also suffer very significant losses of capital as a result of the portfolio and direct investment made in the United States by European banks, insurance companies, and corporations at the peak of the New Paradigm bubble. The blow to European banks, insurance companies, and pension funds could be so great as to require costly government bailouts that would come at a high cost to fiscal stability. On the other hand, the negative wealth effect will take a far milder toll on household wealth in Europe than in the United States, since the equity cult had only begun to gain real momentum in Europe when, in 2000, "the Gods of the Market tumbled, and their smooth-tongued wizards withdrew."[5]

Europe's greatest point of vulnerability remains its persistently high levels of unemployment (see Table 10.6). Some improvement was made during the expansion phase of the business cycle in the late 1990s – but far from enough. The unemployment rate in Europe fell to its best level in 2001, but still remained far too close to double-digit figures in France, Germany, and Italy. By the first quarter of 2002, the unemployment levels had begun to rise again.

Table 10.6 Unemployment: The European scourge, 1999–2002 (Q1) (%)

	1999	2000	2001	2002Q1
France	10.7	9.3	8.6	9.0
Germany	8.4	7.7	7.7	8.0
Italy	11.3	10.4	9.4	9.0
Netherlands	3.2	2.8	2.4	2.5
Spain	12.8	11.3	10.7	11.2
United Kingdom	5.8	5.3	5.0	5.1

Source: OECD.

The high unemployment rate is Europe's greatest economic weakness. It makes it unthinkable that Europe could replace the United States as the "world's engine of economic growth" by adopting a trade deficit policy, similar to that of the United States, that sucks in enormous amounts of cheap manufactured goods from the rest of the world. Europe's still-strong labor unions would not tolerate the social dislocation that such a policy would bring about. So, while Europe will, in all probability, be the part of the world least badly affected by the unwinding of the disequilibrium in the global economy over the coming years, it would be unrealistic and naive to expect Europe to come to the rescue of the global economy. European policymakers who remained dubious about "the American economic model" even at the peak of its glory are very unlikely to attempt to replicate it now that it has become so badly tarnished.

Mexico

Mexico has the ninth-largest economy in the world. Its GDP contributes 2% of global economic output. In 2001, Mexico's exports to the United States fell 3% to US$131 billion. That slowdown was enough to send the economy into recession, despite the fact that Mexico's trade surplus with the U.S. rose 22% to US$30 billion. GDP contracted by 0.3% in 2001 after growth of 6.6% in the prior year. Mexico joined Japan and Taiwan as the only three of the largest 17 economies to experience a recession that year. Such a sharp slowdown caused by such a small fall in its U.S. exports does not bode well for Mexico's economic future.

Nevertheless, Mexico is something of a special case. It is a participant in the North American Free Trade Agreement (NAFTA). When NAFTA was ratified in 1993, it eliminated trade tariffs between Canada, Mexico, and the United States. At the time of ratification, one peso was worth 32 U.S. cents. The following year, the peso started collapsing in value. It has fallen by more than 68% between then and now (see Figure 10.7).

Needless to say, a collapse in the value of its currency, combined with free access to the richest market in the world just north of its border, did wonders for Mexico's exports (see Figure 10.8). Its trade deficit with the United States was also quickly transformed into a very large surplus. By 2001, Mexico's U.S. exports amounted to the equivalent of 21% of its GDP; and its trade surplus with the U.S. grew to the equivalent of 4.9% of its GDP. Its cumulative trade surplus with the United States between 1994 and the first quarter of 2002 was US$148 billion. Beyond any doubt, free trade has been very beneficial to Mexico – up until the present, in any case.

Figure 10.7   Before and NAFTA: Mexican pesos to US$1, 1993–2002

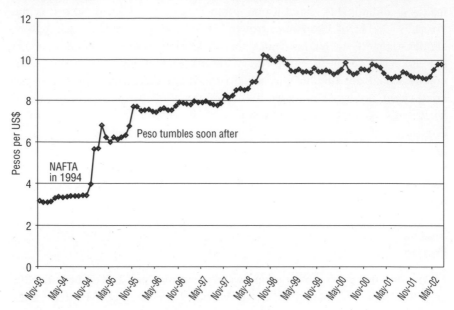

Source: Federal Reserve Economic Data: St. Louis Fed.

Figure 10.8   Mexico: Exports improved after the peso collapsed, 1990–2002 (est.)

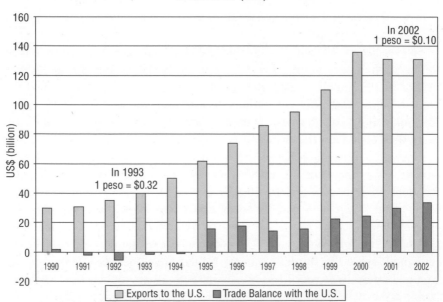

Source: U.S. Census Bureau.

If the trends of the second half of the 1990s were to continue, it would not be long before Mexico's trade surplus with the United States would exceed the US$83 billion trade surplus that China achieved against the U.S. in 2001. Of course, however, if those trends continued, China's U.S. trade surplus would be much, much higher than US$83 billion by the time Mexico reached that mark.

The Mexican economy is adapting itself to its new role as a major supplier of goods to the United States. Large amounts of foreign capital are entering the country. The cumulative financial account surplus was US$79 billion between 1997 and 2000. Investment, consumption, and economic growth were all quite strong during recent years. Government revenues have risen, which has helped the government make progress in resolving the 1994 Mexican systemic banking crisis, estimated to have cost 20% of GDP.

Nevertheless, it remains to be seen how well the Mexican economy will bear up when its exports fall much more sharply in the second phase of the U.S. recession. Very often, a sudden change in the momentum of economic growth brings to light a large number of problems that rapid expansion concealed. One area of weakness is in Mexico's current account. Despite its large trade surpluses with the United States, the country still recorded an overall current account deficit of 3% of GDP in 2000. Large capital inflows on the financial account have funded those deficits, and the IMF has forecast that direct investment into Mexico will average around US$20 billion a year through 2006. If, however, the global economy slows, it would become immediately apparent that Mexico already had more than sufficient capacity to supply the shrinking demand from the north. In that case, direct foreign investment into Mexico could dry up very quickly, forcing a correction of the current account deficit that entailed a reduction in consumption and investment. A slowdown in capital inflows could also give rise to problems in servicing Mexico's US$130 billion in external debt. The country's total reserves (minus gold) amounted to US$35.5 billion in 2000.

It is quite likely that Mexico will be badly whipsawed by the NPR Phase II. The correction of the U.S. current account deficit also represents an awful threat to Mexico. Here, however, in light of the country's proximity to the United States, its very low labor costs, and the extensive ownership of Mexican factories by U.S. interests, Mexico may be among the last of the United States' trading partners to suffer through a contraction of its U.S. trade surplus. If the expansionary trend of that surplus did reverse sharply, it would impose an extraordinarily painful adjustment on Mexico.

CONCLUSION

The inevitable correction of the United States' current account deficit will bring the era of export-led growth to an end and mark the dawn of a difficult new age for the global economy. Most of the United States' major trading partners are already suffering from frail economic health despite the US$400 billion subsidy the U.S. provides to the rest of the world each year through its current account deficit. If a protracted global recession is to be avoided, a new source of global aggregate demand will have to be found to replace that which has been provided by the United States' trade deficit policy up until now. Part Four will outline a strategy that could succeed in doing exactly that. First, however, Chapter 11 will explain why monetary policy – at least as it is traditionally practiced – can play no role in that process.

REFERENCES

1   Robert Rubin, U.S. Treasury Secretary at a White House briefing, June 19, 1998.
2   Standard & Poor's, "Japan Credit Trends 2002: The Downside Deepens," January 31, 2002.
3   Standard & Poor's, "One Step Forward, Two Steps Back: Koizumi's Reform Setbacks," August 2002.
4   OECD, Standardized Unemployment Rates, Q1 2002.
5   Rudyard Kipling, *The Gods of the Copybook Headings* (1919).

Chapter 11

Monetarism is Drowning

... the enormous and mounting U.S. deficits abroad ... flooded the world monetary system, doubling world reserves from the end of 1969 to the end of 1972, i.e., increasing them by as much in this short span of three years as in all previous centuries in recorded history.

— Robert Triffin, 1978/79[1]

INTRODUCTION

Part Four is dedicated to proposing solutions to the current global economic crisis. First, however, this chapter will explain why the monetarist approach of increasing the money supply will not be found among those recommendations.

Tightening the money supply is effective in battling inflation. However, increasing the money supply is no cure for the deflation that results when a credit bubble pops, because it is excessive money supply growth that causes economic bubbles in the first place. To think otherwise is like believing that consuming more alcohol is the cure for drunkenness. The consumption of more and more alcohol will eventually lead to death, just as the unlimited expansion of the money supply will end in the death of the currency system involved. As unpleasant as it may be, the hangover is the period during which the body purges the unnatural toxins that over-stimulated the nervous system during the binge. Similarly, the recession is the period during which equilibrium is restored to the economy after a long period of over-stimulation due to excessive monetary stimulation through credit expansion.

Booms involving periods of extraordinary asset price inflation are episodes of economic drunkenness, where credit is the drink. All those who believe that increasing the money supply in Japan would cure the long, ongoing recession there or that monetary expansion during the 1930s would have prevented the Great Depression, fail to understand, or at least refuse to admit, that the extraordinary booms that preceded those slumps were unnatural and unsustainable economic events originating in too much credit, and that it was those booms themselves that were responsible for the ensuing crises.

215

This is very important to understand, because as the Great End-of-the-Millennium Asset Price Bubble deflates in the United States in the years immediately ahead, deflationary pressures will intensify there, as will the calls for greater monetary stimulation. Unfortunately, there is little doubt that aggressive monetary stimulus cures will be attempted. Interest rates will fall close to zero, as in Japan, and efforts will be made to force the money supply to grow. Those attempts will fail, however. Money supply will not grow at a time when large parts of the economy are incapable of repaying the credit they borrowed during the bubble years.

The failure of those attempts will be the death of monetarism, which claims that any economic difficulty can be overcome simply by adjusting the money supply up or down depending on the circumstances. It will be death through drowning. In this crisis, monetarism, as an economic ideology, will sink under the waves of excess liquidity and drown in an inundation of credit.

▶ "PRINT LOTS OF MONEY"

In 1997, Paul Krugman published an article in a Japanese periodical in which he recommended that the Bank of Japan increase the money supply until prices stop falling and a low level of inflation is achieved. He wrote:

> The simple fact is that there is no limit on how much a central bank can increase the supply of money. Could the Bank of Japan, for example, double the amount of monetary base – that is, bank reserves plus cash in circulation – over the next year? Sure: just buy that amount of Japanese government debt. True, even such a large increase in the money supply might not drive down interest rates very much, since they are already so low. But an increase in Japan's money supply could ease the economic problem in ways other than lower interest rates. It is possible that putting more cash in circulation will stimulate spending directly – that the extra money will simply "burn holes in people's pockets." Or banks, awash in reserves, might become more willing to lend; or individuals, with all that cash on hand, will bypass the banks and find other ways of investing. And even if none of these things happens, when the Bank of Japan increases the monetary base it does so by buying off government debt – and therefore makes room for spending increases or tax cuts.

> So never mind those long lists of reasons for Japan's slump. The answer to the country's immediate problems is simple: PRINT LOTS OF MONEY.[2]

Krugman is a monetarist. Monetarists believe that any economic difficulty can be overcome by increasing or decreasing the supply of money. They believe that inflation can be reined in by tightening the money supply. And they believe that recessions can be overcome by increasing the supply of money in the economy. Milton Friedman, Nobel laureate and advisor to presidents, is the most well-known monetarist. In the early 1960s, he and Anna Jacobson Schwartz published a very lengthy, but interesting, book entitled *A Monetary History of the United States, 1867–1960.*[3] Among many other claims made on behalf of monetarism, this book argued that the deflation of the 1930s (and the entire Great Depression, for that matter) could have been avoided had the Federal Reserve pursued the correct monetary policies by causing money supply to continue to expand, rather than allowing it to collapse as it did when a third of all U.S. banks failed between 1929 and 1932.

Until recently, there had been no opportunity to test Friedman's assertion that expansionary monetary policy could, in fact, overcome deflation. Once prices in Japan's post-bubble economy began to fall, however, Krugman confidently stepped forward and publicized his opinion that the monetarist policy prescription of expanding the money supply was the right cure for Japan's deflationary woes – expressing his astonishment that Japanese policymakers could not understand such a simple concept. "Print lots of money," he advised Japan.

Now, the Bank of Japan has done exactly that in one of the most extraordinary monetary experiments in history. The result? Monetarism has been tested and found wanting. It is now clear that monetarism is not all that it is cracked up to be by Messrs. Krugman and Friedman.

Japan: Money Anyone?

Prices in Japan have been falling for more than three years (see Figure 11.1). Deflation is compounding all that country's other economic problems, and Japanese politicians are desperate to put a stop to it.

As the Japanese recession of the 1990s wore on, the Bank of Japan cut interest rates without restoring sustained economic growth (see Figure 11.2). Then, in March 2001, the central bank fired its last bullet and cut interest rates to virtually zero. It didn't help. Japan fell back into recession. The country was undeniably in a classic liquidity trap. Interest rates were zero, but there were still no profitable investment opportunities in the post-bubble economy that could induce businesses to borrow or banks to lend.

At that time, out of desperation and under very considerable political pressure, the Bank of Japan launched an extraordinary monetary experiment.

Figure 11.1   Japan: Deflation, 1990–2002 (% change in consumer prices over prior year)

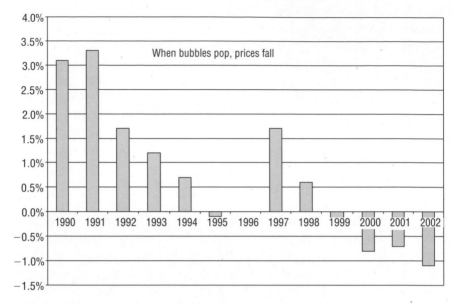

Source: IMF, The World Economic Outlook Database, April 2002.

Figure 11.2   Japan: Central bank discount rates, 1970–2002

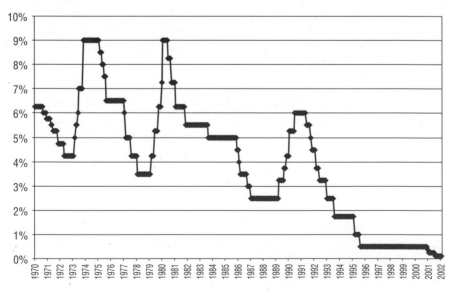

Source: Bank of Japan.

That experiment was explained very frankly in a fascinating speech made by the Governor of the Bank of Japan, Masaru Hayami, on July 24, 2002. That speech is well worth quoting at length.

> In March last year when overnight interest rates reached virtually zero, the Bank, firmly determined to halt the continuing fall in prices, adopted a new framework for money market operations by shifting the operating target to the "quantity" of liquidity, namely the outstanding balance of current accounts held at the Bank. Under the new framework, the Bank has conducted decisive monetary easing which is unprecedented in the history of central banking both at home and abroad.

> As a result, short-term interest rates across the board have declined to virtually zero percent, from overnight call rates to those with three-month and six-month maturity. Medium- to long-term interest rates have also declined to extremely low levels. For example, yields on three-year JGBs are currently at 0.1–0.2 percent, and those on five-year JGBs are at around 0.4 percent. The growth rate of the monetary base, an indicator of the amount of funds provided by the Bank, has been increasing considerably at a rate close to 30 percent year on year. The ratio of monetary base to nominal GDP has been at its highest level in Japan's history, except during World War II.

> Monetary easing has played an important role in preventing deterioration of the economy and has secured financial market stability. This was especially so when the economy was under significant downward pressure following the terrorist attacks in the U.S. and also when concern about financial system stability heightened from the end of December last year to the end of March this year.

> Since April this year, the economy has started to show positive signs, and liquidity demand in financial markets has gradually stabilized reflecting the abatement of concern about financial system stability. However, as mentioned earlier, the economic recovery is still in a nascent stage and there are also risks for the economic outlook. The Bank should therefore continue strong monetary easing to support recent positive movements.

> As I mentioned earlier, it is extremely difficult to revitalize Japan's economy solely by monetary easing when it faces various structural problems. However, the Bank's strong monetary easing will continue to firmly underpin the recovery of the economy by stabilizing financial markets. Furthermore, it is expected that the

effects of the Bank's monetary easing measures will be fully felt when forward-looking economic activity increases as structural reform progresses and efforts to strengthen the financial system bear fruit.[4]

This is a truly extraordinary speech to be given by a central bank governor, particularly a Japanese central bank governor. There is none of the subtle and circuitous locution that one would expect from a Japanese policymaker or that one has become accustomed to hear from Mr. Hayami's American counterpart. The governor is very clear: "... the Bank has conducted decisive monetary easing which is unprecedented in the history of central banking both at home and abroad." Japan's monetary base has been increasing "at a rate close to 30 percent year on year. The ratio of monetary base to nominal GDP has been at its highest level in Japan's history, except during World War II" (see Figure 11.3).

Interest rates are zero and the monetary base is growing at 30% a year. It is a situation that goes far beyond a monetarist's wildest fantasy. The question is: IS IT WORKING? And the answer is: CLEARLY NOT! In his speech, Mr. Hayami acknowledged that the Japanese economy remains weak and clearly stated that "it is extremely difficult to revitalize Japan's economy solely by monetary easing when it faces various structural problems." In light of the Bank of Japan's "decisive monetary easing ... unprecedented in the history of central banking," that statement should be engraved in all

Figure 11.3   Money anyone? Japan's monetary base, 1990–2002

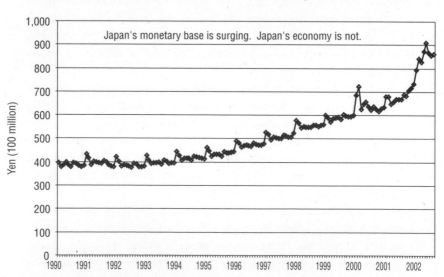

Source: Bank of Japan.

future economic history books as the final nail in the coffin of monetarism. An important plank of monetary theory has been disproved. Central banks can kill inflation and slow the economy by rising interest rates, as Paul Volcker, Mr. Greenspan's courageous predecessor as Fed Chairman, proved in the early 1980s. But central banks cannot cure deflation in a post-bubble economy regardless of how decisive their monetary easing. Pushing on a string is a waste of time (see Figure 11.4).

Lest that message be overlooked, the Bank of Japan also published a paper during the same month as the governor's speech that underscored that point. The paper is entitled "The Effects of Monetary Policy on Firm Investment after the Collapse of the Asset price bubble."[5] The abstract of that paper states:

> This paper investigates what can be learned about the effects of monetary policy on firm investment after the collapse of the asset price bubble in Japan. ... the paper reveals that the monetary easing after the bubble burst worked through the interest rate channel, but not through the credit channel – the credit channel was blocked because of a deterioration in balance-sheet conditions.

Figure 11.4   Japan: Bank current account balances held at the Bank of Japan, 1990–2002

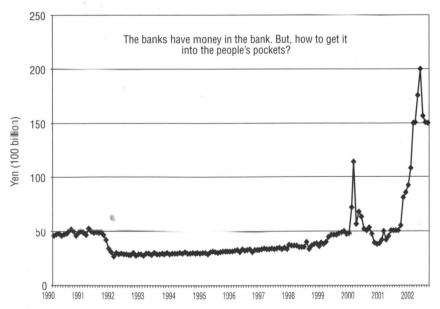

Source: Bank of Japan.

And the paper concludes with this sentence: "Where tighter financial constraints have resulted from a fall in asset prices after the collapse of the bubble, it is far from clear that an easy monetary policy is as effective as the theory suggests."

So, there it is straight from the Bank of Japan. In a post-bubble economy, monetary policy is not effective.

The Bank of Japan put Krugman's advice to the test. They have drastically increased the monetary base. They did not double it over one year, as Krugman suggested would be possible, but they did increase it 36% over one year. All that seems to have resulted from this very aggressive expansion of the money supply is that it has demonstrated the limitations of monetarism. It certainly has not cured deflation or boosted Japan's economy.

The flaw in Krugman's argument – and, by extension, monetary theory – is that it incorrectly assumes that somehow the "extra money" would find its way into "people's pockets." That is because banks, "awash in reserves" though they are, still have not "become more willing to lend." In a post-bubble economy, there are no profitable investment opportunities. In Japan, asset prices are overvalued relative to individual purchasing power and therefore they continue to fall. As for making further investments in the real economy, the opportunities are extremely limited; there is generally excess capacity of almost everything – again stressing that supply is excessive relative to purchasing power, not relative to human wants, which may be infinite. The snag is, there is no way for the "extra money" to get into the hands of the consumers, who, no doubt, would be happy to spend it, if they had it, which they don't. Since the banks aren't lending, and since deflation is not going away, and since the economy is not improving, it is time for Mr. Krugman to admit that he was wrong in this instance, and to admit the limitations of monetary policy in a post-bubble environment. The time has come for him to listen to the Bank of Japan. They put his theory to the test and it didn't work. Full stop. Now it's time for new ideas.

▶ IRRATIONAL MONETARISM?

Will the Fed have any better luck at preventing deflation in the United States? Once it became clear that the U.S. economy was falling into recession in 2001, the Fed cut interest rates 11 times, bringing the federal funds rate down to 1.75% and the discount rate down to 1.25% (see Figure 11.5). Those interest rate reductions, combined with a well-timed tax cut, did help bring about a little dead cat bounce in the economy in the first quarter of 2002. By the second quarter, however, U.S. GDP figures were heading quickly back to earth.

Figure 11.5 The discount rate, 1990–2002

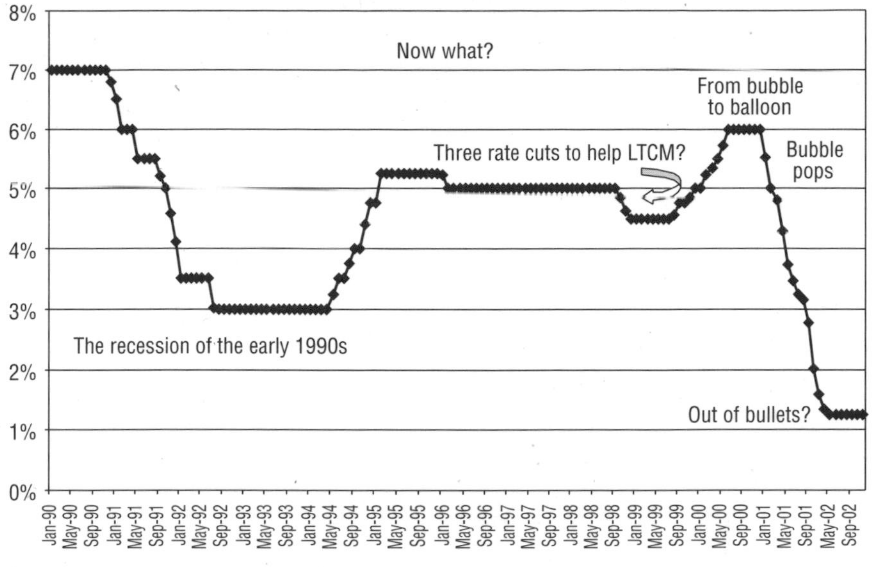

Source: Federal Reserve Statistics, Selected Interested Rates

Yields on 10-year and 30-year Treasury bonds have fallen to levels not seen since the Eisenhower administration (see Figure 11.6), providing an important fillip to the housing market and setting off a refinancing frenzy as mortgage rates follow them down. Nonetheless, the heavily indebted American consumer is showing signs of fatigue. There is a very real danger that prices, which showed very little proclivity to increase even during the final New Paradigm years, may soon begin to fall in absolute terms if rising default rates finally force a reduction in the flow of consumer credit.

How would those "Magi of Money" at the Fed react to deflation in the United States? Interest rates are already very low. Moreover, the monetary base and M2 are both expanding at a sharp clip (see Figure 11.7). M2 is growing at an annual rate of 7.9%, and the adjusted monetary base is growing even faster at 10%. Rarely have those measures of money supply grown more rapidly than at present. Has the Fed run out of monetary bullets

In June 2002, the Board of Governors of the Federal Reserve System circulated a "Discussion Paper" entitled, "Preventing Deflation: Lessons from Japan's Experience in the 1990s."[6] It is very enlightening. Here is an abstract:

> This paper examines Japan's experience in the first half of the 1990s to shed some light on several issues that arise as inflation declines toward zero. Is it possible to recognize when an economy is moving

Figure 11.6   U.S. Treasury bond yields: Ten-year Treasury constant maturity rate, 1953–2002

Source: Federal Reserve Economic Data, St Louis Fed.

Figure 11.7   U.S. money supply growth already accommodating, 1960–2002 (% change from prior year)

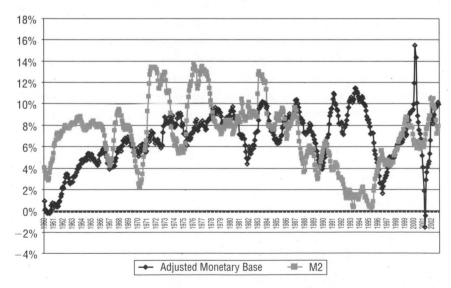

Source: Federal Reserve Economic Data: St. Louis Fed.

into a phase of sustained deflation? How quickly should monetary policy respond to sharp declines in inflation? Are there factors that inhibit the monetary transmission mechanism as interest rates approach zero? What is the role for fiscal policy in warding off a deflationary episode? We conclude that Japan's sustained deflationary slump was very much unanticipated by Japanese policymakers and observers alike, and that this was a key factor in the authorities' failure to provide sufficient stimulus to maintain growth and positive inflation. Once inflation turned negative and short-term interest rates approached the zero-lower-bound, it became much more difficult for monetary policy to reactivate the economy. We found little compelling evidence that in the lead up to deflation in the first half of the 1990s, the ability of either monetary or fiscal policy to help support the economy fell off significantly. Based on all these considerations, we draw the general lesson from Japan's experience that when inflation and interest rates have fallen close to zero, and the risk of deflation is high, stimulus – both monetary and fiscal – should go beyond the levels conventionally implied by baseline forecasts of future inflation and economic activity.

This paper is interesting for a number of reasons. For one thing, it shows that policymakers at the Fed are concerned about the risk of deflation and are "discussing" their options. Second, it may give some indication of how the Fed will respond – that is, even more aggressively – should the risk of deflation increase over the coming months. Next, it could be considered self-serving in that the Fed has already cut the federal funds rate very aggressively to 1.75%, a 40-year low. Finally, in this writer's opinion, this paper demonstrates that the Fed, or, at least those at the Fed who wrote this discussion paper, do not understand that the origin of the economic crisis in Japan (and in the Asia Crisis countries, the United States, and elsewhere around the world) was a credit bubble brought about by the near exponential growth of dollar liquidity since the Bretton Woods system collapsed.

If the Fed fails to grasp the true causes of this crisis and responds with yet more aggressive monetary stimulus, the best outcome that could be anticipated is that it simply is ineffective – as in Japan, where the economy remains trapped in recession despite Japan's aggressive monetary response to its crisis. The outcome could be far worse than that, however. Hyperinflation, a run on the dollar, or both, could result from out-of-control monetary expansion. After all, there is a risk that if cutting interest rates to zero does not prevent deflation, and revving up the printing press just a little does not prevent deflation, then hubris may compel policymakers to run the printing press at full speed until deflation does give way, regardless of the consequences. Once again, an economic crisis caused by too much monetary expansion and characterized by asset price bubbles and excess capacity cannot be cured by yet more monetary expansion.

MG: GLOBAL MONEY SUPPLY

While it is true that you can fight fire with fire, it has never been suggested that you can fight water with water. For a worldwide perspective, it is not helpful to look at M1, M2, M3 or any other measure of money at a national level. MG, the global money supply, is what counts in a global economy, and MG, as measured by international reserve assets, has increased at a mind-boggling rate since the Bretton Woods system broke down.

The world is flooded with financial liquidity (see Figure 11.8), and this excessive liquidity has fueled a global credit bubble that permitted over-investment, brought about excess capacity and asset price bubbles, and now is culminating in deflation. Central banks cannot overcome deflation in this post-bubble environment by lowering interest rates and bumping up the money supply. You can't fight liquidity with liquidity. Monetarism is drowning.

Figure 11.8   MG: The global money supply: Total international reserve assets, 1949–2000

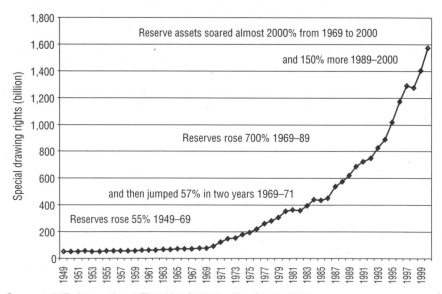

Source: IMF, *International Financial Statistics Yearbook, 2001.*

REFERENCES

1 Robert Triffin, "The International Role and Fate of the Dollar," *Foreign Affairs*, Winter 1978/79.

2 Paul Krugman, "What is Wrong with Japan?" *Nihon Keizai Shimbun*, 1997.

3 Milton Friedman and Anna Jacobson Schwartz, *A Monetary History of the United States 1867–1960* (Princeton, N.J.: Princeton University Press, 1963).

4 "The Challenges Facing Japan's Economy," speech given by Masaru Hayami, Governor of the Bank of Japan, at the Naigai Josei Chousa Kai (The Research Institute of Japan) in Tokyo on July 24, 2002.

5 Takashi Nagahata and Toshitaka Sekine, "The Effects of Monetary Policy on Firm Investment after the Collapse of the Asset price bubble: An Investigation Using Japanese Micro Data," Working Paper 02-3, Research and Statistics Department, Bank of Japan, July 2002.

6 Board of Governors of the Federal Reserve System, International Finance Discussion Papers, No. 729, June 2002, "Preventing Deflation: Lessons from Japan's Experience in the 1990s."

PART FOUR

POLICY TOOLS FOR THE 21ST CENTURY

Chapter 11 explained why monetary policy is helpless to overcome a crisis of excess capacity following the collapse of an economic bubble. As is generally the case in economics, the core problem with the global economy can be explained in terms of an imbalance of supply and demand. During the expansion phase of the cycle, an enormous amount of credit was created around the world. That credit still exists today – in part, as a result of government bailouts of failed financial institutions. This supply of credit greatly exceeds the demand for credit – insofar as effective demand must be backed up by the ability to service, and eventually repay, that debt. Since interest rates are the price of borrowing money, when credit supply greatly exceeds credit demand, the price of money falls to 0%. In a post-bubble economy, only governments borrow from banks. Bank lending to the private sector falls, as has been the case in Japan, Thailand, and Mexico.

The giant U.S. current account deficits are the font of the global credit explosion. The United States' trade deficit policy represents a tragic, brazen flaunting of all classical economic theory and sound economic practice. All that can be said on this subject in defense of the administrations in charge during the last 30 years is that, most probably, that policy evolved by accident rather than by design.

The global credit boom that resulted from the U.S. current account deficit caused worldwide over-investment and over-consumption, as well as asset price bubbles. While credit-induced consumption temporarily absorbed the expanding capacity, an inflection point has now been reached.

Over-investment has created tremendous excess capacity that is now resulting in falling prices. This deflationary pressure, compounded by collapsing asset price bubbles, will inevitably bring about a crash in both investment and consumption on a worldwide scale that leaves only enormous excess capacity and unpaid debts in its wake.

The gap between global aggregate supply and sustainable aggregate demand (supported by real purchasing power) is now so great that, without government intervention, supply must collapse through an extended deflationary process. The process will be extended because industrial capacity does not depreciate quickly.

The right type of coordinated government intervention could prevent the collapse of the global aggregate supply curve by orchestrating an expansion of global aggregate demand. However, that would require forward-looking and courageous policy innovation, because Keynesianism and monetarism, the policy tools of the 20th century, are *en faillite* – bankrupt.

Lessons learned during the evolution of industrial society in the West over the last 200 years must be applied to the new global industrial society that has come into existence at a highly accelerated speed over the last few decades. The conventions and techniques that evolved in Europe and the United States during the 19th and 20th centuries must quickly be applied on a global scale now that a global economy with a global workforce has come into place.

Foremost among the prerequisites that are essential to foster a balanced expansion of global supply and demand is a steadily expanding global minimum wage. There is no way around the fact that aggregate supply can not long expand at a faster rate than the growth in the underlying purchasing power of the public. The absolute necessity of expanding wage rates in the developing (or, rather, industrializing) world, and suggestions as to how that could be achieved, are the topics addressed in Chapter 12.

Next, the international monetary system must be rehabilitated in order to put an end to the explosion of the global money supply that gushes from the U.S. current account deficits. A mechanism to ensure that trade between nations is balanced rather than persistently unbalanced must be put in place to end the destabilizing impact that unbalanced trade has on the global economy. Policymakers must learn to master the global money supply. Chapter 13 will explain why the international monetary system must be modernized in order to effectively serve the needs of the global economy.

It must be understood that the global economy is in a state of extreme and unsustainable disequilibrium. The alternative to developing new sources of global aggregate demand to offset the inevitable contraction in the U.S. current account deficit is a severe and protracted worldwide economic slump. If implemented, the proposals outlined in the final part of this book would remove the source of the global economic disequilibrium by restoring balanced trade, while simultaneously putting in place a new and sustainable source of steadily increasing global aggregate demand.

Chapter 12

A Global Minimum Wage

Because it demands large-scale paradigm destruction and major shifts in the problems and techniques of normal science, the emergence of new theories is generally preceded by a period of pronounced professional insecurity. As one might expect, that insecurity is generated by the persistent failure of the puzzles of normal science to come out as they should. Failure of existing rules is the prelude to a search for new ones.

— Thomas S. Kuhn, 1962[1]

INTRODUCTION

Part One of this book described how the global economy has become destabilized by the United States' enormous current account deficits. Part Two explained why those deficits cannot persist and why a U.S. recession and a collapse in the value of the dollar are now unavoidable. Part Three examined the extraordinarily harmful impact that a recession in the United States and a collapse in the dollar will have on the rest of the world.

Part Four offers recommendations that, if implemented, could help mitigate the damage of the coming worldwide downturn and lay the foundations for more balanced and sustainable economic growth in the decades ahead. If a potentially disastrous global economic slump is to be avoided, a new source of global aggregate demand must be found to fill the gap that will be left when the U.S. current account deficit corrects. This chapter outlines a strategy that could augment global aggregate demand without resorting to government spending or credit creation.

ESTABLISHING EQUILIBRIUM IN THE GLOBAL ECONOMY

There are extraordinary challenges facing the global economy at the beginning of the new millennium, but there are historic opportunities as well. Over the last 20 years, a number of factors, including technological change, trade liberalization, and seemingly insatiable demand in the United States for low-cost imported goods, converged in a way that facilitated rapid industrialization in many developing nations. Within a very compressed period of time, multinational corporations relocated significant portions of their manufacturing facilities to newly industrializing nations, and indigenous entrepreneurs in those countries acquired the machinery and the techniques that enabled them to produce for the OECD markets. The end result was that by the conclusion of the 1990s, a dozen or more countries that had been considered "Third World" in the 1960s had established the kind of advanced system of industrial production that had required centuries to evolve in Europe.

Unfortunately, at the same time, huge differentials in wage rates between the newly industrializing countries and the developed world resulted in trade imbalances of an unprecedented magnitude – and those imbalances created tremendous disequilibrium in the global economy.

The process of industrialization in Europe and, to a lesser extent, in the United States was accompanied by class struggle as the rapidly growing industrial workforce fought for higher wages and better working standards. After generations, and following numerous cycles of revolution and reaction (in Europe), the working class won the right to form unions and to vote. By exercising those rights, they achieved higher wages. Although, at the time, the demands of the industrial workers were viewed as a threat to capitalism, in retrospect it is now clear that the advanced nations never could have reached the current stage of industrialization and economic development had the wages of the majority of the population there not risen. Today's consumer society and service-based economy simply would not exist.

We would be wise to understand that a well-paid workforce is a prerequisite for the development of a fully industrialized economy and apply that lesson to the newly formed global economy. In order to achieve balanced growth on a worldwide scale, the people producing the goods also have to be able to afford to buy them. Today, that is not the case. Industrial workers in many of the world's manufacturing centers earn US$4 to US$5 per day – wage rates that make their products much more price-competitive than any that could be manufactured in developed countries. The overwhelming wage differentials between the developing world and the advanced nations is so great that the international balance of payments can only become increasingly unbalanced under the present regime of relatively free trade.

The existing trade imbalances cannot persist. Already, global demand is not sufficient to absorb global supply, and prices are falling even while governments increase fiscal spending and the money supply in an attempt to support aggregate demand. When the NPR Phase II strikes and the U.S. current account deficit corrects, those imbalances will be enormously exacerbated. Then, either global supply will contract in a protracted deflationary depression or a new source of global demand will have to be found.

This chapter will advocate implementing an internationally agreed program to steadily raise the wage rates of industrial workers in the developing world in order to augment aggregate global demand so that a collapse in aggregate global supply can be avoided. While this idea would not be simple to implement, it is not as far-fetched as it may seem on first impression. It would certainly be far easier than sending a man to the moon, for instance.

This plan would have to clear four major hurdles.

- First, a consensus would have to be reached that steadily increasing wages in the developing world would be a good thing, assuming that it were possible to bring them about through coordinated government intervention.
- Next, an international agreement would have to be reached to implement the idea – to give it a try.
- Then, the mechanics would have to be worked out. Crucially,
  1. an agreement on the initial minimum wage rate would have to be reached; and
  2. the annual rate of increase in the minimum wage rate would have to be agreed upon.
- Finally, verification techniques would have to be devised and put in place to prevent cheating.

Granted, none of these four steps would be easy. On the other hand, there is no reason to consider any of them impossible, either. In short, where there's a will, there's a way.

The rest of this chapter will elaborate on this idea. The following discussion is not intended to be a comprehensive plan, but instead only the outline of a concept. Far-fetched or not, it is hoped that, at the very least, the ideas expressed in this chapter may serve to generate a debate as to how best to replace trade imbalances and credit creation with a new engine of global economic growth suited to a world where further government expenditure risks fiscal crisis and further credit expansion risks monetary chaos.

What is Required?

A means of steadily increasing global aggregate demand that does not rely on deficit spending or expansionary monetary policies is required to ensure balanced and sustainable economic growth in the decades ahead.

Why is Such a Plan Necessary?

This kind of plan is necessary because excessive credit creation has brought about an imbalance in global supply and demand that is culminating in intense deflationary pressure. In recent years, the overheated U.S. economy has provided a subsidy to the rest of the world through its large current account deficits. Those deficits have been an important source of global aggregate demand. They cannot persist, however. When they correct, the gap between supply and demand will widen tremendously. The outcome could be a protracted, deflationary worldwide depression.

Moreover, the differential in wage rates between the economically advanced countries and the newly industrializing nations is so great that trade imbalances can only continue to widen so long as exchange rates remain at current levels. Extraordinarily large movements in currency values would be required to end those imbalances. For example, even a 50% depreciation of the dollar against the Chinese yuan would not be sufficient to establish balanced trade between the United States and China, given the tremendous difference in the wage rates in those two countries. The disequilibrium in the international balance of payments is expanding and destabilizing the global economy. A program to boost wages in the developing world would help restore balanced trade and global economic equilibrium.

Why Can't This Problem be Resolved through Market Forces?

Wage rates are very low in the developing world relative to those in industrialized countries, and demographic trends may push them lower in absolute terms in the decades ahead.

In developing countries, industrial jobs generally pay higher wages than most other kinds of employment. However, there are many more people in the workforce than there are factory jobs. Consequently, there is little pressure for wages to rise. Moreover, demographic trends in most developing countries mean that the size of the workforce will increase much more rapidly than the number of factory jobs over the next 20 years. Therefore, wage rates in the industrial sector are more likely to fall in developing countries than to rise, if left to the law of supply and demand. In dollar terms, wages have already fallen across much of the world during the last 10 years, due to the numerous currency devaluations.

THE PROPOSAL

Raise the wage rates of industrial workers employed in export industries in developing countries through coordinated government intervention. At present, factory wages are approximately US$4 per day or less in most developing countries. An increase of US$1 per day each year would cause the earnings (and purchasing power) of industrial workers to more than triple to US$14 per day over a 10-year period.

Why Begin With Industrial Workers in the Export Sector?

Since the goal is to increase global aggregate demand, why focus only on the wages of industrial workers employed in export industries? To succeed, this program would have to meet three criteria: (1) it would have to be enforceable; (2) it would have to affect a large enough group to have an impact on global aggregate demand; (3) however, the targeted group could not be so large that increasing their wages would destabilize the economies of the participating countries.

It would be useless and counterproductive to attempt to raise all wages in developing countries. Any such agreement would be impossible to enforce. Furthermore, if it were attempted, it would cause an inflationary shock across the developing world and, if it were strictly enforced, it would probably result in rising unemployment in those countries as employers attempted to rein in costs by hiring fewer people.

These problems are avoided by narrowing down the focus to only industrial workers employed in exporting industries. The number of people affected would be sufficiently large to have an impact on the global economy, since a very large portion – and perhaps the majority – of the world's manufacturing jobs are already located in the developing world, while the rest soon will be if present trends continue.

This arrangement could also be enforced by requiring that all industrial imports entering any country be accompanied by evidence verifying that those products had been made using labor that had been paid a wage rate equivalent to or higher than the agreed upon minimum wage rate. Where sufficient evidence was lacking, import duties could be applied as a penalty and an enforcement mechanism.

Raising the wages of industrial workers in exporting industries would also put upward pressure on wage rates in other parts of the economy. As the earnings of factory workers increased, more people would seek factory jobs.

Eventually, other employers would also be compelled to increase the wages they offered in order to retain staff. In this way, higher wages in one part of the economy would naturally lead to increasing wages in other sectors as well.

How Would it Help?

Increasing wages in the developing world would augment global aggregate demand. It would succeed in putting more money in people's pockets, something that traditional monetary policy is incapable of doing in a post-bubble environment. Purchasing power would increase in line with wage growth. Industrial workers employed in export industries would begin to spend more as their wages increased. Their spending would boost domestic consumption in the developing countries. There would also be a multiplier effect from that expenditure that would reverberate throughout those economies. As wages in the selected industrial jobs continued to rise year after year, they would begin to exert upward pressure on the wages in other parts of the economy as well. This scheme would allow the developing world to foster a domestic demand-driven economy and help wean those countries from their heavy reliance on export-led growth.

As consumption expanded in the newly industrializing countries, so would demand for imported goods, an important development that would help restore balanced trade in the world.

Given the magnitude of the wage gap between the developed world and the developing world, this scheme could remain in place and continue to boost global aggregate demand for decades before wage rates in the poorer countries caught up with those in the economically advanced nations. This plan would create a sustainable source of expanding global aggregate demand. Moreover, it would augment demand without, in any way, relying on either government deficit spending or expansionary monetary policies.

Who Would Pay?

The private sector would pay the higher wage rates and most probably pass on their increased cost to the consumer. The cost would not be particularly high, however. Furthermore, any decrease in profit margins that did ensue would be offset by the higher sales volumes that would result from the boost that higher wages in the developing world would give to global aggregate demand.

Let's take an example of a tennis shoe company that manufactures its shoes in Vietnam and sells them primarily in the United States. Of course, the shoes are made on a production line. But let us assume that, on average, one worker can produce one pair of shoes per day and that the worker is currently paid US$5 per day – a very high rate by Vietnamese standards. Let's also assume that the tennis shoes are sold for US$100 per pair.

Now, to increase the worker's pay from US$5 per day to US$6 per day would increase that worker's purchasing power by 20%. A 20% increase in purchasing power would have a very powerful effect on the worker's lifestyle. Adding US$1 to the retail price of the shoes would add only 1% to their price, an amount unlikely to be noticed by the American consumer who would end up paying much more than US$1 in financing charges for buying the shoes with a credit card, anyway. In this example, the profit margins of the tennis shoe company would be unchanged and the inflation rate on the (imaginary) tennis shoe price index would increase by 1%.

There are two other scenarios that should be considered. In the first scenario, as global aggregate demand expanded following the increase in wages in the developing countries, it is likely that many more people would buy tennis shoes from the company in question than they otherwise would have. In that case, sales volume would increase and profits would rise.

In the other scenario, nothing is done to increase wages in the developing world. In that case, the global economy would endure a protracted and severe economic slump when the U.S. current account deficit corrects. Consequently, far fewer people would buy tennis shoes. Profits would fall. The tennis shoe company's share price would fall (further). Management stock options would become worthless and the management team would be fired – because that's the way it works in a laissez-faire environment when economic bubbles pop.

THE ILLUSTRATION

At this stage, it would be useful to flesh out this proposal with some rough numbers in order to demonstrate how an increase in wages in the developing world would boost global aggregate demand.

It is first necessary to estimate the number of workers employed in export industries in developing countries. The International Labor Organization's online database, LABORSTA, provides a detailed breakdown of labor statistics for most countries in the world. Table 12.1 shows the number of workers employed in the manufacturing sector for several of the most important exporting nations in the developing world.

Data are not available for India, but the total number of industrial workers in the other eight countries shown in this table amounts to 121 million. Of course, the majority of those workers would be employed in companies manufacturing solely for the domestic market. They would not be directly affected by any proposal to raise the wages of workers employed in

Table 12.1 Industrial workers in the developing world, 2001

	Millions
China	80.4
India	n.a.
Indonesia	11.5
Brazil	8.3
Mexico	7.5
Thailand	4.8
Vietnam	3.3
Philippines	2.8
Malaysia	2.1
Rest of the world	?

Source: International Labor Organization, LABORSTA database.

exporting industries. The precise number who would be affected is not known, but an estimate of 40 million seems like a reasonable approximation.

Taking that number as a starting point, Table 12.2 shows the effect on global demand that would come about as a result of increasing the wage rate of those workers by US$1 a day each year for the next 10 years. In year one, a US$1 a day increase in wages for 40 million workers would increase global aggregate demand by US$48 billion, assuming they worked 300 days a year and a multiplier effect of 4 times. In year two, the increase in global aggregate demand would be US$102 billion, since the workforce would receive US$2 a day more than they otherwise would have. The only point that requires clarification is the increase in the estimate for the multiplier. Over the 10-year period, the estimate for the multiplier is steadily increased because it is believed that the rise in the wages of the workforce in the exporting industries would slowly begin to drive up wages in other sectors of the economy, as other employers would find it necessary to raise their wage offers somewhat in order to hold on to their workers, who would otherwise gravitate toward the higher-paying exporting jobs. The rapidly expanding domestic demand that would result from the rising wages in the export sector would make it possible to lift wages across other industries as well without causing a decline in overall profitability. Consequently, it is assumed that the multiplier would increase from 4 times in year one to 6.25 times in year 10. As these assumptions are offered as rough estimates only, the reader should feel free to adjust them.

Given the assumptions outlined above, the calculations in the preceding table indicate that increasing the wage rates of industrial workers employed in exporting industries from US$4 per day to US$14 per day over a 10-year period would augment aggregate demand in the developing world by US$750 billion in year 10 alone. That amount is the equivalent of approximately two-thirds of China's 2001 GDP. An increase in the

Table 12.2 A US$750 billion boost to global demand by year 10

Year	No. of workers (mn)	Wage increase p.a. (US$ per day)	Wage rate (US$ per day)	Cumulative wage increase vs satus quo (US$ per day)	Days worked p.a. (days)	Direct wage increase vs. status quo (US$ mn)	Multiplier (times)	Total increase in income p.a. vs. status quo (US$ mn)
1	40	1	5	1	300	12,000	4.00	48,000
2	40	1	6	2	300	24,000	4.25	102,000
3	40	1	7	3	300	36,000	4.50	162,000
4	40	1	8	4	300	48,000	4.75	228,000
5	40	1	9	5	300	60,000	5.00	300,000
6	40	1	10	6	300	72,000	5.25	378,000
7	40	1	11	7	300	84,000	5.50	462,000
8	40	1	12	8	300	96,000	5.75	552,000
9	40	1	13	9	300	108,000	6.00	648,000
10	40	1	14	10	300	120,000	6.25	750,000

developing world's domestic demand of that magnitude would have a profound impact on the global economy and on the international balance of trade. For example, it would be more than sufficient to offset an orderly correction in the U.S. current account deficit, as shown in Table 12.3.

The inevitable correction of the United States' half a trillion dollar a year current account deficits poses a terrible threat to the global economy during the years immediately ahead. At present, that deficit provides an extraordinary subsidy to the rest of the world. The shock will be equally extraordinary when that deficit begins to return to balance. If a very severe global economic slump is to be avoided, an alternative engine of economic growth will have to be found. Steadily increasing wages in the developing world could serve as the next engine of global economic growth.

Table 12.3 Crisis prevention: Global aggregate demand expands even while the U.S. current account deficit corrects

Year	U.S. current account deficit (US$ bn)	Change in U.S. current account deficit vs. status quo (US$ bn)	Total increase in developing world income p.a. vs. status quo (US$ bn)	Combined impact on global aggregate demand (US$ bn)
0	500	0	0	0
1	450	−50	48	−2
2	400	−100	102	2
3	350	−150	162	12
4	300	−200	228	28
5	250	−250	300	50
6	200	−300	378	78
7	150	−350	462	112
8	100	−400	552	152
9	50	−450	648	198
10	0	−500	750	250

The Arguments Against, Refuted

There are many arguments that can be made against a scheme to augment global aggregate demand by orchestrating higher wages in the developing world. The strongest one might be expressed as follows: "There isn't going to be a severe global economic slump; therefore, there is no need to bother with such a complicated plan." If it is correct that there will not be a slump, then it is also true that there is no justification to attempt to boost wages anywhere – or, at least, not for the reasons expressed in these pages.

However, it is difficult to believe that the global economy will not suffer when the U.S. current account deficit corrects; and it is harder still to believe that the deficit will not correct.

It could be argued that this scheme would be inflationary. It should be hoped that it would be inflationary. The world is entering a deflationary slump because of an overabundance of supply relative to purchasing power. Higher wages are required to rectify this imbalance by augmenting purchasing power and thereby global aggregate demand. If inflation returns, that would be a sign of success. If the rate of inflation became too high, subsequent wage increases could be reduced or postponed.

It will be argued that a minimum wage rate causes fewer people to be employed. Regardless of whether or not that is true in a developed economy, it would not be true in this case. The ability to manufacture most of the world's manufactured goods in newly industrializing countries using very low-cost labor is a development that emerged very quickly and very recently. It is of tremendous historic importance. Shifting the world's manufacturing base to the developing world is an innovation that has greatly reduced the cost of labor as a percentage of the total cost of bringing a product to market. Wage rates are 90–95% less in most of the developing world relative to those paid in most OECD nations. If wages rise by US$1 per day over the next year in Indonesia, multinational companies are not going to pack up and move back to Düsseldorf or Seattle. Nor are they going to invest heavily in new plant and equipment to reduce the head count in their Indonesian factories. At Indonesian wage rates, why bother?

Increasing the wages of industrial workers in the developing world will not cost jobs. It will *generate* jobs, as the increased purchasing power of those people begins to spark domestic-driven economic expansion in those countries. The shift in the global manufacturing base to the developing world had brought about a collapse in the cost of industrial labor relative to the rate that had been paid previously. It would be a serious mistake to attempt to wring the last drop of savings that could be generated from this extraordinary development. It would be far wiser to take advantage of this historic opportunity to kick-start domestic demand-driven economic growth in the developing world by paying wages somewhat above what the market would bear.

It will be argued that it can't be done. Hogwash! We are living in an age of organizational miracles and technological marvels. At a time when the riddles of DNA are being unwound and cloning is yesterday's news, when banks trade more than US$100 trillion worth of derivatives contracts each year, more than 100 years after minimum wages were first introduced at a national level, do not doubt that a minimum wage program of this kind could be devised and implemented on a global scale. It *could* be done.

The weakest argument against this plan would be one that opposed it on the grounds that it interferes with market forces and therefore must be a bad thing. If laissez-faire practices ever held sway in the real world, it was certainly a very long time ago. In the modern world, the economy functions within a framework that is very far removed from anything vaguely resembling a laissez-faire model. The political economy of the 20th century was built around a long list of things that could not be described as laissez-faire-like in the least. For example:

- central banks;
- paper money issued by governments;
- income tax;
- fiscal stimulus;
- monetary stimulus;
- steel tariffs;
- agricultural subsidies;
- child labor laws;
- minimum wage laws in the economically advance countries;
- anti-monopoly laws;
- the International Monetary Fund; and
- all social safety nets, including the U.S. Social Security system, which is neither laissez-faire nor solvent.

For centuries, as challenges in the economic sphere arose, interventionist solutions were formulated to resolve them. So it must be today. The sudden emergence of a global economy has made it possible to pay industrial workers in the developing world very low wages to produce things for consumption in the economically wealthy parts of the world. Not surprisingly, that development has resulted in very large trade imbalances, as the rich buy more from the poor than the poor buy from the rich. Those trade imbalances have created credit bubbles that have destabilized the global economy and resulted in a rash of systemic banking failures around the world and intense deflationary pressures. The economic challenge facing this generation is that this global economic disequilibrium is about to unwind in a severe deflationary depression unless a new source of aggregate demand can be found to replace the demand that the United States' overheated economy has been generating up until now but which it is incapable of continuing to generate in the future. Leaving the resolution of this challenge up to market forces is certain to produce a very painful outcome. We can do better than that. Foresight, imagination, courage, and willpower – in other words, effective leadership – would do the trick.

FOUR BIG STEPS

Step 1: Forming the Consensus

There was a time not so long ago when attempting to control economic output through increasing or decreasing either government expenditure or the amount of credit in the economy would have been considered mad. There can be little doubt that any proposal that calls for government intervention in the global economy will meet with a similar reception, regardless of how obvious some kind of intervention is required. The most difficult part of stimulating the global economy through raising wage rates in the developing world would be achieving a consensus that such a thing is theoretically possible in the first place.

It is remarkable, but nonetheless true, that well-educated people who, until recently, were quite willing to believe that a new economic paradigm had put an end to the business cycle and therefore justified price-to-earnings multiples of 100 times or more for countless Nasdaq stocks, would laugh outright at the concept that a minimum wage could be implemented on a worldwide basis, despite the fact that similar legislation already exists at the national level almost everywhere around the world.

This first step of building a consensus would be the hardest. It would be necessary first to convince a few people in positions of the highest authority that such a plan was both necessary and efficacious. Top-down consensus building would be much faster and much more likely to succeed than attempting to build a consensus up from the grass-roots level.

A very careful case would have to be made to overcome all the doubts that would naturally arise to greet such an unprecedented approach to economic management. Everything after step 1 would be a piece of cake.

Step 2: International Agreement

While it would be naïve to suggest that any international agreement involving a large number of countries would be easy to reach, step 2 would be considerably easier than step 1. The negotiations necessary to reach an agreement such as this could be conducted through a special session of the World Trade Organization, or they could be conducted outside any existing framework in order to keep the talks focused and brisk. The World Bank could be helpful in disseminating the idea and in collecting feedback through its ongoing dialog with all the governments of the world. If a consensus had truly already been reached (step 1), then convening an international meeting or even reaching an agreement (in principle) to implement such an arrangement would not be all that difficult. Working out the mechanics of the scheme, step 3, and the verification process, step 4, would be tougher.

Step 3: The Mechanics

Step 3 would involve reaching an agreement on two things: the initial minimum wage rate, and how quickly that wage rate should be increased in subsequent years. Different wage rates currently prevail in various developing countries. It would be important to harmonize those rates as quickly as possible, so that no one country would have a competitive wage advantage over the others. At present, one of the factors that keep wage rates from rising in developing countries is the fear that businesses would relocate to countries with lower wage rates. For example, if labor costs rise to US$6 a day in Thailand, plants might move to Vietnam where the cost of labor is far less than that.

Harmonization of wage rates across the developing world would probably have to be phased in over, say, a 10-year period, with rates rising more quickly in the countries with the lowest labor costs during the first few years until they were on par with those countries with higher wage rates. For example, it should be agreed that by the end of the first 10 years, the wage rates for industrial workers would be increased (at a constant rate of change each year) to a minimum of US$14 per day, regardless of whether in year one wage rates were US$3 per day in country A and US$6 per day in country B, etc.

Careful consideration would have to be given to the harmonization rate to be targeted, as well as the rate at which those wages should increase in subsequent years after wage harmonization had been established. The goal would be to raise the wage rates of industrial workers in developing countries enough to boost global aggregate demand without raising them so much that they cause inflation to become a concern. An initial harmonization rate of US$14 per day by year 10, followed by a 5–10% annual increase thereafter, could be appropriate or, at least, could serve as benchmarks around which a serious debate could begin. If wage increases in this range proved insufficient to achieve the desired goal of augmenting global aggregate demand, they could be raised. Similarly, if they proved to contribute to economic overheating and inflation, these targets could be lowered or phased in over a longer period of time.

Phase 4: Verification

The success of this scheme would very much depend on verifying that the industrial workers were, in fact, being paid (at least) the agreed upon minimum wage. The temptation to cheat in order to gain a competitive advantage would be very strong. A foolproof verification system would have to be devised to provide assurance to all parties that there were no ways around the rules.

Establishing a trustworthy verification system would not be as difficult as might be imagined. Minimum wage rates are already enforced at a national level in most countries. Means could be devised to enforce them at an international level as well.

For instance, verification, testing, and certification companies such as the SGS Group already provide the important service of verifying that the quality and quantity of international commodity shipments meet the correct specifications. These firms verify that each shipment of rice from Thailand to Europe, for example, matches the agreed upon quantity. They also test the shipment to determine that the number of broken grains of rice does not exceed a previously agreed upon percentage. These types of companies could also be used to verify that manufactured goods being imported into a country had been produced using properly paid labor.

Plant inspections would be necessary. The system employed to enforce the collection of value added taxes could also aid in the verification process, as could the methods used to enforce existing import quotas. There would also be strong incentives for rival businesses to report violations committed by business competitors. However, in the age of the Internet, the most effective means of preventing cheating would be to encourage the industrial workers themselves to report wage violations. Internet cafes are becoming ubiquitous even in the developing world. Factories producing for export could be required to educate their workforce on their right to receive a minimum wage, and be required to distribute an email address to their employees (*iambeingunderpaid@wto.org*, for example) that the employees could use to report underpayment of wages. It is very hard to keep a secret, even when it is known by only two people. When the secret is known by 100 or more people working in a factory, it is impossible to keep – particularly when the secret is that all those people are being paid too little.

Of course, violations would still occur. Just as people cheat on their income taxes, many factory owners would attempt to circumvent the requirement to pay higher wages. However, strong penalties, including heavy fines and the loss of export licenses, would serve as a deterrent. Over time, enforcement techniques would achieve the desired result.

It is true that verification would be complicated and laborious. Law enforcement usually is. That does not make it impractical. A global economy will require some global regulations. A global minimum wage is a good place to start.

OLD TOOLS HAVE TO BE REPLACED

In recent decades, policymakers have attempted to direct, control, and support the global economy by manipulating exchange rates. Since at least the Plaza Accord in 1985, governments have intervened in currency markets, causing currencies to rise and fall, in order to achieve certain economic policy objectives. This could be described as global economic management through currency manipulation.

During the 1990s, in order to boost weak economies in many regions of the world, many currencies were allowed to fall or made to fall relative to the dollar. Although that strategy was generally successful in the short term, that immediate success was achieved by generating huge trade imbalances that may exact a heavy long-term price when they correct.

Today, the global economy is still weak, but the United States' strong dollar/trade deficit policy can no longer be relied on to provide further subsidies to the rest of the world. The dollar cannot be allowed to strengthen further given that the U.S. current account deficit is already approaching 5% of U.S. GDP. In fact, a sharp fall in the value of the dollar now appears inevitable, although it is not yet clear whether it will be orchestrated by government intervention or come about as the result of a panic on the currency markets.

Therefore, coordinated government intervention designed to alter the global economy should not be seen as something new. Instead, it should be recognized that the primary tool that has been used by governments to bring about adjustments in the global economy over the last two decades – that is, currency manipulation – is now incapable of providing any further stimulus to the global economy.

When one tool becomes ineffective, a new tool must be found. Coordinated intervention to raise wage rates in the developing world would be more complicated than currency manipulation. On the other hand, however, it is very likely that it would prove to be much more effective in boosting global aggregate demand over the long run.

> ## IF UNANIMITY IS LACKING ...

Forming a consensus that this approach is necessary and desirable would be the most difficult part of implementing this plan. In fact, reaching such a consensus could easily prove to be impossible. The business community in OECD countries could object for fear that higher wages in the developing world would cut into the profitability of their companies. They need to be made to understand that a protracted global economic slump lies ahead unless remedial action is taken. If nothing is done, their businesses and their standard of living will suffer. That eventuality could be avoided if a consensus can be reached to orchestrate higher wages and, by extension, higher purchasing power in the newly industrializing parts of the world.

Misgivings in the developing world would center on concerns over the verification process. The only conceivable reason that any government would object to a plan designed to raise the wages of its people in a deflationary age is for fear that other countries could cheat by paying their workforce less in order to gain an unfair trade advantage. These concerns could be alleviated by assigning government officials from the developing world a leading role in overseeing the implementation of the verification process.

While unanimous agreement would unquestionably create the best environment to implement an ambitious scheme such as this one, a lack of complete agreement would not necessarily make implementation impossible. Alternative scenarios could also be imagined where this plan could be put into effect even if important players refused to cooperate.

For example, if the leaders of the developing countries believed this strategy would help them, but the industrialized countries did not concur, there would be nothing to stop the developing world from forming a labor cartel, just as the oil-producing countries created an oil cartel through OPEC. Like oil, a cheap industrial workforce has become absolutely necessary to sustain the prosperity of the developed world, and especially that of the United States. The economically advanced countries have no domestic source of low-cost labor. If the developing world presented a united front and cooperated fully, they could orchestrate higher wage rates for the workers in their export industries even if the rest of the world didn't like it.

Similarly, if the importing nations agreed that wages in the developing world should rise, even though the developing countries themselves disagreed, the developed nations could unilaterally mandate that importers verify the payment of specified minimum wages or else face import duties or outright prohibition. In this scenario, unanimous agreement among the advanced nations would not be necessary. In fact, should the United States decide to act entirely on its own, it still could have a profound impact on wage rates around the world, given the enormous amount that it imports from the rest of the world.

 ## A CAVEAT

A global minimum wage is needed and feasible. However, it must be recognized that if a policy to boost wages in the developing world is implemented, the impact of sharply rising global aggregate demand would take a heavy toll on the global environment. Counter-measures would have to be designed and implemented to offset that damage. Chapter 13 contains suggestions as to how such measures could be financed.

 ## REFERENCE

1   Thomas S. Kuhn, *The Structure of Scientific Revolutions* (Chicago: University of Chicago Press, 1962).

Chapter 13

Controlling the Global Money Supply

One thing of which we are confident is that the history of money will continue to have surprises in store for those who follow its future course — surprises that the student of money and the statesman alike will ignore at their peril.

— Milton Friedman and Anna Jacobson Schwartz, 1963[1]

The international monetary system that evolved after the breakdown of the Bretton Woods system in the early 1970s is badly flawed. It lacks a mechanism to prevent persistent trade imbalances. That has made it possible for the United States to incur enormous current account deficits totaling a cumulative US$3 trillion since 1980. Those deficits have acted as an economic subsidy to the rest of the world, but they have also flooded the world with dollars, which have replaced gold as the new international reserve asset. Those deficits have, in effect, become the font of a new global money supply. Each year that the United States incurs a current account deficit, international reserves increase by approximately the amount of that deficit. During the 20 years between 1949 and 1969, international reserves rose by 55%. Since 1969, when the Bretton Woods system began to break down, international reserve assets have increased by 1,900%. This near-exponential increase in the global money supply (MG) has been the most important economic event of the last half-century. It has sparked off economic booms in the surplus nations as they amass dollar reserves, and it has sparked off an economic boom in the United States as those dollar surpluses re-enter the United States to acquire dollar-denominated assets. In every case, boom turns to bubble and then the bubble pops. Banking systems, unable to withstand the volatility in asset prices, are collapsing all around the world in unprecedented numbers. Despite these problems, the global economy has grown dependent on exporting to the United States. In 2001, the U.S. current account was the equivalent of 1.3% of the world's entire economic output. When that deficit corrects, as it inevitably must, the global economy will suffer an extraordinary shock.

There are two important challenges facing policymakers in addressing these problems in the global financial architecture. The first is to devise a plan to reform the international monetary system in a way that prevents the persistent trade imbalances that are ultimately responsible for the extreme disequilibrium in the global economy today. The second challenge will be to implement that plan in a manner that does not result in economic breakdown. A third, broader challenge confronting world leaders will be to devise a new economic growth engine to replace the stimulus that up until now has been generated by the U.S. current account deficits. Chapter 12 laid out one plan that could help address this third challenge by augmenting global aggregate demand through orchestrating higher wage rates in the developing world. This chapter will consider how the international monetary system could be reformed in a manner that would eliminate its inherent flaws and support global economic expansion at the same time.

Today, global money supply is being determined by the United States' current account deficits. In addition to being destabilizing, this system is neither sustainable nor easily controlled. It is not sustainable because the United States cannot continue going deeper into debt to the rest of the world indefinitely. It is not easily controlled because the disbursement of MG takes place as a result of trade imbalances and capital flows that are far too complex to easily direct. This is really no way to run a global economy.

A new international monetary accord is needed. The new system must prevent persistent trade imbalances, and it must put in place a mechanism that would allow the growth of the global money supply to be controlled and allocated in an orderly and rational manner.

▶ CONTROLLING MG

Under the gold standard, governments had very little control over the global money supply. Then, the world's monetary base was comprised (primarily) of gold. Global money supply only increased when additional gold was dug up from the ground. This was not ideal, because the supply of newly mined gold was erratic. When major new goldfields were discovered, gold reserves expanded substantially. At other times, the supply of gold barely increased from one year to the next. During these periods, complaints were heard that a shortage of gold was stifling economic growth.

By the end of World War II, the United States had accumulated most of the world's gold reserves. The international monetary framework that was created at the Bretton Woods Conference in 1944 established a system of fixed exchange rates that was designed, in part, to get around this uneven distribution of the world's gold stock. The U.S. dollar and all other currencies were fixed at a certain price to a certain quantity of gold. Consequently, all the currencies were also fixed at an unchanging ratio to one another. The Bretton Woods system was a quasi-gold standard because other countries were guaranteed the right to convert their dollars into gold at an exchange rate of US$35 for one ounce of gold.

After the war, there was considerable concern that there was an insufficient supply of dollars abroad to support economic recovery. The dollar shortage was one of the most pressing economic issues of that time. The Marshall Plan partially alleviated this problem in the late 1940s and early 1950s as US$13.4 billion entered Europe for the purposes of economic assistance. However, concerns over the shortage of dollars persisted throughout the 1950s and into the 1960s. Strong arguments were made in support of putting in place a mechanism to increase the supply of international reserves. Eventually, in 1968, it was agreed at the 23rd annual meeting of the International Monetary Fund to create a new reserve currency to be called special drawing rights that would supplement gold and dollars as international reserves.

However, by the time this agreement was reached, the dollar shortage had already ceased to be a problem. By the late 1960s, overseas investments by American corporations, as well as U.S. development and military aid, had resulted in a growing amount of foreign-held dollars. Soon, a number of countries felt they held too many dollars. When they attempted to convert those dollars into gold, President Nixon suspended dollar convertibility in order to protect the United States' gold reserves. With that act, the Bretton Woods system fell apart and a system of floating exchange rates began to emerge.

Later, as we have seen, when the United States began to run very large current account deficits in the early 1980s, the world became flooded with U.S. dollars and international reserve assets surged at a rate that would have been inconceivable to the classical economists of the 18th and 19th centuries or even to John Maynard Keynes and Harry Dexter White, the architects of the Bretton Woods system. Suddenly, very dramatically, and completely by accident, the world economy shifted from a monetary system anchored by a physical asset, gold, to one that was completely unanchored by anything. The age of paper money had arrived with a bang. And, as discussed at length in these pages, the bang turned to boom and the boom is now turning to bust.

That brings us up to the present. The problem today is that the global money supply has run amok. Arrangements must be made to bring it back under control. The first step in this process is to enact measures that prevent persistent, multi-year trade imbalances. Lord Keynes, in the plan he drew up in preparation for the Bretton Woods Conference, recommended that fines be imposed on countries with current account deficits and on those with current account surpluses, in order to discourage both.[2] This proposal was part of his plan for an International Clearing Union. That plan, the Keynes Plan, was presented at Bretton Woods as the British proposal for the post-war monetary system.

The Keynes Plan was rejected by the Americans, who were calling the shots at Bretton Woods in 1944. Nonetheless, his proposal to fine countries for imbalances on their current account could be employed to put an end to the enormous trade imbalances that are now destabilizing the global economy. Deficit countries and surplus countries would both be fined in order to ensure that they both took the necessary actions to restore balance to their balance of payments. Keynes suggested the fine should be 1% of the deficit or surplus. That could be effective. If not, the percentage could be increased progressively each year until balance was restored.

Policymakers need to put in place a system that ensures that equilibrium on the current account is maintained. Establishing a mechanism to fine countries with deficits or surpluses could be an effective means of achieving that objective. Alternative methods could also be devised. It is not necessary to work out the details here. The current account deficits are destabilizing the global economy by creating runaway global money supply growth. They must be put to a stop. There are many ways that could be accomplished. It should be done without delay.

Then What? The Hair of the Dog That Bit You

Of course, turning off the taps of the global money supply after so many years of rapid monetary expansion would provide a terrible shock to the global economy. Steps would have to be taken to soften the blow. The goal is not to stop the global money supply from increasing at all. It is to gain control of its rate of growth and to slow it down to a pace that is supportive of economic expansion but not so excessive that it is destabilizing. Therefore, a new method of providing sufficient liquidity expansion would have to be put in place. Special drawing rights (SDRs) could fill that role.

As mentioned above, the global community agreed to the creation of SDRs in 1969 in order to ensure sufficient international liquidity at a time when it was believed that a shortage of dollars was restricting economic growth. Once the United States stumbled on to its trade deficit policy, dollar liquidity exploded and SDRs were no longer required. Consequently, they never evolved into the primary reserve assets that many had hoped they would. Nonetheless, there is no reason they could not be used now to allow the global money supply to continue expanding after the U.S. current account deficits are brought under control.

It is interesting to see how SDRs are described by the IMF itself. The IMF factsheet on special drawing rights reads (in part) as follows:[3]

> In 1969, the IMF created the SDR as an international reserve asset, to supplement members' existing reserve assets (official holdings of

gold, foreign exchange, and reserve positions in the IMF). The SDR is valued on the basis of a basket of key national currencies and serves as the unit of account of the IMF and a number of other international organizations.

Why was the SDR created?

The Bretton Woods fixed exchange rate system came under pressure in the 1960s because it contained no mechanism for regulating reserve growth to finance the expansion of world trade and financial development. Gold and the U.S. dollar were the two main reserve assets at the time, but gold production had become an inadequate and unreliable source of reserve supply, and the continuing growth in U.S. dollar reserves required a persistent deficit in the U.S. balance of payments, which in itself posed a threat to the value of the U.S. dollar. For these reasons, it was decided to created a new international reserve asset under the auspices of the IMF.

Only a few years after the creation of the SDR, the Bretton Woods system collapsed, however, and the major currencies shifted to a floating exchange rate regime. This development, along with the growth in international capital markets, which facilitated borrowing by creditworthy governments, lessened the need for SDRs.

Today, the role of SDRs as a reserve asset is limited: by end-April 2002, SDRs accounted for less than 1.25 percent of IMF members' non-gold reserves. And while some private financial instruments are denominated in SDRs, efforts to promote its use in private markets have had limited success. Hence, the SDR's main function is to serve as the unit of account of the IMF and some other international organizations. In this respect, it is used almost exclusively in transactions between the IMF and its members.

What this means is that a system is already in place that allows the IMF to create international reserve assets in the form of SDRs. It is rather hard to believe that such an ambitious and complicated scheme was ever agreed upon by the international community. Nonetheless, it is fortunate that it now exists. SDRs could be made into an important economic policy tool.

The IMF could allocate SDRs with the specific intent of supporting economic expansion around the world. A supplement to global liquidity would certainly be necessary once new arrangements were in place to end trade imbalances. After years of very rapid expansion of MG, the world would experience the monetary equivalent of cold turkey if global monetary expansion ceased all at once when the U.S. current account deficit disappeared. SDRs could be allocated in sufficient amounts to allow the global economy to wean itself off its dependence on the U.S. deficits and the reserve assets that those deficits generate. If you will, SDRs could serve as a kind of monetary methadone to assist the world to free itself from its dollar addiction.

It will not go unnoticed that this proposal must be categorized as monetarism applied on a global scale. Nor will it have been forgotten that earlier chapters of this book argued repeatedly that a crisis caused by excessive monetary expansion cannot be cured by still further monetary expansion. An analogy was even employed that compared the global economic crisis to a hangover brought on by the consumption of too much credit. That is all true. This proposal to allocate SDRs in order to ease the transition while the global money supply is being brought under control should be considered a treatment of the "hair of the dog" variety. It is widely known that a little drink the morning after a big night can do wonders for an aching head. Once the trade deficit taps are turned off and the torrent of global money supply slows to a trickle, the world will badly need a monetary Bloody Mary. It was a role SDRs were created to fill.

Effective Allocation

SDRs could be allocated in any quantities found desirable, so long as they did not cause too much inflation. Furthermore, they could be allocated in a manner that would overcome the inability of traditional monetary policy to effectively cure deflation in a post-bubble environment. As shown in Chapter 11, traditional monetary policy has not been effective in Japan, because the increased money supply created by the Bank of Japan has become stuck in the banks and does not make its way into the people's pockets. The banks can't find enough solvent customers to lend to, and the public can't find enough viable investment opportunities to inspire them to borrow and invest. There is no reason why the newly created SDRs have to be handed over to central banks. A wide variety of ways could be devised to distribute these funds so that they were assured of having the desired effect of stimulating the global economy.

Joseph Stiglitz and George Soros have recommended that SDRs be allocated in a manner that supports developmental goals. During the first quarter of 2002, Joseph Stiglitz, Nobel laureate and former chief economist of the World Bank, advocated "the provision of new liquidity at the international level" to assist global development. In an article published in *Economic Times*,[4] he wrote:

One idea (to support global development) receiving attention is a new form of global money akin to the IMF's Special Drawing Rights (SDRs). SDRs are a kind of global money, issued by the IMF, which countries agree to accept and exchange for dollars or other hard currencies.

Instead of holding their reserves in dollars, a new form of global money – "global greenbacks" – could be issued which countries could hold in reserve. The money would be given to developing countries to finance their development programs as well as global public goods like environmental projects, health initiatives, humanitarian assistance, and so on.

There are a variety of institutional arrangements by which these global greenbacks could be issued. The IMF (responsible for issuing SDRs) could issue them, or a new institution could be created to decide on quantity and allocations. A new institutional arrangement might entail the creation of a set of trust funds – say, for education or health, or the environment – with competition among countries for projects helping to promote these objectives.

Mr. Stiglitz made similar remarks at a Roundtable Discussion held by the Institute for International Economics in February 2002.[5] George Soros also spoke at that forum.[6] Mr. Soros stated:

My proposal relates to a special issue of SDRs that has already been authorized by the IMF in 1997 and approved by 72% of the membership; all it needs is the approval of the U.S. Congress to attain the 85% supermajority that is necessary to make the issue effective. The special issue amounts to about US$27 billion, of which about US$18 billion would be donated.

Mr. Soros went on to recommend that President Bush

... ask Congress to approve the 1997 special issue on the condition that the rich countries agree to donate their SDRs to a trust fund that would be used for the provision of public goods on a global scale. In the first instance the public goods would consist of public health, education, and the strengthening of legal systems. The global fund for fighting infectious diseases like AIDS would be a case in point.

The donations scheme would be tried out, in the first instance, in implementing the special issue already authorized by the IMF in 1997. If the trial is successful, the scheme could be scaled up.

The SDR donation scheme has only one drawback: it is complicated and difficult to understand. It combines two forms of assistance. One, developing countries receive an addition to their foreign currency reserves. That is as close to a free lunch as you can get; it is free as long as you don't eat it. Two, developed countries donate their allotments for the provision of public goods like health, education, and the rule of law, on a global scale. Could there be a better combination? The IMF authorizes the issue of SDRs if there is a global need for liquidity. The developing countries have such a need and the need is becoming more acute as the reverse flow of capital from emerging markets persists. The developed countries do not need additional monetary reserves because they can borrow from the financial markets but they do need to increase their contribution to global welfare. By donating their SDR allocations both needs can be met.

Mr. Stiglitz and Mr. Soros are quoted here to demonstrate that SDRs could be used to increase the global money supply if the international community agreed that it should be so. Moreover, their remarks are also exemplary in that they demonstrate that these men are not afraid to think "outside of the box" in order to resolve the pressing issues of the day.

Golden Fetters

In 1992, Barry Eichengreen published a book entitled *Golden Fetters: The Gold Standard and the Great Depression 1919–1939*[7] in which he argued that England's attempt to return to the gold standard in the second half of the 1920s had disastrous deflationary consequences that led to the Great Depression a few years later. It is an interesting and well-researched book with important lessons for policymakers considering tinkering with the international monetary system.

England's attempt to reintroduce the gold standard may be described as an attempt to shove the credit genie back in the bottle after he had already escaped. It was an impossible task. The bottle broke. *Golden Fetters* demonstrates how.

The book falls short, however, for failing to grasp the real origin of the economic crisis. The Great Depression did not come about because it was necessary to re-establish control over credit expansion. It came about because credit expansion had run out of control in the first place when the suspension of the gold standard rules set off an explosion of international credit creation. Mr. Eichengreen seems to completely fail to understand that long before England attempted to go back on the gold standard, the global economy had already become completely destabilized by the global credit boom during the dozen years that followed the breakdown of the gold standard. That is an extraordinarily important thing not to understand.

While the analysis contained in *Golden Fetters* does not provide an adequate explanation for the causes of the Great Depression, it does demonstrate why the global economy cannot simply revert to the rules it functioned under during the gold standard or the Bretton Woods era. Any attempt to regain control over the runaway growth of the global money supply will have deflationary consequences that must be anticipated and overcome. The allocation of SDRs would be an effective means to offset the deflationary impact that will accompany the elimination of the U.S. current account deficit and the inevitable restoration of balanced international trade.

THE IMF-GCB

The International Monetary Fund was created at the Bretton Woods Conference to provide short-term loans and policy advice to countries with balance of payments deficits, in order to prevent the kind of competitive currency devaluations that exacerbated the economic crisis of the 1930s. How times have changed. The world economy no longer functions within the framework of fixed exchange rates. Now, when a country experiences an economic crisis (as occurs with increasing frequency), the IMF generally encourages the government of that country to devalue its currency against the dollar in order to boost that country's exports. The IMF also lends enormous sums that enable that country to avoid defaulting on its international debt obligations.

In a sense, the IMF has already begun to resemble a global central bank (GCB). When it bails out distressed countries, it also bails out the international financial institutions (FIs) with exposure to that country. By so doing, the IMF prevents the global money supply from contracting in the same way that a central bank prevents its national money supply from contracting when it bails out a failed bank or banking system at the national level. On the one hand, by bailing out crisis-hit countries and the FIs that lend (too much) to them, the IMF has prevented any of the myriad economic crises of recent years from turning into a global crisis. On the other hand, however, by bailing out the FIs and thereby keeping the global money supply intact, the IMF has created other problems. First, it has created moral hazard. By demonstrating again and again that it will bail out the international FIs, the IMF has made the FIs less fearful of loss, which, in turn, has made them more aggressive lenders. Their loans have played an important role in destabilizing the countries that eventually call on the IMF for help. A second problem that has arisen from the IMF bailouts is that they have been so successful at preserving the global money supply that an overabundance of money and credit has become a serious problem. The surfeit of capital has resulted in asset price bubbles, economic overheating, and, by financing over-investment, deflationary pressures at the consumer and wholesale level all around the world.

It is well understood that there is a global economy. It must now become understood that there is also a global monetary base and a global money supply. Either the supply of that money is going to be controlled in an orderly and rational way, or it is going to continue destabilizing the global economy, as it has for the last two decades. A GCB is required to control a global money supply.

The IMF has the organizational structure and many of the policy tools needed to carry out the role of a quasi-GCB. However, there are three important tasks that the IMF must now master if it is going to succeed in that role. First, the IMF must gain control over the global money supply – that is, over the creation of international reserve assets. Second, it must learn how to allocate the future supply of global liquidity in quantities that are neither excessive nor too sparse. Finally, it must learn how to allocate the global money supply in a way that both ensures global economic stability and, simultaneously, supports the global development agenda.

These are ambitious goals, but far from impossible. The necessary tools are in place. All that is required is leadership and sufficient political will to create a rational international monetary system capable of meeting the needs of a global economy. Time is not on our side.

REFERENCES

1   Milton Friedman and Anna Jacobson Schwartz, *A Monetary History of the United States, 1867–1960* (Princeton, N.J.: Princeton University Press, 1963).
2   The Keynes Plan, February 11, 1942. Reproduced in *The International Monetary Fund 1945–1965, Twenty Years of International Monetary Cooperation. Volume III: Documents.*
3   IMF website: *Special Drawing Rights, A Factsheet*, August 20, 2002.
4   Joseph Stiglitz, "Global Greenbacks," *Economic Times*, March 22, 2002.
5   Joseph Stiglitz, "Sustained Development Finance to Fight Poverty," remarks at the Roundtable on "New Proposals on Financing for Development," February 20, 2002. Held at the Institute for International Economics.
6   George Soros, "Special Drawing Rights for the Provision of Public Goods on a Global Scale," remarks at the Roundtable on "New Proposals on Financing for Development," February 20, 2002. Held at the Institute for International Economics.
7   Barry Eichengreen, *Golden Fetters: The Gold Standard and the Great Depression 1919–1939* (New York: Oxford University Press, 1992).

PART FIVE

The Evolution of a Crisis

The New Paradigm technology bubble popped in 2000. The following year, the United States went into a mild recession and U.S. imports contracted by 6%. That drop in U.S. demand caused a severe economic slowdown around the world. Stock markets crashed, global commodity prices plunged, and government budget deficits blew out as tax revenues declined. By 2002, the United States faced the threat of deflation for the first time since the Great Depression. Part Five begins by examining how policymakers responded to that threat through the application of extraordinary stimulus – fiscal and monetary, conventional and otherwise. It then considers the nature, sustainability, and consequences of the global reflation that stimulus produced. Finally, it reflects on the few remaining policy options still available to respond to the new and much more severe global economic slump that will occur in the years immediately ahead as the U.S. dollar sinks further and the United States' current account deficit corrects.

Members of the Federal Reserve Board are terrified of deflation – and well they should be. Once interest rates have fallen to 0%, the Fed is left without any conventional means of providing further stimulus to the economy. Chapter 14 examines how far the Fed is prepared to go to prevent deflation from occurring in the United States, as well as its unorthodox contingency plans for overcoming deflation if it does spread to America.

When the strong dollar trend of the late 1990s broke, private investors scurried to get their money out of the U.S. and out of dollars. Suddenly, not only did the U.S. need to fund a half a trillion dollar a year current account deficit, but also a deficit of several hundred billion dollars more on its financial account. Chapter 15 analyzes how the United States was able to avoid a balance of payments crisis during the run on the dollar in 2003. Money creation on an unprecedented scale was required to avert the crisis.

Large U.S. tax cuts, historically low U.S. interest rates, and what amounted to a global helicopter drop of money by the Bank of Japan all acted in unison to boost aggregate demand in the United States, which, in turn, produced a remarkable surge in global economic growth. Chapter 16 describes how a 21% increase in U.S. imports and a 40% deterioration in the U.S. current account deficit over two years bought the world a few more years of prosperity.

Before the collapse of the Bretton Woods international monetary system, the demand for money determined the level of interest rates, since the supply of money was fixed. That is no longer the case. Now that governments are free to create as much money as they please, it is the relationship between the demand for money and the supply of money that counts. This is a profound change, especially in light of the explosion of the global money supply. Understanding interest rates in the age of paper money is the subject of Chapter 17.

On November 19, 2004, Fed Chairman Alan Greenspan made a speech in which he explained why large U.S. current account deficits cannot be sustained over the long run. That speech sent the dollar tumbling. Chapter 18 explores why the Fed has begun to talk down the dollar, and examines the possibility that the U.S. current account deficit has become so large that it has caused the Fed to lose control over U.S. interest rates.

The rapid expansion of the U.S. current account deficit, and the parabolic surge in the global money supply that accompanied it, created a powerful, but transitory, global economic boom in 2003 and 2004. Chapter 19 takes a fresh look at why the global economy will suffer a severe and protracted economic slump when that deficit inevitably corrects. The lack of consumer price inflation during the boom was an ominous portent of the deflation that will accompany the bust.

A correction in the U.S. current account deficit will cause the floor to drop out from under global prices and threaten the world with a 1930s-style deflationary depression. Chapter 20 explains why policymakers in the United States are likely to respond to that event through large-scale fiscal stimulus financed by central bank monetization of government debt, something quite close to what Fed Governor Ben Bernanke described as "a helicopter drop of money." It also explains why such a policy response is bound to bring about the collapse of the dollar standard.

Chapter 14

Deflation: The Fed's Greatest Fear

Preparing Desperate Measures

Indeed, there is an especially pernicious, albeit remote, scenario in which inflation turns negative against a backdrop of weak aggregate demand, engendering a corrosive deflationary spiral.

— Alan Greenspan, 2003[1]

Although they will never say so publicly, the Fed is terrified of deflation. During the past six years, Japan has been stuck in a deflation-induced liquidity trap. Overnight interest rates are 0%. Two-year government bonds yield nine basis points. Ten-year government bonds yield 1.34%. The banks are flooded with excess deposits and, still, there is no demand for money. Bank lending has contracted during each of the last eight years. Under such conditions, a central bank becomes helpless, losing all power to provide any further stimulus to the economy. The possibility that the same thing could happen in the United States is the Fed's worst nightmare. And, according to Fed Governor Bernanke, it is a scenario the Fed "would take whatever means necessary to prevent."[2] For a full discussion on deflation, see Chapter 8.

During 2002, deflation posed a grave threat to the U.S. economy for the first time since the Great Depression. The implosion of the New Paradigm bubble and the recession that accompanied it had undermined aggregate demand and exacerbated excess industrial capacity domestically. Meanwhile, a surge in imports from ultra-low-wage developing economies exerted relentless downward pressure on the overall price structure of the country. The Fed had cut the federal funds rate to a 41-year low of 1.75% and still the economy was not responding. Moreover, the market had begun to fear that the Fed was "out of bullets."

Officially, the Fed's position was that there was only a remote possibility that the United States would fall into deflation; however, since the damage that would result from that scenario would be "especially pernicious," as Chairman Greenspan once put it, steps should be taken to ensure against it anyway.[3]

In June 2002, the Board of Governors of the Federal Reserve System published a Discussion Paper entitled "Preventing Deflation: Lessons from

Japan's Experience in the 1990s."[4] The abstract of that paper is reproduced on pages 223 and 225, but its conclusion bears repeating here:

> ...we draw the general lesson from Japan's experience that when inflation and interest rates have fallen close to zero, and the risk of deflation is high, stimulus – both monetary and fiscal – should go beyond the levels conventionally implied by baseline forecasts of future inflation and economic activity.

Two and half years later, it is now completely clear that it was exactly this policy prescription that U.S. policymakers were pursuing at that time to combat the threat of deflation: stimulus – both monetary and fiscal – that went beyond levels conventionally implied by baseline forecasts.

We know now that the Fed was eventually to cut the federal funds rate to 1%, while the Bush administration was to push through three tax cuts worth nearly US$190 billion between 2001 and 2003. Aggressive as those measures were, they are still measures of a conventional nature.

From the perspective of mid-2002, the question confronting those in charge of preventing deflation must have been **how far beyond** the conventional levels implied by the base case the economic policy response could go. The government budget had already swung back into a large deficit, and the federal funds rate was at a 41-year low. How much additional stimulus could be provided? A further increase in the budget deficit seemed

Figure 14.1   United States: Government budget balance, 1980–2004

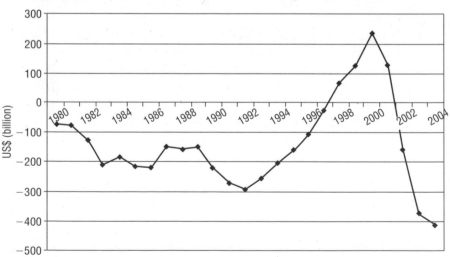

Source: Office of Management and Budget, Executive Office of The President of the United States.

likely to push up market-determined interest rates, causing mortgage rates to rise and property prices to fall, which would have reduced aggregate demand that much more. And, with the federal funds rate at 1.75% in mid-2002, there was limited scope left to lower it further. Moreover, given the already very low level of interest rates, there was reason to doubt that a further rate reduction would make any difference anyway.

It was at that time that the world began to learn about unorthodox monetary policy and when the expression "the Bernanke put" entered the lexicon of the financial markets. It is very important to understand the types of unconventional policy tools the Fed considered employing at the time, not only because of the impact the discussion of those policies had on financial markets then, but even more so because they are the policies that the Fed may yet feel forced to deploy if the threat of deflation re-emerges, which is much more likely than is generally recognized.

In a speech entitled "Deflation: Making Sure 'It' Doesn't Happen Here,"[5] delivered on November 21, 2002, Federal Reserve Governor Ben Bernanke explained to the world exactly how far beyond conventional levels the policy response could go. It was surely one of the most remarkable speeches ever made by any central banker, and it is well worth quoting at length.

Governor Bernanke began by stating:

> I believe that the chance of significant deflation in the United States in the foreseeable future is extremely small, for two principal reasons. The first is the resilience and structural stability of the U.S. economy itself. ... The second bulwark against deflation in the United States, and the one that will be the focus of my remarks today, is the Federal Reserves System itself. The Congress has given the Fed the responsibility of preserving price stability (among other objectives), which most definitely implies avoiding deflation as well as inflation. I am confident that the Fed would take whatever means necessary to prevent significant deflation in the United States and, moreover, that the US central bank, in cooperation with other parts of the government as needed, has sufficient policy instruments to ensure that any deflation that might occur would be both mild and brief.

He then spelled out what those policy instruments include:

> Because central banks conventionally conduct monetary policy by manipulating the short-term nominal interest rate, some observers have concluded that when that key rate stands at or near zero, the central bank has "run out of ammunition" – that is, it no longer has the power to expand aggregate demand and hence economic activity. It is true that once the policy rate has been driven down to zero, a

central bank can no longer use its *traditional* means of stimulating aggregate demand and thus will be operating in less familiar territory.

However, a principal message of my talk today is that a central bank whose accustomed policy rate has been forced down to zero has most definitely *not* run out of ammunition. As I will discuss, a central bank, either alone or in cooperation with other parts of the government, retains considerable power to expand aggregate demand and economic activity even when its accustomed policy rate is at zero.

Like gold, U.S. dollars have value only to the extent that they are strictly limited in supply. But the U.S. government has a technology, called a printing press (or, today, its electronic equivalent), that allows it to produce as many U.S. dollars as it wishes at essentially no cost. By increasing the number of U.S. dollars in circulation, or even by credibly threatening to do so, the U.S. government can also reduce the value of a dollar in terms of goods and services, which is equivalent to raising the prices in dollars of those goods and services. We conclude that, under a paper-money system, a determined government can always generate higher spending and hence positive inflation.

Of course, the U.S. government is not going to print money and distribute it willy-nilly. Normally, money is injected into the economy through asset purchases by the Federal Reserve. To stimulate aggregate spending when short-term interest rates have reached zero, the Fed must expand the scale of its asset purchases or, possibly, expand the menu of assets that it buys.

So what then might the Fed do if its target interest rate, the overnight federal funds rate, fell to zero? One relatively straightforward extension of current procedures would be to try to stimulate spending by lowering rates further out along the Treasury term structure – that is, rates on government bonds of longer maturities. There are at least two ways of bringing down longer-term rates, which are complementary and could be employed separately or in combinations. One approach ... would be for the Fed to commit to holding the overnight rate at zero for some specified period. ... A more direct method, which I personally prefer, would be for the Fed to begin announcing explicit ceilings for yields on longer-maturity Treasury debt (say, bonds maturing within the next two years). The Fed could enforce these interest rate ceilings by committing to make unlimited purchases of securities up to two years from maturity at prices consistent with the targeted yields. If this program were successful, not only would yields on medium-term Treasury securities fall, but (because of links operating through expectations of future interest rates) yields on longer-term public and private debt (such as mortgages) would likely fall as well.

Of course, if operating in relatively short-dated Treasury debt proved insufficient, the Fed could also attempt to cap yields of Treasury securities at still longer maturities, say three to six years. Yet another option would be for the Fed to use its existing authority to operate in the markets for agency debt (for example, mortgage-backed securities issued by Ginnie Mae, the Government National Mortgage Association).

… a second policy option, complementary to operating in the markets for Treasury and agency debt, would be for the Fed to offer fixed-term loans to banks at low or zero interest, with a wide range of private assets (including, among others, corporate bonds, commercial paper, bank loans, and mortgages) deemed eligible as collateral.

The Fed can inject money into the economy in still other ways. For example, the Fed has the authority to buy foreign government debt, as well as domestic government debt. Potentially, this class of assets offers huge scope for Fed operations, as the quantity of foreign assets eligible for purchase by the Fed is several times the stock of U.S. government debt.

Now, out of this long and truly extraordinary speech comes the most interesting part. Governor Bernanke went on to say:

Each of the policy options I have discussed so far involves the Fed's acting on its own. In practice, the effectiveness of anti-deflation policy could be significantly enhanced by cooperation between the monetary and fiscal authorities. A broad-based tax cut, for example, accommodated by a program of open-market purchases to alleviate any tendency for interest rates to increase, would almost certainly be an effective stimulant to consumption and hence to prices.

A money-financed tax cut is essentially equivalent to Milton Friedman's famous "helicopter drop" of money.

So, there you have it. The Fed is not out of bullets. It could print money and buy Treasury bonds to push down the yields at the long end of the yield curve, thereby driving down mortgage rates and inflating the U.S. property bubble further. Or, it could print money and use that money to buy newly issued government bonds to finance a broad-based tax cut, enabling the government to provide the economy with a fiscal jolt without any risk that the increase in government debt would drive up interest rates.

In May 2003, Governor Bernanke visited Japan and conducted a series of meetings with officials at the Bank of Japan (BOJ), the Ministry of Finance (MOF), and the Financial Services Agency. While there, he made a speech entitled "Some Thoughts on Monetary Policy in Japan."[6] His message was familiar:

> My thesis here is that cooperation between the monetary and fiscal authorities in Japan could help solve the problems that each policymaker faces on its own. Consider for example a tax cut for households and businesses that is explicitly coupled with incremental BOJ purchases of government debt – so that the tax cut is in effect financed by money creation.

The importance of Governor Bernanke's speeches was not lost on the bond market. A highly visible governor of the Federal Reserve System had stated publicly that, in his opinion, the Fed would do whatever it took to keep the U.S. from falling into a deflationary recession, even if that meant printing money and buying Treasury bonds to drive down their yields at the long end.

This came to be known as "the Bernanke put," meaning that many investors and speculators came to the conclusion that they could buy bonds without fear of price declines because they understood Governor Bernanke to have said that the Fed would step in and buy them if the bond prices started to fall (and the yields to rise).

Not surprisingly, participants in the bond market responded by buying government bonds. The yield on the 10-year U.S. Treasury bond fell to 3.1% in mid-2003, the lowest in four and a half decades. Just *talking* about "unorthodox" measures had driven down yields at the long end of the yield curve, apparently validating the Fed's ability to fight against the possibility of deflation even with the federal funds rate at such low levels.

But then something the bond market had not anticipated happened. In Congressional testimony on July 15, 2003, Fed Chairman Alan Greenspan made the following remarks:[7]

> Inflation developments have been important in shaping the economic outlook and the stance of policy over the first half of the year. With the economy operating below its potential for much of the past two years and productivity growth proceeding apace, measures of core consumer prices have decelerated noticeably. Allowing for known measurement biases, these inflation indexes have been in a neighborhood that corresponds to effective price stability – a long-held goal assigned to the Federal Reserve by the Congress. But we can pause at this achievement only for a moment, mindful that we

face new challenges in maintaining price stability, specifically to prevent inflation from falling too low.

This is one reason the Federal Open Market Committee (FOMC) has adopted a quite accommodative stance of policy. A very low inflation rate increases the risk that an adverse shock to the economy would be more difficult to counter effectively. Indeed, there is an especially pernicious, albeit remote, scenario in which inflation turns negative against a backdrop of weak aggregate demand, engendering a corrosive deflationary spiral.

Until recently, this topic was often regarded as an academic curiosity. Indeed, a decade ago, most economists would have dismissed the possibility that a government issuing a fiat currency would ever produce too little inflation. However, the recent record in Japan has reopened serious discussion of this issue. To be sure, there are credible arguments that the Japanese experience is idiosyncratic. But there are important lessons to be learned, and it is incumbent on a central bank to anticipate any contingency, however remote, if significant economic costs could be associated with that contingency.

The Federal Reserve has been studying how to provide policy stimulus should our primary tool of adjusting the target federal funds rate no longer be available. Indeed, the FOMC devoted considerable attention to this subject at its June meeting, examining potentially feasible policy alternatives. However, given the now highly stimulative stance of monetary and fiscal policy and well-anchored inflation expectations, the Committee concluded that economic fundamentals are such that situations requiring special policy actions are most unlikely to arise.

BANG! In that last sentence, Chairman Greenspan completely undermined the Bernanke put. Immediately, bond prices plunged and within days the 10-year bond yield rose from 3.1% to 4.6%. Fortunes were lost. The bond market was in shock. What had happened?

Had the economy really improved so much that there was no longer any need to contemplate unorthodox monetary policies? Or, did Chairman Greenspan worry that so much talk of printing money and buying Treasury bonds had caused the bond market to become carried away in driving bond yields down too low? Or, was it simply that the Fed no longer had to consider printing money in order to buy bonds, since the Bank of Japan (in cooperation with the Japanese Ministry of Finance) had begun to do exactly that, and on a mind-bogglingly large scale?

Between January 2003 and the end of March 2004, the BOJ "printed" ¥35 trillion, which the MOF used to buy US$320 billion. With those dollars, the Japanese authorities bought U.S. dollar-denominated assets, most probably U.S. Treasury bonds and agency debt. (In Japan, it is the MOF that carries out currency market intervention, even though it is the BOJ that creates the money used to conduct that intervention. For the sake of simplicity, the intervention discussed over the following pages will be referred to as the BOJ/MOF intervention.)

Was the BOJ/MOF conducting Governor Bernanke's unorthodox monetary policy on behalf of the Fed? There is no question that the BOJ created money on a very large scale, as the Fed would have been required to do under Bernanke's scheme. Nor can there be any question that the money created was used to buy an increasing supply of U.S. Treasury bonds being issued to finance the kind of broad-based tax cuts Bernanke had discussed. Moreover, was it merely a coincidence that the really large-scale BOJ/MOF intervention began during May 2003, while Governor Bernanke was visiting Japan? Was the BOJ simply serving as a branch of the Fed, as the Federal Reserve Bank of Tokyo, if you will?

Although the possibility of that kind of cooperation between the Fed and the BOJ/MOF should not be completely ruled out, there is another, much more likely explanation for the BOJ's actions. Facts suggest that when the strong dollar trend of the late 1990s broke and went into reverse, private investors sold dollars and bought yen in such large quantities that the Japanese monetary authorities were forced to print and sell yen in enormous quantities in order to prevent a very sharp appreciation of the Japanese currency. In other words, the BOJ/MOF intervention was forced upon them by private-sector capital flight out of the dollar that, in effect, amounted to a run on the U.S. currency.

▶ REFERENCES

1   Testimony of Federal Reserve Board Chairman Alan Greenspan, Federal Reserve Board's semiannual monetary policy report to the Congress, before the Committee on Financial Services, U.S House of Representatives, July 15, 2003.
2   Remarks by Federal Reserve Board Governor Ben S. Bernanke, before the National Economists Club, Washington, D.C., November 21, 2002, "Deflation: Making Sure 'It' Doesn't Happen Here."
3   Testimony of Federal Reserve Board Chairman Alan Greenspan, Federal Reserve Board's semiannual monetary policy report to the Congress, before the Committee on Financial Services, U.S. House of Representatives, July 15, 2003.
4   Board of Governors of the Federal Reserve System, International Finance, Discussion Papers, No. 729, June 2002, "Preventing Deflation: Lessons from Japan's Experience in the 1990s."

5   Remarks by Federal Reserve Board Governor Ben S. Bernanke, before the National
    Economists Club, Washington, D.C., November 21, 2002, "Deflation: Making Sure
    'It' Doesn't Happen Here."
6   Remarks by Federal Reserve Board Governor Ben S. Bernanke, before the Japan
    Society of Monetary Economics, Tokyo Japan, May 31, 2003, "Some Thoughts on
    Monetary Policy in Japan."
7   Testimony of Federal Reserve Board Chairman Alan Greenspan, Federal Reserve
    Board's semiannual monetary policy report to the Congress, before the Committee
    on Financial Services, U.S. House of Representatives, July 15, 2003.

Chapter 15

The Run on the Dollar, 2003

*If we stay as we are, with no coordination [to stop the decline of the dollar],
one can imagine a catastrophic economic situation at the global level.*

— French Finance Minister Herve Gaymard, 2004[1]

During the strong dollar trend of the late 1990s, foreign investors, both private and public, invested heavily in the United States. Those investments put upward pressure on the dollar and on U.S. asset prices, including stocks and bonds. The trend became self-reinforcing. The more capital that entered the U.S., the more the dollar and dollar-denominated assets rose in value. The more those assets appreciated, the more foreign investors wanted to own them. Because of the large sums entering the country, the United States had no difficulty in financing its giant current account deficit, even though that deficit nearly tripled between 1997 and 2001.

By 2002, however, with the U.S. current account deficit approaching 5% of U.S. GDP, it became increasingly apparent that the strong dollar trend was unsustainable. The magnitude of the current account deficit made a downward adjustment in the value of the dollar unavoidable. At that point, the strong dollar trend gave way and the weak dollar trend began (Figure 15.1). Foreign investors who had invested in U.S. dollar-denominated assets during the late 1990s naturally wanted to take their money back out of the United States once it became clear that a sharp correction of the dollar was underway. Moreover, many U.S. investors, and hedge funds in particular, also began selling U.S. dollar-denominated assets and buying non-U.S. dollar-denominated assets to profit from the dollar's decline.

The change in the direction of capital flows can be seen very clearly in the breakdown of Japan's balance of payments. Figure 15.2 shows the balance on Japan's current account and financial account, the two principal components of Japan's balance of payments, going back to 1985. Traditionally, Japan runs a large current account surplus and a slightly less large financial account deficit, with the difference between the two resulting in changes (usually additions) to the country's foreign exchange reserves.

Beginning in 2003, however, there was a startling change in the direction of the financial account (see Figure 15.3). Instead of large financial outflows from Japan to the rest of the world, there were very large financial

Figure 15.1   The end of the strong dollar trend,
Dollar Index (DXY), 1997–2004

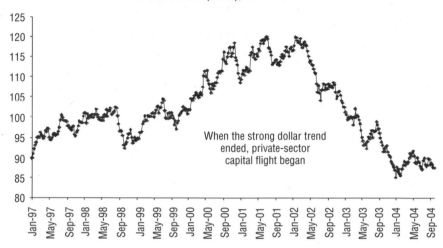

When the strong dollar trend
ended, private-sector
capital flight began

Source: Bloomberg.

Figure 15.2   Japan: Current account and financial account,
1985 to the present

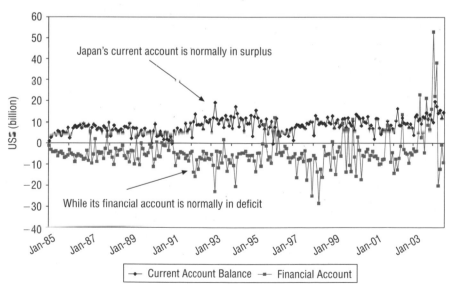

Japan's current account is normally in surplus

While its financial account is normally in deficit

→ Current Account Balance ■ Financial Account

Source: CEIC.

Figure 15.3   Japan: Financial account, 1985 to the present

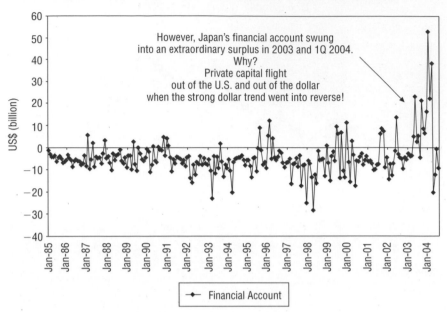

Source: CEIC.

inflows. For instance, in May 2003, Japan's financial account reflected a net inflow of US$23 billion into the country. The net inflow in September was US$21 billion. These amounts increased considerably during the first quarter of 2004, averaging US$37 billion a month.

The inflow of so much capital into Japan was largely responsible for the surge in the Japanese stock market that began in the first half of 2003 (see Figure 15.4). Higher share prices, in turn, made it possible for Japan's major banks to raise badly needed capital. Thus, Japan was able to put the capital entering (or re-entering) the country to very good use.

But why did Japan, which normally exported capital, suddenly experience net capital inflows on a very large scale in the first place? The most likely explanation is that very large amounts of private-sector money began fleeing the dollar and seeking refuge in the relative safety of the yen.

The capital inflows into Japan at that time were massive, even relative to Japan's traditionally large annual current account surpluses. In order to prevent the yen from appreciating very sharply, the BOJ/MOF began to intervene very aggressively in the foreign exchange markets.

During the 15 months between January 2003 and March 2004, the BOJ/MOF spent ¥35 trillion to acquire US$320 billion in the foreign exchange markets to slow the yen's appreciation against the dollar (see Figure 15.5).

Figure 15.4 Nikkei Index

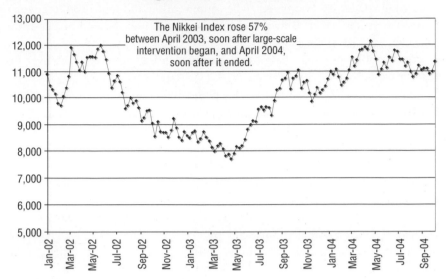

The Nikkei Index rose 57% between April 2003, soon after large-scale intervention began, and April 2004, soon after it ended.

Source: Bloomberg.

Figure 15.5 Japan: Foreign exchange intervention required to purchase the capital fleeing the dollar

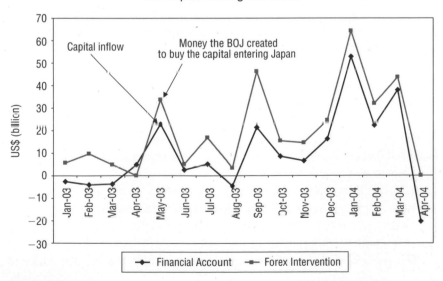

Source: CEIC.

This amounted to more than all the BOJ/MOF intervention during the preceding 10 years combined. The intervention did not stop the yen's appreciation altogether. Between the end of 2001 and the end of 2004, the yen increased by 19% against the dollar. Nevertheless, it held the yen's rise to considerably less than that of the euro, which increased by 51% over the same period.

The BOJ/MOF intervention stopped when the Fed indicated that it would begin tightening, which corresponded to a higher reading on the Producer Price Index (PPI) and to bond market fears that the Fed was behind the curve. Interestingly, when the BOJ/MOF intervention stopped, a sharp correction occurred in commodity prices and, for that matter, across all asset classes except for the dollar, which bounced when higher U.S. interest rates seemed to be on the cards.

The aggressive BOJ/MOF intervention in the currency markets was extensively covered in the financial press at the time. However, the real significance of that event was almost entirely overlooked. In order for the MOF to spend ¥35 trillion, the BOJ first had to *create* ¥35 trillion. This was money creation on a scale never before attempted in peacetime.

To put this into perspective, ¥35 trillion is approximately 1% of the world's annual economic output (which could be thought of as global GDP). It is roughly the size of Japan's annual tax revenue base, or nearly as large as the loan book of UFJ, one of Japan's four largest banks. It amounts to the equivalent of US$2,500 for every person in Japan and, in fact, would amount to US$50 per person if distributed equally among the entire population of the planet.

Having acquired US$320 billion, the MOF needed to invest those dollars in dollar-denominated assets in order to earn a return. In all probability, it invested them in U.S. Treasury bonds or agency debt. By doing so, the BOJ/MOF provided an extraordinary amount of stimulus to the U.S. economy and, consequently, to the global economy.

During the fiscal year ending September 30, 2004, the U.S. budget deficit climbed to a record US$413 billion, up from a deficit of US$158 billion two years earlier. Despite the US$255 billion deterioration in the budget deficit over those two years, the average interest rate on 10-year U.S. government bonds was lower in 2004 than in 2002. It is quite certain that the US$320 billion the BOJ/MOF acquired with its freshly created yen played a very important role in financing the sharp deterioration in the U.S. budget deficit at interest rates that proved low enough to allow U.S. property prices to continue inflating at a rapid clip.

It is remarkable how much this process resembled the "money-financed tax cut" Governor Bernanke had discussed as a policy option available to the Fed during his speech in November 2002.[2] Recall he felt certain that "a broad-based tax cut, for example, accommodated by a program of open-market purchases to alleviate any tendency for interest rates to increase, would almost certainly be an effective stimulant to consumption and hence to prices." Indeed, events were to prove that he was absolutely correct in that belief.

By financing the expanding U.S. budget deficit at low interest rates, the money created by the BOJ played a crucial role in supporting the strong global economic expansion during 2003 and 2004. In fact, the Bush tax cuts and the BOJ money creation that financed them (at very low interest rates) were the two most important elements driving the strong global economic expansion during that period. Combined, they produced a very powerful global reflation. The process seems to have worked in the following way.

U.S. tax cuts and low interest rates fueled consumption in the United States. In turn, growing U.S. consumption shifted Asia's export-oriented economies into overdrive. China played a very important part in that process. With a trade surplus vis-à-vis the United States of US$124 billion, equivalent to 9% of its GDP in 2003 (rising to above 10% in 2004), China became a regional engine of economic growth in its own right. It used its large trade surpluses with the U.S. to pay for its large trade deficits with most of its Asian neighbors, including Japan. The recycling of China's U.S. dollar export earnings explains the incredibly rapid "reflation" that began across Asia in 2003 and that was still underway at the end of 2004. Even Japan's moribund economy began to reflate.

Whatever its motivation, Japan was well rewarded for creating money and buying U.S. Treasury bonds with it. Whereas the BOJ had failed to reflate the Japanese economy directly by expanding the domestic money supply, it appears to have succeeded in reflating it indirectly by expanding the global money supply through financing the sharp increase in the MOF's holdings of U.S. dollar foreign exchange reserves (see Figure 15.6).

Japan's helicopter drop of freshly printed money into the United States acted as an important prop to the global economy in a second crucial way as well. When the strong dollar trend broke, had the BOJ/MOF not bought the dollars that the private sector sold in such large quantities, the United States would have faced a balance of payments crisis, in which, in addition to having to fund a half a trillion dollar a year trade deficit, it would have had to find a way to fund a deficit of several hundred billion on its capital account as well.

Any other country facing a large shortfall on its balance of payments would have experienced a reduction in its foreign exchange reserves. The United States, however, maintains only a limited amount of such reserves; only US$75 billion as at the end of 2003, far too little to fund the private capital outflows occurring at that time.

Figure 15.6 Japan: International reserves
(minus gold), 1967 to the present

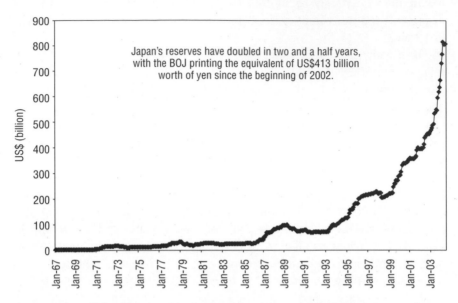

Source: International Monetary Fund, *International Financial Statistics*.

Once those reserves had been depleted, market-determined interest rates in the U.S. would have begun to rise, in all probability popping the U.S. property bubble and throwing the country into recession. Under that scenario, a reduction in consumption in the United States would have undermined global aggregate demand and created a severe worldwide economic slump.

As discussed in earlier chapters, the U.S. current account deficit more or less finances itself since the central banks of the surplus countries buy the dollars entering their countries to prevent their currencies from appreciating, and then recycle those dollars back into U.S. dollar-denominated assets in order to earn interest on them.

Large-scale private-sector capital flight out of dollars presented the recipients of that capital with the same choice. The central bank of each country receiving the capital inflow had the choice of either printing their domestic currency and buying the incoming capital, or else allowing their currency to appreciate as the private sector swapped out of dollars. The European Central Bank chose to allow the euro to appreciate. The Bank of Japan and the People's Bank of China chose to print yen and yuan and accumulate the incoming dollars to prevent their currencies from rising. If some central bank had not stepped in and financed the private-sector capital flight out of the dollar, then sharply higher U.S. interest rates most likely would have thrown the world into a severe recession. It is quite likely that this consideration also played a role in influencing the actions of the Japanese monetary authorities during this episode.

REFERENCES

1   French Finance Minister Herve Gaymard. Speaking on a visit to a General Motors factory in Strasbourg, France, on the need for the U.S., Europe, and Asia to work together to stem the decline of the dollar against the euro, December 23, 2004.
2   Remarks by Federal Reserve Board Governor Ben S. Bernanke, before the National Economists Club, Washington, D.C., November 21, 2002, "Deflation: Making Sure 'It' Doesn't Happen Here."

Chapter 16

The Great Reflation

Globalization presumes sustained economic growth. Otherwise, the process loses its economic benefits and political support.

— Paul A. Samuelson[1]

L arge U.S. tax cuts, historically low U.S. interest rates, and what amounted to a global helicopter drop of money by the Bank of Japan all acted in unison to boost aggregate demand in the United States, which, in turn, produced a remarkable surge in global economic growth.

U.S. property prices responded to this extraordinary stimulus by rising at the fastest rate in decades, as can be seen in Figure 16.1. By the third quarter of 2004, home prices were increasing at a double-digit annualized rate in more than half of the 50 U.S. states. For the country as a whole, the average price increase for a home was 13%. That represented the highest housing price inflation since the late 1970s. The late 1970s were characterized by a broad-based increase in prices in the United States that resulted from the second oil shock. That is not the case at present. Consumer

Figure 16.1   OFHEO house price index for the United States, quarterly, 1976 to the present

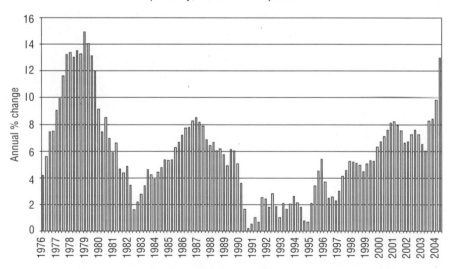

Source: Office of Federal Housing Enterprise Oversight.

price inflation is very muted and has been for years. The current surge in home prices is unique and, therefore, all the more worrying in that it is taking place in the absence of significant CPI-level inflation.

Rapid inflation in property prices created a wealth effect that allowed the American public to finance additional consumption by extracting equity from their homes. Additional consumption meant additional imports. As a consequence, by 2003, the U.S. current account deficit, after a brief pause in 2001, had once again begun to act as the world's engine of economic growth (see Figure 16.2).

It should be recalled that during the New Paradigm bubble years, imports into the United States had surged, expanding by 33% between 1998 and 2000 alone. However, in 2001, when U.S. imports contracted by 6%, the global economy quite nearly tipped into crisis. The economic growth rates of all the United States' major trading partners decelerated abruptly. Stock markets spiraled downward, commodity prices fell, and government finances came under strain all around the world. The consequences of the US$78 billion decline in U.S. imports that year are described in detail in Chapter 9.

U.S. imports remained depressed in 2002, increasing only 2%. Over the following two years, though, driven by an extraordinary burst of stimulus – monetary and fiscal, conventional and otherwise – imports into the United States leapt 21.5% to US$1.4 trillion, and the U.S. trade gap blew out to US$629 billion (see Figure 16.3).

Figure 16.2 United States: Current account balance, 1980–2004E

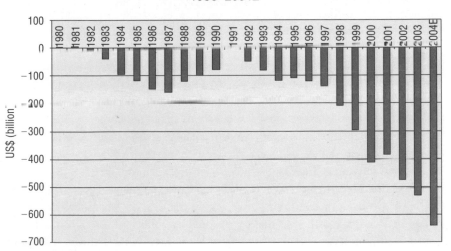

Source: Federal Reserve Economic Data, St. Louis Fed.

Figure 16.3 Imports into the United States, 1960–2004

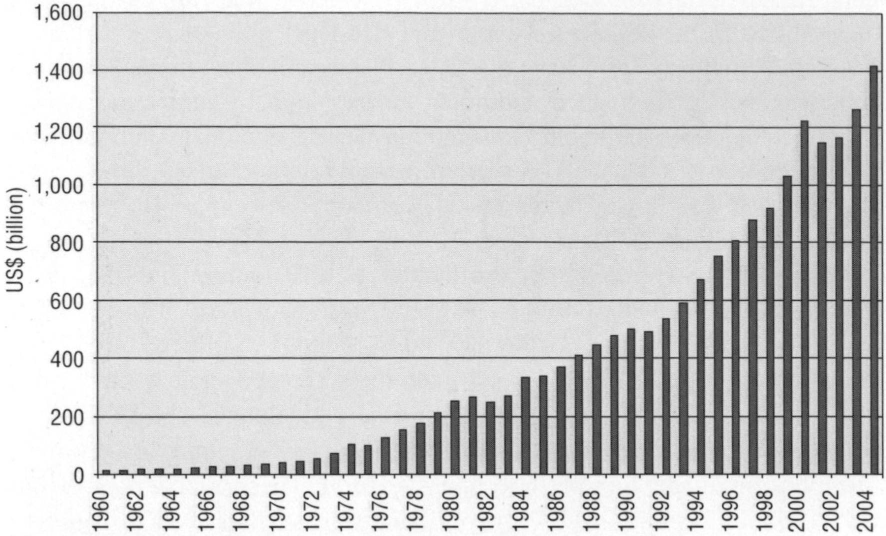

Source: Federal Reserve Economic Data, St. Louis Fed.

Between 2000 and 2004, imports into the U.S. increased by US$190 billion. The growth in imports from China accounted for nearly 40% of that increase. Astonishingly, China's exports to the United States practically doubled over those four years to an estimated US$160 billion in 2004 (see Figure 16.4).

As a result of its surging exports to the United States, China came to play an important role in the great global reflation that has occurred over the last few years. In fact, its role has become so significant that it deserves to be considered in some detail.

Over a very short space of time, China has become a powerful force in international trade. Unlike the United States, however, China does not pay for its imports with credit. China has become an important trading partner for many countries around the world, but few of those countries would be willing to accept Chinese government bonds as payment for goods and services rendered, in the same way that they accumulate U.S. Treasury bonds. China must pay in cash. The source of that cash is a very large balance of payments surplus.

There are three main elements of that surplus: China's trade surplus with the United States, foreign direct investment (FDI), and hot money entering China in anticipation of a revaluation of the Renminbi. In 2004, China's trade surplus with the U.S. will amount to approximately US$160 billion. FDI into China is estimated to reach approximately US$60–70 billion. On top of that, a

Figure 16.4   China: Trade surplus with the United States, 1990–2004

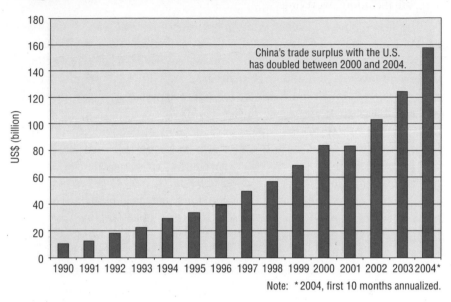

Note: *2004, first 10 months annualized.

Source: U.S. Department of Commerce, U.S. Census Bureau.

Figure 16.5   China: International Reserves (minus gold), 1980–2004

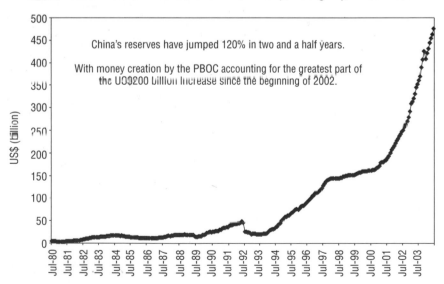

Source: International Monetary Fund, *International Financial Statistics*.

large amount of hot money will also enter the country, with estimates ranging from US$20 billion to US$70 billion.

Because China's currency is pegged to the dollar, China's central bank, the People's Bank of China (PBOC), is compelled to buy every dollar that enters (and remains) in the country. To do so, the PBOC has to create equally large amounts of Renminbi. The increase in China's foreign exchange reserves gives a rough indication of the scale of money creation undertaken by the Chinese authorities (see Figure 16.5).

Money creation on that scale, however, causes economic overheating. China's experience has proved no exception to that rule. By early 2004, China's money supply growth was expanding at an annual rate of 23% and commercial bank loans were increasing at a similar rate. Between September 2002 and the end of 2004, bank loans in China increased by 44%, taking the ratio of loans to GDP to 145%, one of the highest in the world. See Figure 16.6. The growth rate in industrial production peaked at 23% in February 2004.

Capital inflows of the magnitude that China is experiencing make economic management difficult. Therefore, it has been in China's interest to export as much of the incoming capital as possible. This has occurred through expanding the country's imports. Although China's trade surplus with the United States was US$124 billion in 2003, its overall trade surplus with the whole world was only US$45 billion, meaning that China's trade

Figure 16.6   China: Commercial bank loans to GDP, 1986 to 2004E

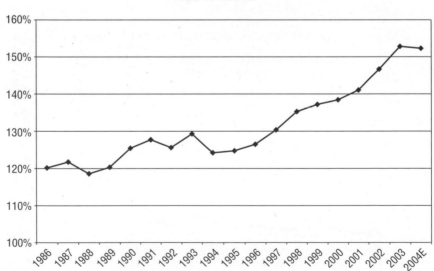

Source: CEIC and *China Statistics Yearbook*.

deficit with the rest of the world (excluding the United States) was US$79 billion that year, up eightfold relative to 1998 (see Figure 16.7).

While China's demand for imports was, in a sense, only a derivative of its trade surplus with the United States (and of the foreign direct investment attracted to China as a result of China's export competitiveness), nonetheless, that demand has begun to have a significant, even profound, impact on the global economy over the last few years. Chinese demand for imports spans the spectrum from high-tech machine tools from Japan and Korea, to steel and cement from India and Thailand, to palm oil and soybeans from Malaysia and Brazil. In fact, increasing demand from China is believed to have played a very considerable role in the 50% surge in global commodity prices between November 2001 and March 2004 (see Figure 16.8).

Of course, China is not the only country able to finance its imports from third countries as a result of having a trade surplus with the United States. Far from it. Intra-Asian trade – and for that matter, *all* international trade – is facilitated and expanded because most countries in the world do have a large trade surplus with the United States that they use to buy products from other countries.

Therefore, as the U.S. current account deficit expanded from 3.8% of U.S. GDP a year in 2001 to 4.8% in 2003 and an estimated 5.4% in 2004,[2] the rest of the world benefited tremendously. The countries that gained the

Figure 16.7 China: Trade deficit with the rest of the world (excluding the United States), 1997–2003

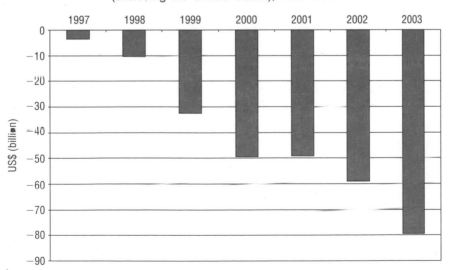

Sources: U.S. Department of Commerce, U.S. Census Bureau, and CEIC.

Figure 16.8   Commodity price index, 1997–2004

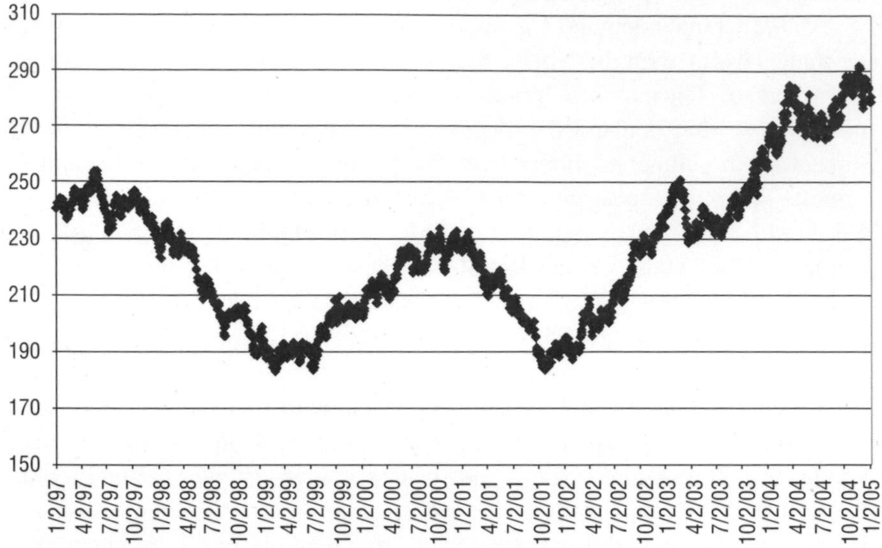

Sources: Bloomberg and Reuters CMB Index.

most were those where the central bank created, and then sold, its own currency to prevent it from appreciating against the dollar. The extent of such intervention can be gauged by the expansion of each country's foreign exchange reserves. For example, between the beginning of 2002 and September 2004, India's foreign exchange reserves increased by 152%, Korea's by 70%, Malaysia's by 86%, Singapore's by 34%, Thailand's by 35%, and Russia's by 181% (see Figure 16.9).

Surging exports, combined with the expansion of the domestic money supply that accompanies the accumulation of foreign exchange reserves, created a powerful reflationary mix for those countries. (The processes through which the expansion of international reserves leads to the formation of an economic bubble is the subject of Part One of this book.) Five out of the six countries shown in Figure 16.9 experienced accelerating economic growth over that period. Only Korea's economy failed to accelerate due to the unwinding of excesses within its banking systems.

Moreover, what was true for those countries individually was true for the world as a whole. Surging trade and a surging supply of paper money brought about the fastest rate of global economic growth in nearly 30 years in 2004.

It is important to understand that, at the same time, this surge in the supply of paper money also put unexpected downward pressure on U.S.

Figure 16.9 Surging foreign exchange reserves
(selected countries), 1998–2004

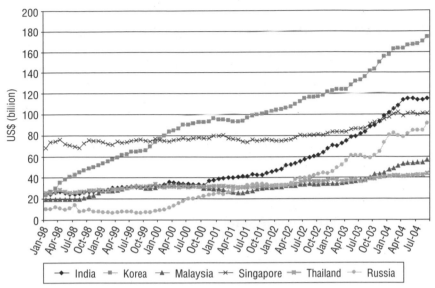

Sources: International Monetary Fund, *International Financial Statistics*.

interest rates despite a blowout in the U.S. government's budget deficit to a record US$413 billion in the fiscal year ending September 30, 2004. In the post-Bretton Woods era of fiat money, the supply of paper money is just as important as the demand for paper money in determining interest rates.

REFERENCES

1   Paul A. Samuelson, Think exist.com, http://en.thinkexist.com/quotes/paul_a._samuelson/2.html.
2   Office of Management and Budget, Mid-Session Review, July 2004.

Chapter 17

Understanding Interest Rates in the Age of Paper Money

... prevailing exchange rates will not lead to a material letup in our trade deficit. So whether foreign investors like it or not, they will continue to be flooded with dollars. The consequences of this are anybody's guess. They could, however, be troublesome – and reach, in fact, well beyond currency markets.

— Warren Buffett, 2004[1]

In early July 2004, the yield on 10-year U.S. treasury bonds was 4.9% and market participants were nearly unanimous in expecting it to move considerably higher. They were spectacularly mistaken. The yield fell below 4% in late September. During that period, the world's central banks were creating too much paper money to allow interest rates to rise. In this new age of fiat money, the rules have changed. From now on, the supply of money will be at least as important as the demand for it in determining interest rates.

Before the breakdown of the Bretton Woods system, interest rates were determined by the supply and demand for money. That is still true today. There is one very important difference, however. Then, there was a limited amount of money and governments did not have the power to create it at will. Today, governments can create as much money as they want. This convenience makes global economic management very much easier (at least in the short run). Then, if governments spent more than their tax revenues, government borrowing pushed up interest rates and crowded out the private sector. Today, that is no longer true ... not for the U.S. government anyway. Today, the interest rate on the 10-year U.S. Treasury bond is determined primarily by the relationship between the demand for money from the U.S. federal government and government-sponsored enterprises (GSEs) such as, Fannie Mae, and the amount of paper money created by the United States' trading partners, which, in turn, to a large extent, is determined by the size of their trade surplus with the United States. Capital markets were stunned by the sharp drop in 10-year Treasury bond yields that occurred during the third quarter of 2004. The explanation for that unexpected decline is simply that the supply of paper money outstripped the demand for it as government and agency debt expanded less than the U.S. current account deficit. Consider the data in Table 17.1.

Table 17.1 The demand for and supply of paper dollars

The increase in U.S. federal government and agency debt relative to the U.S. current account deficit (US$ billion)

	2002	2003				2004		
	4Q	1Q	2Q	3Q	4Q	1Q	2Q	3Q
Federal government (1)	3,637	3,701	3,807	3,914	4,033	4,169	4,210	4,293
Q/Q increase		64	106	107	119	136	41	83
Q/Q % increase		1.8%	2.9%	2.8%	3.0%	3.4%	1.0%	2.0%
Government-sponsored enterprises (1)	2,350	2,406	2,454	2,569	2,594	2,599	2,657	2,684
Q/Q increase		56	48	115	25	5	58	27
Q/Q % increase		2.4%	2.0%	4.7%	1.0%	0.2%	2.2%	1.0%
Agency & GSE mortgage pools (1)	3,159	3,227	3,289	3,371	3,489	3,506	3,520	3,544
Q/Q increase		68	62	82	118	17	14	24
Q/Q % increase		2.2%	1.9%	2.5%	3.5%	0.5%	0.4%	0.7%
Total govt. + GSE + Agency & GSE mortgage pools (1)	9,146	9,334	9,550	9,854	10,116	10,274	10,387	10,521
Q/Q increase		188	216	304	262	158	113	134
Q/Q % increase		2.1%	2.3%	3.2%	2.7%	1.6%	1.1%	1.3%
U.S. current account deficit	127	138	134	132	127	147	164	165
as % of increase in govt. debt		216%	126%	123%	107%	108%	400%	199%
as % of increase in total govt. & agency debt		73%	62%	43%	48%	93%	145%	123%

Note: (1) Amounts outstanding at end of period.
Sources: Flow of Funds 3Q 2004, U.S. Federal Reserve and Bureau of Economic Analysis.

The table shows the amount of debt outstanding for (1) the federal government, (2) government-sponsored enterprises, (3) agency and GSE mortgage pools, and (4) the three combined. It also shows the quarter-on-quarter increase in debt for each of the above. Finally, the table provides the size of the U.S. current account deficit for the last eight quarters.

Strong economic growth resulted in higher than expected tax revenues in the United States during the first half of 2004. Consequently, the increase in U.S. government debt slowed very sharply beginning in the second quarter (see Figure 17.1). In July, the President's Office of Management and Budget revised down its estimate of the U.S. budget deficit by US$76 billion for fiscal year 2004 to US$445 billion, from its original estimate of US$521 billion made five months earlier due to stronger-than-expected tax revenue growth. The actual figure came in considerably lower still, at US$413 billion.

At the same time, the GSEs became considerably less aggressive in expanding their balance sheets. The intensifying scrutiny of the accounting practices of Fannie Mae and Freddie Mac seem likely to have been a factor behind their reduced appetite for debt. In any case, the combined growth in federal government debt and agency-related debt slowed very considerably in 2004 relative to 2003 (see Figure 17.2).

The trend in the size of the U.S. current account deficit moved in the opposite direction, however (see Figure 17.3).

Figure 17.1   United States: Government debt, quarterly increase

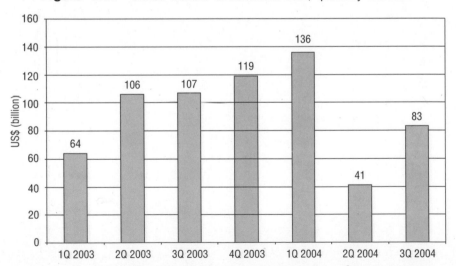

Source: *Flow of Funds* 3Q 2004, U.S. Federal Reserve and Bureau of Economic Analysis.

Figure 17.2 United States: Government debt plus agency debt, quarterly increase

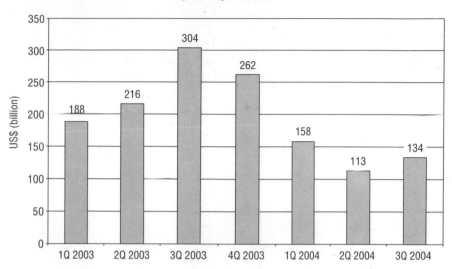

Source: *Flow of Funds*, U.S. Federal Reserve.

Figure 17.3 United States: Current account deficit by quarter

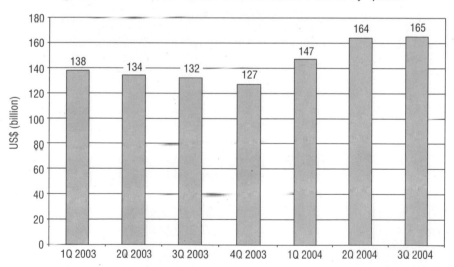

Source: Bureau of Economic Analysis.

The central banks of most of the United States' trading partners printed as much money as was necessary to acquire all the dollars entering their economies in order to prevent their currencies from appreciating, and with those dollars they bought U.S. Treasury bonds and agency debt. However, as can be seen in Figures 17.4 and 17.5, beginning in the second quarter of 2004, the increase in the amount of new debt being offered by the government and GSEs was insufficient to meet the demand for it.

Figure 17.4 Total increase in U.S. government debt and agency debt versus the U.S. current account deficit

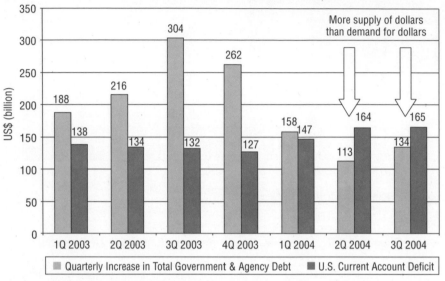

Sources: Flow of Funds, Federal Reserve, Bureau of Economic Analysis.

Figure 17.5 The U.S. current account deficit as a percentage of the quarterly increase in total U.S. government debt and agency debt

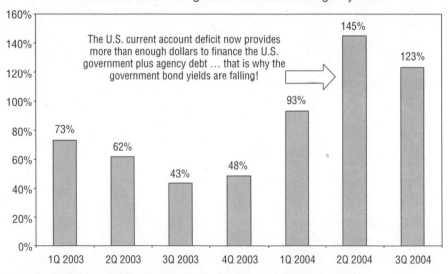

Sources: Federal Reserve, *Flow of Funds*; Bureau of Economic Analysis.

For this reason, market-determined interest rates fell, even though the Fed had begun increasing the federal funds rate in June. More paper money was being created as a result of the rapidly expanding U.S. current account deficit than was needed to fund the budget deficit and the GSEs' demand for credit. This surfeit of money also explains why the interest rate spread on corporate bonds over Treasuries fell to multi-year lows during that period.

Classical economic theory taught that changes in the demand for money determined the level of interest rates, since the supply of money was fixed. Today, that is no longer true. Keep an eye on the supply. It's exploding! (see Figure 17.6).

Figure 17.6 Total international reserves (minus gold), all countries, 1965 to September 2004

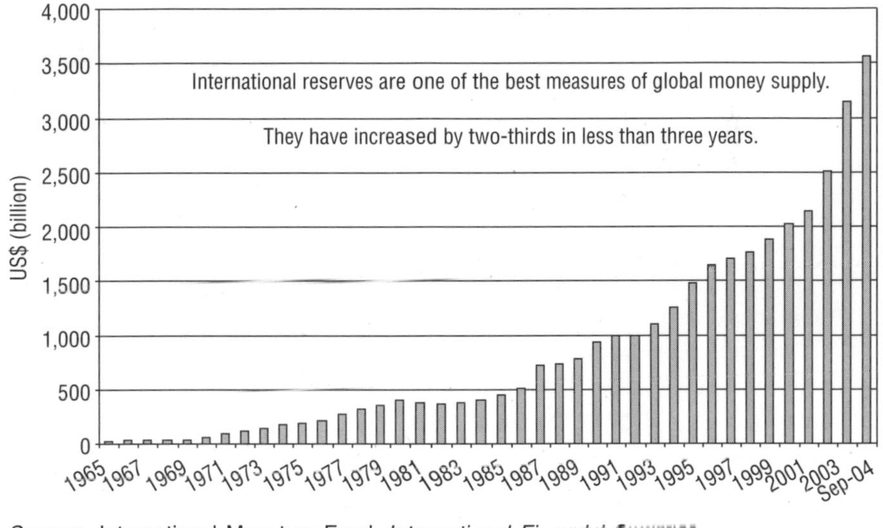

Source: International Monetary Fund, *International Financial Statistics*.

REFERENCE

1 Warren Buffett, Letter to Shareholders, Berkshire Hathaway Inc., 2003 Annual Report.

Chapter 18

What's Worrying the Chairman?

Has the Fed Lost Control over Interest Rates?

If something cannot go on forever, it will stop.

— Herbert Stein[1]

O n November 19, 2004, Fed Chairman Alan Greenspan made an uncharacteristically blunt speech at the European Banking Congress in Frankfurt[2] that sent the dollar tumbling. He said that the rest of the world would not be willing to finance a large U.S. current account deficit forever and called into question the rest of the world's appetite for dollars. This may well prove to be the speech for which he is remembered by posterity, capping his tenure as the world's most influential central banker during an epoch of irrational exuberance that he did not prevent and was unable to control. He said:

> Current account imbalances, per se, need not be a problem, but cumulative deficits, which result in a marked decline of a country's net investment position – as is occurring in the United States – raise more complex issues. The U.S. current account deficit has risen to more than 5% of GDP. Because the deficit is essentially the change in net claims against U.S. residents, the U.S. net international investment position excluding valuation adjustments must also be declining in dollar terms at an annual pace equivalent to roughly 5% of U.S. GDP.
>
> The question now confronting us is how large a current account deficit in the United States can be financed before resistance to acquiring new claims against U.S. residents leads to adjustment. Even considering heavy purchases by central banks of U.S. Treasury and agency issues, we see only limited indications that the large U.S. current account deficit is meeting financing resistance. Yet, net claims against residents of the United States cannot continue to increase forever in international portfolios at their recent pace. Net debt service cost, though currently still modest, would eventually become burdensome. At some point, diversification considerations will slow and possibly limit the desire of investors to add dollar claims to their portfolios.

Net cross-border claims against U.S. residents now amount to about one-fourth of annual U.S. GDP.

This situation suggests that international investors will eventually adjust their accumulation of dollar assets or, alternatively, seek higher dollar returns to offset concentration risk, elevating the cost of financing of the U.S. current account deficit and rendering it increasingly less tenable. If a net importing country finds financing for its net deficit too expensive, that country will, of necessity, import less.

It seems persuasive that, given the size of the U.S. current account deficit, a diminished appetite for adding to dollar balances must occur at some point. But when, through what channels, and from what level of the dollar? Regrettably, no answer to those questions is convincing.

Greenspan's remarks stunned the financial markets. Such straight talk from Chairman Greenspan on *any* subject is highly unusual, but on the topic of the dollar it was almost flabbergasting – particularly since, as a matter of policy, the Fed does not comment on the dollar, *ever*. Within the U.S. government, only the Treasury Secretary is permitted to discuss the value of the currency.

So, why did Mr. Greenspan choose this time to draw attention to the long-run impossibility of financing the U.S. current account at current exchange rates? He pointed to the deterioration of the net international investment position of the United States, but that is hardly news. As can be seen in Figure 18.1, it has been going on since Ronald Reagan was president.

Information on the net international investment position of the country is released by the Commerce Department only once each year, during June.[3] As an aside, it is interesting to note that during 2002 and 2003, the net debt of the U.S. increased by only US$340 billion, even though the U.S. current account expanded by more that US$1 trillion. Significant revisions to estimates of the value of U.S.-owned assets abroad accounted for the discrepancy.

Be that as it may, the deterioration in the country's net international investment position does not seem to be so alarming as to necessitate such an uncharacteristically blunt speech by Chairman Greenspan on a subject as sensitive as the value of the dollar. He, himself, said there was no problem financing it at present. Foreign central banks (although not foreign private-sector investors) appear to have an unlimited appetite to buy dollars to prevent their currencies from appreciating, so as to protect their countries' trade surpluses. Will they stop acquiring dollars and watch their economies be thrown into recession as their currencies rapidly appreciate, just because the net international investment position of the United States has reached a

Figure 18.1   United States: Net international investment position
(at market costs), 1982–2003

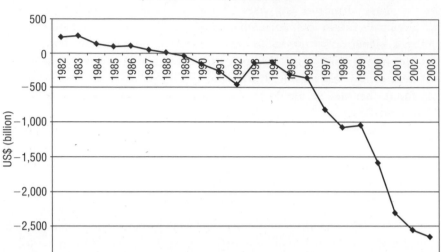

Source: U.S. Department of Commerce, Bureau of Economic Analysis.

deficit equivalent to 25% of U.S. GDP? Why would 25% be the threshold
that would trigger a change in their behavior? Why not 75% of U.S. GDP?
Or 150%? When there is only one buyer in the market, vendor-financing will
carry on for quite a long time even after the first signs of deterioration in that
buyer's financial health have become apparent. And so it is in this case. If
the United States' trading partners, particularly those in Asia pursuing an
export-led model of economic growth, stop financing the U.S. current
account deficit, the U.S. will import less and their export-dependent
economies will be thrown into crisis.

There is a widespread misconception that the United States relies on the
savings of other countries to finance its current account deficit. This is
incorrect. During recent years, at least, the U.S. current account deficit has
been financed primarily by money newly created by the central banks of
other countries. Newly issued paper money is not the same thing as a
country's savings. The companies that earn money by exporting to the U.S.
keep their savings. It is only that they keep them in their domestic currencies
after having sold the dollars they earned from exporting to their central bank.
In fact, the banking systems of the export-oriented economies all across Asia
are burdened by *too much* savings. Deposits are accumulating in the banks
more quickly than there are viable lending opportunities and, consequently,
interest rates have fallen to historic lows.

Therefore, it is not a matter of the U.S. using up all the rest of the world's savings to fund its deficit. It is a matter of that deficit being financed by the central banks of the United States' trading partners. And, for their part, Asian central banks, in particular, have consistently demonstrated their ability and willingness to create money in order to finance the U.S. current account deficit. Given that nothing has occurred to call into question their determination to continue doing so, there is no reason to expect that behavior to change any time in the near future. What else, then, could be worrying Chairman Greenspan?

He does not seem to be concerned about the loss of jobs in the United States, even though the trend of moving manufacturing jobs to low-wage countries is now being followed by a trend to outsource service sector jobs abroad as well. In fact, in his Frankfurt speech, the unambiguous remarks quoted above were preceded by an erudite preamble – more typical of Greenspan – identifying the diminution of "home bias" during recent years as the reason behind the radical expansion of the U.S. current account deficit; comments which helped to obscure, without completely denying, the obvious fact that the deficit has been caused by the desire of Americans and non-Americans alike to buy their goods from the lowest-cost producers, who for the most part do not manufacture their products in the United States.

Mr. Greenspan even concluded his remarks by calling for yet more product and labor market flexibility in the United States and elsewhere. He cited labor mobility as the reason that interstate trade imbalances are resolved without provoking crises within the United States. It is not quite clear what purpose he intended that example to serve, however, since it is unlikely he meant to advocate unrestricted labor migration between the United States, with a population of 300 million, and the developing world, with its population of over four billion.

He *is* concerned about a protectionist backlash against free trade, as he has made clear on many occasions. However, with the U.S. presidential elections just completed and little opportunity for voters to express their frustration over job losses until the next election in 2008, that would not have been reason for expressing concern over the current account deficit now. What else could be on his mind?

It may be that he is growing concerned that he and his colleagues at the Fed are losing control over interest rates, and, therefore, over the broader economy. The Fed began raising the federal funds rate in June 2004. Since then it has increased rates by 25 basis points on five occasions, by a total of 125 basis points, to 2.25%. Despite that, the market-determined rate on 10-year government bonds has actually fallen over that period by 25 basis points to 4.25%. That cannot be what the Fed had hoped for when it began raising rates.

The explanation for this unexpected outcome can be found in the imbalance between the amount of dollars being accumulated by the central banks of the United States' trading partners and the issuance of new U.S. government and agency debt (see Figures 17.4 and 17.5).

The former can be thought of as the supply of paper dollars, while the latter represents the demand for paper dollars. When there is more supply of paper dollars than demand for paper dollars, as has been the case since the second quarter of 2004, interest rates fall.

Many countries around the world accumulate large stockpiles of dollars as a result of their trade surpluses with the United States. The central banks of most of those countries print their own currency and buy those dollars in order to prevent their currencies from appreciating when the private-sector companies that earned the dollars exchange them for the domestic currency on the foreign exchange markets. The central banks then invest the dollars they have acquired into U.S. dollar-denominated debt instruments, preferably U.S. Treasury bonds or agency debt, in order to earn a return. If the amount of dollars accumulated by foreign central banks exceeds the amount of new debt being issued by the U.S. government and the U.S. agencies during any particular period, then the central banks will buy existing government and agency debt instead of newly issued debt. By acquiring existing debt, they push up the price and push down the yield. That seems to explain why long bond yields have been falling since mid-2004 even though the Fed has been increasing interest rates at the short end of the yield curve.

If this reasoning is correct, the implications are quite disturbing given current trends in the current account deficit and the budget deficit. If the U.S. current account deficit continues to expand from its level of approximately US$650 billion in 2004, as seems likely so long as the dollar remains at existing exchange rates, then the amount of paper dollars that foreign central banks wish to invest in U.S. government debt will continue to expand. Meanwhile, the U.S. budget deficit is widely expected to be lower in FY2005 (approximately US$350 billion) than in FY2004, when it was US$413 billion. That means the government will issue less new debt this year than it did last year. Presumably, the same will be true of Fannie Mae and Freddie Mac, in light of the accounting scandals in which they have become embroiled. Under such circumstances, there will not be enough new government and agency debt issued to satisfy the demand of foreign central banks. Consequently, they are likely to buy existing debt instead, which will have the effect of pushing up the price of those bonds and driving their yields down even further … regardless of what the Fed does to the federal funds rate.

Mortgage rates are determined by the yield on 10-year Treasury bonds in the United States. Therefore, if foreign central bank buying drives down the yield on Treasury bonds, it would also push down mortgage rates, which in turn would cause the rate of increase in U.S. property prices, already the fastest in 25 years during the third quarter of 2004, to accelerate still further. Higher property prices would allow yet more equity extraction which, in turn, would stimulate U.S. consumption further. Additional consumption would pull in more imports and exacerbate the U.S. current account deficit. And, a larger current account deficit would put yet more dollars in the hands of foreign central banks, who would then look for still more dollar-denominated assets in which to invest them.

In other words, if the U.S. current account continues to widen faster than the U.S. budget deficit, it could drive yields on government bonds, and therefore the interest rates on mortgages, so low that it creates an asset bubble in the United States that the Fed could not control.

What policy options are still open to global policymakers to prevent the current imbalances from leading to a cycle of spiraling economic overheating along the lines described above? Mr. Greenspan told his Frankfurt audience that the U.S. government should reduce its budget deficit in order to reduce the country's current account deficit. Specifically, he said:

> U.S. policy initiatives can reinforce other factors in the global economy and marketplace that foster external adjustment. Policy success, of course, requires that domestic savings must rise relative to domestic investment.
>
> Reducing the federal budget deficit (or preferably moving it to surplus) appears to be the most effective action that could be taken to augment domestic savings.

But, what would happen if the U.S. government *did* balance its budget? It is possible that the U.S. current account deficit would expand less quickly, although that was not the case in the late 1990s when the government's budget actually went into surplus while the U.S. current account deficit continued to worsen. It is even possible that the U.S. current account deficit would contract a little. For the sake of argument, then, imagine that the budget deficit is balanced and the U.S. current account deficit is reduced from US$650 billion a year to US$500 billion a year. At present, foreign investors own approximately 50% of the US$4 trillion in U.S. government debt that is held by the public. Under the circumstances just described, within four years, foreign investors could end up owning all outstanding U.S. government debt. After that, they would have no choice but to invest their annual surpluses into other dollar-denominated assets, such as agency debt, corporate debt, equities, property, bank loans, etc. Such a scenario would cause extraordinary asset price inflation, both directly as foreign investors bought more and more U.S. assets, and indirectly as their acquisition of bonds drove down interest rates, providing still more unwanted stimulus to the U.S. economy. Perhaps Mr. Greenspan should be careful what he wishes for. After all, the last time the government budget was in surplus corresponded with the rise of the New Paradigm bubble.

Regardless, then, of whether the U.S. government reduces its budget deficit or not, it would appear that the rapidly expanding U.S. current account deficit has begun to undermine the ability of the Fed to determine the level, or even the direction, of interest rates in the United States. Moreover, if the present trend in the current account deficit is left unchecked, the investment of ever larger amounts of dollar surpluses by foreign central banks into U.S. dollar-denominated assets threatens to produce asset price bubbles and economic overheating in the United States which the Fed would have no power to control. Seen from this perspective, there is little wonder that the Fed has begun to talk down the dollar.

It is also worth noting that the extraordinary accumulation of dollar reserves has begun to impact third party countries, as well. When investors diversify out of dollars and into euros, for instance, they then invest those euros in euro-denominated debt instruments and thereby push up bond prices and push down bond yields in Europe. Soon, this could make economic management there more difficult, too.

▶ REFERENCES

1   Herb Stein's Unfamiliar Quotations, Stein's Law, first pronounced in the 1980s, arising first in discussion of the U.S. balance of payments.
2   Remarks by Federal Reserve Board Chairman Alan Greenspan, at the European Banking Congress 2004, Frankfurt, Germany, November 19, 2004.
3   U.S. Department of Commerce, Bureau of Economic Analysis.

Chapter 19

After Reflation, Deflation

Inflation has been somewhat elevated this year, though a portion of the rise in prices seems to reflect transitory factors.

— FOMC Statement, August 2004[1]

The great global reflation that has occurred since the economic downturn of 2001 was accomplished through an incredible expansion of the U.S. current account deficit and the global money supply. However, Chairman Greenspan's speech on November 19, 2004, and the deafening silence from the U.S. Treasury Department that followed it, suggests that the U.S. government has finally recognized the dangers posed to the global economy by the runaway U.S. current account deficit. It now seems likely that steps will be taken by the United States to reduce that deficit. If those steps fail, a continued explosion of the global money supply could lead to uncontrollable asset price inflation around the world, as described in the previous chapter. On the other hand, if those steps succeed, the reduction in the deficit will produce a severe global recession, characterized by worldwide deflation.

The U.S. current account deficit can only be reduced if the U.S. imports less from the rest of the world, or if the rest of the world imports more from the United States. Given the high wage rates in the United States relative to the wage rates in developing countries, U.S. manufactured goods are not cost-competitive in the global marketplace. That loss of competitiveness may now spread to large parts of the service sector as India gears up to become the world's outsourcing center. Consequently, it is very unlikely that the rest of the world will begin importing more goods or services from the United States, at least not on a scale sufficient to achieve a significant reduction of the deficit.

The adjustment, then, if there is to be one, will occur as a result of the United States importing less from the rest of the world. The impact on the global economy of a reduction in U.S. imports can be discerned from the experience of 2001. When the United States went into a mild recession that year, imports into the U.S. declined by US$78 billion. As described in Chapter 9, the impact of that decline in U.S. demand on the rest of the world was quite severe.

With imports contracting by US$78 billion that year, the U.S. current account deficit improved, but only by US$28 billion. That is because when the United States reduced its imports from the rest of the world, its trading partners also reduced their imports from the United States. In 2002, imports into the U.S. began to recover, increasing by US$19 billion, but U.S. exports declined by a further US$37 billion, and so the U.S. current account deficit worsened once again.

Figure 19.1 illustrates the problem policymakers will face as they attempt to bring the destabilizing U.S. current account deficit under control. Overall, between 2000 and 2004, imports into the U.S. increased by US$191 billion. U.S. exports, however, rose by only US$14 billion during that time. There is no question that the United States has the ability to reduce the amount it imports. Any number of measures could be taken to ensure a reduction in the amount of goods the country buys from abroad. It is almost equally certain, however, that when the U.S. does reduce the amount that it buys from abroad, the rest of the world will respond by lowering their demand for U.S. exports. Consequently, a significant reduction in the overall current account imbalance will be very difficult to achieve.

Difficult or not, it is inevitable that the U.S. current account imbalance will correct, as even Chairman Greenspan is now pointing out.[2] That which can't go on forever will stop. When the deficit does begin to contract, a

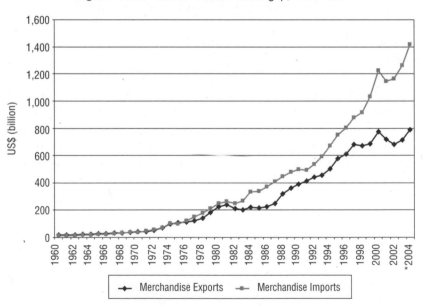

Figure 19.1 United States: Trade gap, 1960–2004

Source: Federal Reserve Economic Data, St. Louis Fed.
Note: *2004 = 6 months annualized.

global recession will be unavoidable. The global economic downturn of 2001 that resulted from a US$78 billion decline in U.S. imports was, in all probability, only a mild prelude relative to the adjustment that lies ahead.

Over the last two years, the world has grown only more dependent on exporting to the United States. Those countries that have benefited most from the reflationary boom are likely to suffer the most when that boom gives way to bust. China is particularly vulnerable now, having experienced a boom of truly historic proportions in recent years.

In the late 1980s, Japan was forced by the United States to accept "voluntary" quotas on its automobile and semiconductor exports to the U.S. Soon thereafter, the Japanese economy went into a recession from which it has yet to recover. It is quite possible that a similar fate is in store for China. China won't be allowed to continue growing its trade surplus with the United States forever. Unless measures have been taken before then to wean the Chinese economy off its dependence on exporting to the United States, when its trade surplus with that country stops expanding, extraordinary challenges will arise to confront policymakers there. To begin with, if China's trade surplus with the U.S. is capped, the huge amount of direct foreign investment that is currently flowing into China would slow to a trickle, since most of those investments are being made in enterprises focused on exporting to the United States. Then, instead of being confronted with excessive capital inflow leading to runaway money supply growth, as was the case in early 2004, the situation could be reversed. Greatly reduced capital inflows could result in insufficient money supply growth. Many mistakes and problems can be covered over given enough incoming cash flow. When that cash flow begins to contract, however, very serious economic flaws can be expected to emerge. When China's trade surplus with the U.S. stops expanding, China could find itself burdened with excess industrial capacity, a bankrupt banking system, and insufficient fiscal resources to pull itself out of a deflation-induced liquidity trap similar to the one confronting Japan today. China's imports from the rest of the world would then plunge dramatically, with a knock-on effect felt from South Korea to Brazil.

The surest way to prevent such a scenario from taking place would be for the Chinese government to strictly enforce steadily increasing wage rates across the country's export-oriented industrial sector, thereby igniting a surge in domestic demand strong enough to push the Chinese economy to a higher plane of economic development. Higher wage rates at the bottom of the pyramid of China's workforce would also be a much more certain way of correcting the trade balance between China and the United States than a revaluation of the Chinese currency would be, since a higher exchange rate alone would not necessarily end up putting more money in the hands of the industrial workforce producing the products.

The Chinese government has demonstrated remarkable skill in transforming China from a very poor country 25 years ago into a great economic success story today. There is reason to believe that they could meet with the same success now in transforming the economy from one reliant on exporting to one capable of sustainable growth driven by domestic demand. The key to doing so is a government-directed upward adjustment to the country's wage structure. Until Chinese workers can afford to buy the things they produce, balanced trade between the high-wage countries and China is not possible in the absence of trade barriers (see Chapter 12).

The Japanese economy will also be badly affected when the U.S. current account deficit begins to correct. A great deal of progress has been made in improving the balance sheets of Japanese corporations, and the giant Japanese asset bubble has been largely deflated by a 60% collapse in the stock market and a 70% collapse in land prices. Nevertheless, it should not be forgotten that the Japanese economy is still mired in deflation. Moreover, the economy is on a drip of fiscal life support amounting to 8% of GDP a year, without which it would have fallen into depression years ago.

Japan has benefited greatly from the global reflationary boom of 2003 and early 2004. Above-trend GDP growth in 2003 gave rise to hope that the post-bubble slump had finally ended and that a self-sustaining cycle of domestic demand-driven growth was underway. During the second and third quarter of 2004, however, Japan's economy stopped growing; and that was at a time when the U.S. current account deficit was still expanding rapidly. It is quite certain that a significant reduction in the U.S. current account deficit would deepen Japan's ongoing economic crisis.

Europe, while less vulnerable than China or Japan, would not escape unscathed from the global recession that a reduction in U.S. imports would cause. Meanwhile, all the commodity-exporting countries would suffer as commodity prices sink back toward their 2001 lows, if not lower.

As for the United States, a *large* reduction in its current account deficit would reverse the current problem of too many dollars in the hands of foreign central banks chasing an insufficient supply of new Treasury bonds and agency debt. In that case, market-determined bond yields could rise, sending the over-inflated property market crashing. Even a less exceptional reduction in the deficit that simply left the 10-year bond yield at the existing level could suffice to undermine consumption there, since property prices would stabilize – or, more probably, deflate – if interest rates remain flat rather than continuing the downtrend of the last many years.

And what of the outlook for the global price level? By March 2004 the global reflationary process had driven commodity prices 50% above their

2001 low. Higher commodity prices had begun to push up the Producer Price Index (PPI) in the United States, and even to spill over into slightly higher consumer prices. The bond market began to take fright that inflation was rebounding. Calls began to be heard that the Fed should begin to tighten. Some commentators even said the Fed was "behind the curve," meaning that it had already waited too long to increase interest rates and that it would now be difficult to bring inflation back under control.

At that time, the Fed began signaling to the market that it would start increasing rates in the near future. The first rate hike came in late June, soon after the March and April employment reports showed the strongest job creation since the economic downturn began. In the Federal Open Market Committee statements that accompanied the first two rate hikes, the Fed acknowledged there were signs of increased inflationary pressure; however, it described those pressures as being "transitory."[3]

FOMC statements are concise, usually consisting of only a few paragraphs each. Every word in those statements is scrutinized by the financial markets in an attempt to understand what the Fed's next move may be. The Fed understands this very well. It chooses its words with extreme care. It used the word "transitory" in two consecutive FOMC statements in June and August to describe the inflationary pressures that had provoked the Fed into tightening.

Events were to prove that they knew exactly what they were talking about. The commodity price index peaked at the end of March, and was still below its March high at the end of 2004. The sharp correction in commodity prices that began in April 2004 corresponded with the end of the BOJ/MOF spree of money creation and currency market intervention, which ceased at the end of March, and with the late April announcements by Chinese government officials of a round of policy measures designed to cool down China's seriously overheated economy.

Soon thereafter, the reduction in commodity prices filtered through into lower PPI- and CPI-level inflation. In fact, when the U.S. GDP numbers were released for the third quarter of 2004, they revealed that the core inflation for personal consumption expenditure, one of Mr. Greenspan's favorite measures of inflation, had increased by only 0.7%, the lowest increase since 1962.

So, in retrospect, it is now clear that the world economic slump of 2001 was overcome through an extraordinary global reflationary process which created strong, but transitory, commodity price inflation that just barely impacted prices at the CPI level. The question arises, though, was it a good thing or a bad thing that prices rose so little during the boom? If the strongest global economic growth in nearly 30 years brought about only a mild and transitory increase in consumer prices, what will happen when the global economy slows again?

Globalization is the reason that consumer prices in the U.S. have risen so little. Globalization is exerting tremendous downward pressure on the price of manufactured goods because of the rapid increase in the amount of goods being produced in, and exported by, ultra-low-wage countries. It is highly probable that the downward pressure on the prices of manufactured goods will intensify in the years ahead and, more likely than not, begin to spill over into downward pressure on prices in the service sector as well once the outsourcing of services gets underway in earnest.

As the U.S. current account deficit expanded by 66% between 2001 and 2004, the global money supply also exploded by more than two-thirds over the same period due to money creation by the central banks in the surplus countries. That explosion of the global money supply has created a short-term boom effect that reflated the global economy. That boom will prove to be transitory, much like the transitory increase in commodity prices that accompanied it. While this liquidity-induced boom is transitory, the liquidity itself is not. The equivalent of well over US$1 trillion of paper money has been created by the world's central banks over the last three years. That money has entered the global economy and is seeking to earn a return on investment. Unfortunately, the more money there is that is looking for a return, the more difficult it is to achieve that return. Too much money creation leads to too much capital chasing a limited number of investment opportunities. After the initial transitory boom wears off, the newly created money that caused it remains behind and continues to look for opportunities to earn a return that no longer exist. If no money-making opportunities can be found, the money will go into government bonds and drive their yields lower. If this process carries on long enough, interest rates on government bonds will eventually fall to zero. That is what has occurred in Japan; and based on the current trajectory in global money supply growth (as reflected in the increase in total international reserves), the same thing will soon take place everywhere else in the world as well. When central banks create too much money relative to opportunities to invest that money profitably, the cost of renting (borrowing) that money falls to zero. It is as basic as the law of supply and demand. The only twist is that large-scale money creation first produces an unsustainable economic boom that lingers for a while before giving way to a deflationary bust.

Of course, this is not the first time governments have created fiat money on a large scale. It has occurred many times in the past. Each time the result was the collapse of the currency system involved. This time will be no different.

REFERENCES

1   Board of Governors of the Federal Reserve, The Federal Open Market Committee (FOMC) Statement, August 10, 2004.
2   Remarks by Federal Reserve Board Chairman Alan Greenspan, at the European Banking Congress 2004, Frankfurt, Germany, November 19, 2004.
3   Board of Governors of the Federal Reserve, The Federal Open Market Committee (FOMC) Statements, June 30, 2004 and August 10, 2004.

Chapter 20

Bernankeism

Anticipating the Policy Response
to Global Deflation

*Like gold, U.S. dollars have value only to the extent that they are strictly limited
in supply. But the U.S. government has a technology, called a printing press (or,
today, its electronic equivalent), that allows it to produce as many U.S. dollars
as it wishes at essentially no cost.*

— Fed Governor Ben Bernanke, 2002[1]

The Fed would already be faced with its worst nightmare, deflation in the
United States, had the price of oil not risen above US$50 a barrel
following the U.S. invasion of Iraq. Globalization is exerting tremendous
downward pressure on the U.S. cost structure that can only intensify in the
years ahead as service sector jobs follow manufacturing jobs offshore. A
correction in the U.S. current account deficit will cause the floor to drop out
from under global prices and threaten the world with a 1930s-style
deflationary depression. The following paragraphs will consider how
policymakers in the United States are likely to respond to that event.

America's free trade policy, which it has pursued for decades, is
obviously flawed. Free trade between countries with enormous wage rate
differentials, and within an international monetary system entirely lacking in
any mechanism to prevent large-scale, persistent trade imbalances, is
untenable. However, U.S. policymakers are afflicted by the collective
hypnosis of conventional wisdom which has taught them that free trade is
good and must always be good under any and all circumstances. It is
anyone's guess as to how much longer those in charge of economic policy
in the U.S. will cling on to this strange idea.

Meanwhile, it is almost certain that they will respond to the approaching
crisis by applying the two great economic policy tools of the last century:
Keynesianism and monetarism. The abuse of those tools will prolong and
exacerbate the death throes of the dollar standard.

The first recourse will be to employ more fiscal stimuli. With prices
falling, and in light of the extraordinary amount of paper money that has
been created in recent years (see Figure 20.1), interest rates will be very low

Figure 20.1 Global money supply under the dollar standard, total international reserves (minus gold), all countries, 1965 to September 2004

Source: International Monetary Fund, *International Financial Statistics*.

and there will be little difficulty in paying interest on a much larger amount of government debt. It would not be surprising to see the U.S. budget deficit surpass US$1 trillion by 2007 or 2008 if the U.S. current account has come down significantly by that time.

If, at that point, the U.S. current account deficit has been reduced, foreign central banks would not have a sufficient inflow of dollars to finance such a large deterioration in the U.S. budget deficit, even assuming that Fannie Mac and Freddie Mac have ceased issuing any new, competing, debt of their own.

The Fed, however, as Governor Bernanke explained, has already put considerable thought into how to deal with such a contingency and stands ready, in Bernanke's opinion, to support "a broad-based tax cut" through "a program of open-market purchases to alleviate any tendency for interest rates to rise."[2]

How long could such "cooperation between the monetary and fiscal authorities"[3] underpin the global economy? For quite a number of years, most probably. Economic cycles play themselves out over very long periods of time. Moreover, U.S. policymakers will use every last tool at their disposal to prevent, or at least delay, a global depression. An economic system underpinned by large-scale fiscal stimulus financed by central bank monetization of government debt could hardly be described as capitalism (perhaps the term "Bernankeism" would be appropriate) but, with any luck, it could stave off disaster for a considerable length of time.

Nevertheless, despite the best efforts of policymakers to keep the dollar standard alive and to stave off the depression that would most probably follow its collapse, ultimately, one of the following scenarios is likely to overwhelm even Bernankeism:

1. A protectionist backlash against free trade, resulting in a trade war similar to that which occurred during the Great Depression.
2. A U.S. asset price bubble (as interest rates fall toward zero) that drives property prices so high they can't be financed even at very low interest rates. This is similar to what occurred in Japan at the end of the 1980s.
3. A meltdown of the under-regulated US$200 trillion derivatives market. (Two hundred trillion U.S. dollars is roughly six times global GDP.)
4. A loss of nerve on the part of policymakers that deters them from undertaking ever more unorthodox economic policies, resulting in a "deer in the headlights" kind of policy freeze.
5. A decline in interest rates to 0%, or very near 0%, as in Japan at present.

Any one of the first four scenarios could undermine the dollar standard, but the final scenario, where interest rates fall very near 0%, would certainly deal it a fatal blow. From that point, the only option left to stimulate aggregate demand would be to drop paper money from helicopters. That too would fail, however, for who would accept paper dropped from helicopters in exchange for real goods and services? Hyperinflation would quickly set in. Economic transactions would then be conducted through barter rather than via the medium of a debased script. Eventually, a gold standard would re-emerge.

Exactly how these events will unfold is impossible to forecast; nevertheless, the eventual outcome is within sight. The dollar standard is inherently flawed and increasingly unstable. Its demise is imminent. The only question is, will it be death by fire – hyperinflation – or death by ice – deflation? Fortunes will be made and lost, depending on the answer to that question.

REFERENCES

1 Remarks by Federal Reserve Board Governor Ben S. Bernanke, before the National Economists Club, Washington, D.C., November 21, 2002, "Deflation: Making Sure 'It' Doesn't Happen Here."
2 Remarks by Federal Reserve Board Governor Ben S. Bernanke, before the National Economists Club, Washington, D.C., November 21, 2002, "Deflation: Making Sure 'It' Doesn't Happen Here."
3 Remarks by Federal Reserve Board Governor Ben S. Bernanke, before the Japan Society of Monetary Economics, Tokyo Japan, May 31, 2003, "Some Thoughts on Monetary Policy in Japan."

Conclusion

In this book, I have been critical of some of the monetarist prescriptions currently in vogue as to how to fight deflation. Nevertheless, I would like to make it clear that I do not consider myself to be either a Keynesian or a monetarist, but rather both, in so far as each has its place and proper role. As far as I can determine, Keynesianism was never actually practiced. Keynes believed that governments should maintain a balanced budget over the long run, but that deficit spending should be used to boost the economy during recessions. When the economy recovered, he advocated that those expansionist policies be followed by fiscal austerity and government surpluses. The latter half of that policy was never attempted. Over the last 50 years, governments have generally adopted fiscal stimulus measures and run large budget deficits during good times and bad. The budgets never balanced. Now, when a strong dose of deficit spending would undoubtedly be useful, concerns about the sustainability of government debt have begun to undermine the impact that fiscal stimulus would otherwise have had. A long-running and profligate government spending spree – which was inaccurately labeled Keynesian – is to blame.

As for monetarism, it is effective under certain circumstances. Increasing interest rates will bring down inflation. However, monetary policy is not an appropriate tool today to use against deflation, since this global deflation came about as a result of excessive global money supply growth in the first place. We have a global economy. International reserve assets are one measure of the global money supply. International reserves have grown at a near exponential rate since the Bretton Woods system broke down; and global credit has expanded more or less as a function of that increase in international reserves. Too much credit permitted over-investment, excess capacity, and ultimately falling prices and deflation. The monetary history of the last 30 years has been the history of monetarism run amok. We have long known that a little too much expansion of the money supply causes inflation. We know now that much too much expansion of the money supply ultimately ends in deflation. It is really tremendously ironic.

As Chinese leader Deng Xiaoping (1904–97) once said, "It doesn't matter if the cat is black or white, so long as it catches mice." Essentially, I agree. I am for any policy that works. But the policy must work over the long run. It cannot simply be a short-term fix that creates even greater problems for the future. It is with this principle in mind that I have proposed the establishment of a global minimum wage as a means of increasing global aggregate demand, and the establishment of a global central bank to regulate the global money supply. Both will be required to resolve the dollar crisis.

Increased aggregate demand is required to absorb the existing excess capacity that came about due to out-of-control global money supply growth. The steadily increasing demand that a rising global wage rate would bring about is also necessary to ensure that an equilibrium is maintained between the rapid increase in supply that our techno-industrial global economy can produce and effective worldwide demand, which boils down to nothing more or less than purchasing power.

A global central bank is necessary to prevent runaway money supply growth from creating asset price bubbles, over-investment, and deflation. The judicious allocation of the increase in the global money supply through the use of special drawing rights could also make an important contribution in the struggle against poverty, infectious diseases, and environmental degradation.

Just as I do not consider my economic views to be either Keynesian or monetarist, I do not view my policy recommendations as either leftist or right-wing or, for that matter, either particularly pro-free trade or anti-globalization. A steadily rising global wage rate would benefit everyone. It would be effective in putting money in the pockets of the people working in industrial jobs in the newly industrializing countries, and it would be effective in staving off a global depression that would wipe out the money in the stock portfolios of the public in developed nations. Similarly, a global central bank is just the most effective means of ensuring worldwide monetary stability.

We have a global economy. In the 21st century, it cannot be "us against them." We really are in this together – economically, socially, and even environmentally. We now must put in place global policies that are appropriate for a new, global era. It is just a matter of seeing the big picture and mastering it. I am supremely confident that humanity is up to this task.

Index